UNDER THE BLUE BERET

UNDER THE BLUE BERET

A U.N. Peacekeeper in the Middle East

TERRY "STONEY" BURKE

DUNDURN
TORONTO

Editor: Jennifer McKnight
Design: Jennifer Scott
Printer: Webcom

Library and Archives Canada Cataloguing in Publication

Burke, Terry, 1947-
     Under the blue beret : a U.N. peacekeeper in the Middle East / by Terry "Stoney" Burke.

Issued in print and electronic formats.
ISBN 978-1-4597-0832-7 (pbk.).--ISBN 978-1-4597-0833-4 (pdf).--ISBN 978-1-4597-0834-1 (epub)

1. Burke, Terry, 1947-. 2. United Nations--Peacekeeping forces--Middle East. 3. Peacekeeping forces, Canadian--Middle East. 4. Social conflict--Middle East. I. Title.

U55.B8458A3 2013   355.3'570956   C2013-900829-2   C2013-900830-6

1   2   3   4   5   17   16   15   14   13

  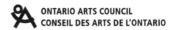

We acknowledge the support of the Canada Council for the Arts and the Ontario Arts Council for our publishing program. We also acknowledge the financial support of the Government of Canada through the Canada Book Fund and Livres Canada Books, and the Government of Ontario through the Ontario Book Publishing Tax Credit and the Ontario Media Development Corporation.

Care has been taken to trace the ownership of copyright material used in this book. The author and the publisher welcome any information enabling them to rectify any references or credits in subsequent editions.

J. Kirk Howard, President

Printed and bound in Canada.

Visit us at
Dundurn.com | Definingcanada.ca | @dundurnpress | Facebook.com/dundurnpress

Dundurn
3 Church Street, Suite 500
Toronto, Ontario, Canada
M5E 1M2

Gazelle Book Services Limited
White Cross Mills
High Town, Lancaster, England
LA1 4XS

Dundurn
2250 Military Road
Tonawanda, NY
U.S.A. 14150

To Brigitte
My one true constant
Thank you for always being there for me

CONTENTS

INTRODUCTION

As I think back to my time in Germany, I can't help but feel that it had all gone by so quickly. The 1960s were drawing to a close and I was about to return to Canada. I would like to say I was looking forward to going back, but after five years in Germany, it actually felt like I was leaving home for a place I no longer knew.

It seemed that everything about my life had changed, in just the blink of an eye. When I left London in the mid sixties, I was a mere eighteen years old. The law may have considered me an adult, but in my mind I was still a kid, with hardly a care in the world. We were paid every two weeks, but I was usually broke within a day or two. My most valuable possession was a reel-to-reel tape player, which I had picked up second hand for forty bucks. All I had achieved during that first year in Germany was an increased tolerance toward the local beer. Everything I owned could fit neatly into a kit bag and a barrack box.

Now here I was, just five years later, and it would take a full two-and-half-ton-truck just to get all our belongings to the air terminal in Düsseldorf.

I could never put my finger on the exact moment it happened, but somewhere in those intervening years I had become an adult, with grown-up responsibilities. I had a wife, a two-year-old daughter, and a newborn son, all relying on me to do the right thing.

* * *

Our first year of marriage presented its own unique set of difficulties. Our tiny upstairs flat sat hidden away in a narrow alley, just a few hundred metres from the main railroad station, in downtown Soest. Most nights we would awake to the sound of a loud whistle, as yet another train prepared to leave the station. The owners of the house were a couple in their eighties and they lived right below us. The long winter months were particularly rough. Our apartment had no heat or hot water and our toilet was shared with the landlord downstairs. The two tiny rooms were nothing to look at, but it was all we could afford on a corporal's pay.

The bedroom had enough space to hold a double bed and a crib for our baby girl. Later, when our son came along, we would have to jam another crib in the corner, next to the bedroom door.

Soon after dawn each morning, I would dress quickly and throw on a coat before heading to the kitchen to try to get the fire going in the big iron stove. Once I lit a match under the kindling wood and newspaper, all I could do was hop around on the cold linoleum floor while I waited for the flames to finally take hold. Next I could carefully add a few small pieces of coal and wait as the heat started to build. Soon I could open the kitchen door and let the heat find its way through to the bedroom. Once the kettle warmed up, I could fill the plastic basin to wash and shave before heading off to work.

Keeping the baby warm and dry was always a challenge, but somehow she seemed to thrive. Each morning I would tiptoe into the bedroom to say goodbye and there she would be, smiling up at me from beneath her triple layer of blankets.

Life had never been easy for my wife, Brigitte. She had been born during a time of great devastation.

The American bombers would come by day and the British by night. By the beginning of 1944, there was little left of the once picturesque town of Quedlinberg. The town's location near the Polish border made it a major rail hub for resupply trains moving toward the eastern front.

Each evening Brigitte's mother would bundle up her seven children and move to the underground bunker to wait out the endless bombing raids. At first light the older boys would head for the farmers' fields in search of food. On a good day they might be fortunate enough to dig up a few seed potatoes or even the occasional turnip.

By spring the skies grew quiet. There was nothing left to bomb. The town lay in ruins and the railroad tracks running east were little more than a series of massive craters and twisted steel. Now there was another terror to deal with.

At first there was only the sound of artillery in the distance, but soon the Russian Army was right on their doorstep. They paused only long enough to destroy anything that remained. Brigitte's sister was barely twelve years old and would have to remain hidden in a closet, just waiting and hoping for the Russian troops to move on towards Berlin. She did manage to evade detection, but many women, both young and old, were not so fortunate.

The war may have ended in May, but the hardship continued. The family found themselves trapped deep inside the Russian sector and every day presented new dangers. Food was always scarce and the older children would often sneak in behind the army kitchen and sift through the garbage, looking for anything edible to take home to their mother.

Brigitte's father had been captured on the Russian front, but after months in captivity he finally came home. His ordeal had left him only a shell of his former self. He died in the early 1950s.

One night, shortly before midnight, Brigitte's mother shook her awake and told her to get dressed. She was just ten years old, but she knew the significance of the moment. All were busy dressing, but no one made a sound. Outside a truck waited to take them on the first leg of their journey. The house that had been in their family for generations would have to be abandoned. They could take only what each person could carry. When the sun rose the following morning the truck pulled over to the side of the road. They had managed to cover over eighty kilometres, but the road ahead was far too dangerous to drive any further. The rest of the journey would have to be done on foot. There was still over thirty-two kilometres to travel before they reached the safe zone.

It was late in the summer of 1954 when Brigitte's family began their long journey. The Berlin Wall had not yet been built, but there were still many real dangers awaiting them as they approached the border area. During daylight they remained under cover, in the forest. By night they continually moved to the northwest, always taking care to avoid the numerous roadside checkpoints. After three days they finally spotted a Union Jack flying above a checkpoint. Brigitte still remembers the moment they realized they were in the British Sector of West Germany. It was one of the few times she ever saw her mother cry.

After all they had gone through together, I knew Brigitte had a special bond with her brothers and sisters. She was heartbroken when no one from her family came to our wedding. It was almost two years later and still they chose to stay away. They all believed that somehow Brigitte would finally come to her senses and realize she had made a mistake when she married me. None of them referred to me by name. I was simply the "Canuck" who had taken their sister away from her family.

Brigitte's mother would visit from time to time, but only during the day when I was away at work. These visits usually ended moments after I walked through the door.

It was early in January 1969 when the padre called me in to tell me my father had passed away. Almost as soon as her family heard I had gone back for the funeral they immediately began to sow the seeds of doubt in Brigitte's mind. "That is the last you will ever see of him," they told her over and over again. I knew deep down that Brigitte believed in me, but still it must have been difficult to find she was alone with the baby. All she could do was sit, waiting in that tiny, damp apartment, never really knowing when I would return.

Brigitte tried to hide all that had happened while I was away, but I could see the relief in her eyes the moment I walked through the door.

It would take a full ten years before any one of her seven brothers and sisters would finally accept the fact that Brigitte and I were together for good and nothing they could say or do would change that.

Even when we shook hands for the first time, I still harboured a good deal of ill feelings toward all of them for the years of grief they had brought to their sister. Only after I saw the smile on Brigitte's face could

I finally let all that resentment go. At last our children could get to know their aunt and uncles and Brigitte had her family back. That was all that really mattered.

It had been an eventful few days, but Brigitte and the kids seemed to be taking it in stride. I had hoped we could all get some much needed sleep, but there wasn't a single free seat on the plane. The flight attendant did not look pleased as I went about the task of removing the armrests. That left just enough room for Brigitte to sit next to the window, while the children lay down across the open seats. After squatting a while on the outside armrest, I managed to find a cardboard box that just fit nicely in the corner, next to the kitchen galley. The big container was not a particularly comfortable seat, but it would have to do for the next ten hours.

We had been on the go since six o'clock that morning, so it didn't take very long for the children to settle down. Every so often I would glance over the seat and watch them as they slept. How could these two tiny children possibly comprehend how their young lives were about to change? By the time the aircraft reached the Atlantic coastline, even Brigitte managed to close her eyes and get some much needed rest. I did doze off a few times, but I was far too nervous to get any real sleep. There were so many unanswered questions racing through my mind.

Naturally Brigitte was nervous about the prospect of meeting my family for the first time. Everything she knew of them was based upon the few photos I had and the many stories I told her about my past. All of that seemed rather abstract. Now, in just a matter of hours, everything would become very real.

I had seen all of my brothers and sisters just a few months earlier, when I came home for my father's funeral, but I felt a certain level of unease at the prospect of seeing them all again. I had certainly been treated well by everyone during that January week I had spent in Toronto. Much of our time together was spent reminiscing about the past, but soon the conversation would turn to things more current. All I could do was sit there and listen. The past was an experience we could all share, but I knew nothing of their current lives. I never regretted my decision to leave, but still I realized that I had missed so much that could never be gotten back.

The instant the plane touched down I knew that Brigitte's first impression of Canada was not going to be a good one. For months I had been bragging to her about the wonderful Canadian climate. Every time it rained in Germany, I would regale her with stories of the warm, dry summers and the cold, crisp winters she would find in Canada. I may have exaggerated just a little.

It was a late November evening when our Yukon aircraft began its final approach into the Trenton Airport. The weather had taken a turn for the worse soon after we entered Canadian airspace. I tried to let the children sleep, but the flight attendant had become rather insistent that I replace the missing armrests and return to my seat. We all buckled in for what was turning into a very bumpy ride. Once the wheels touched ground, we could actually hear the pellets of rain and sleet bounce off the body of the airplane as we taxied toward the terminal. By the time we carried the children down the ramp and across the tarmac we were all soaked through to the skin.

Considering the time change, we had been on the go for roughly thirty-six hours. Now our ordeal was almost over. I could already see my brother Michael waving to us from the other side of the rope barrier. Those last few steps would have to wait just a while longer. We were all soaking wet, but still we would have to stand and wait patiently while Canadian customs scanned through our mountain of paperwork. Most of the passengers were cleared and gone within minutes, but it would take over an hour to check and ensure our many documents were in order.

At last the customs officer reached under the counter and, in one swift motion, he stamped Brigitte's passport. She was still a German, but from this point on, her and the children would be considered "landed immigrants."

Our week-long stay in Toronto could not have gone better. Any fears I had about Brigitte's acceptance by my family were soon forgotten. They could not have been kinder to her and the children. Every day they took her someplace new. There was always a language barrier but somehow they all found ways to communicate and made us all feel welcome. As my seven days leave drew to a close, I began to notice that Martina and Eric had managed to pick up quite a few English words.

In my single days I had only bothered to learn a few of the more common German phrases. As far as I was concerned, there was really only one phrase that mattered: "*Guten abend, ein bier bitte.*" Once I learned to say, "Good evening, one beer please," to the bartender, what more could I possibly need? After I met Brigitte, I soon got past the laziness and set about the task of learning to communicate. After all, this was her country and therefore it was up to me to learn her language. Soon we were speaking nothing but German whenever I was home.

I knew that the children would adapt to English quickly once we settled down in London. I assumed that the process would take longer with Brigitte, but eventually she would master this newfound language. Neither one of us were overly concerned. Even if it took a while, I was always right there to help her along.

Soon after our arrival in London, I discovered a fault in our logic. Brigitte would have just ninety days to learn the fundamentals of English. After that she would be alone for a very long time.

The winter of 1970 can best be described in one word: nasty. In the latter part of January, London was hit by a record-breaking snowstorm. The city was shut down. With the exception of the odd snowmobile, the streets were completely abandoned.

The snowplows were working around the clock, but still the snow kept coming. When it finally stopped, the entire city was buried under a mountain of snow.

According to the radio reports, there were serious problems happening throughout the region and little could be done to help. The airwaves were filled with stories of car accidents and all types of medical emergencies that went unanswered because wheeled vehicles simply couldn't move.

There were a total of twenty M113 armoured personnel carriers (APCs) in Wolseley Barracks, and by the end of day two all of them were deployed to the key points throughout the city.

The APC was a tracked vehicle and could traverse almost any type of terrain. The large box-like vehicle could easily carry paramedics, police, or even a crew of firefighters. An accident victim or a pregnant woman might not have been comfortable riding in the back of this big noisy monster, but it would always get them to their destination.

My three-day shift was spent in a fire hall on the west side of the city. Our first morning was spent doing practice loading drills. By noon we could be fully dressed, with the engine running and everyone on board, in fewer than seven minutes. My job was to command the vehicle and guide the driver to the scene of the incident. Once we arrived, we just stood back while the firefighters went about their business. Thankfully we never had to deal with a major blaze. The few incidents we did attend were all minor and easily dealt with by the fire crew.

The winter was far from over, but by early February life in the city finally got back to normal.

Our apartment on Thompson Road was small but comfortable. To the casual observer, our surroundings may have seemed quite ordinary, but to me it felt like luxury. No more would I have to get up early just to build a fire and heat water. The simple act of turning up the thermostat and having instant heat or being able to get hot water from a tap just made life seem so much easier.

Martina and Eric were still too young for school, but between television and playing with the neighbourhood kids, they were already conversing in an odd mixture of German and English. During our first few days in London, Brigitte had been quite hesitant to venture out on her own. It would take a little time, but once she got over the sheer size of the supermarket and mastered Canadian money, she found the whole process of buying groceries a lot less intimidating.

We may not have had very much, but we were getting by. Most months we had just enough money to stretch between paydays and, with a little effort, we could put a tiny amount aside to buy a car sometime in the distant future.

For a while it seemed that all my worries had been for nothing. Our little family was adjusting to life in Canada. Like everyone else, we had our share of problems, but all in all, life was good and we were happy.

By mid-December Brigitte was already busy decorating the apartment for our first Christmas in Canada. Every evening I would look forward to coming home. As I started up the stairs to our third-floor apartment I could already pick up the smell of supper cooking on the stove. When I walked through the door, the kids would run to help me take off my boots before I tracked any dirt or snow into the house.

My military life began to settle into a familiar routine. After five years in pioneer platoon, I was once again back in an infantry company, doing the job of a rifleman. No more did I have to concern myself with explosives and mine warfare. Now my days were spent relearning all the basic skills necessary to become an effective infantry soldier.

I had been in Alpha Company less than a week when I first heard the rumour. My initial reaction was to ignore what was being said. After all, as any soldier would tell you, the military was always rife with all manner of rumours.

It was the week before Christmas and work in the battalion was slowly winding down for the holidays. As we fell in for morning inspection, you could sense the mood of guarded optimism throughout the group. Soon we could all look forward to getting a few days off, but first there was the matter of sorting out the duty roster. We all understood that certain key duties had to be done, regardless of the time of year. Each night there still had to be ten men patrolling the base on fire watch. The kitchens would remain open, and that would require another dozen men. When you added duty staff for each of the five companies, plus the battalion headquarters, it would take a total of forty or more men to cover all of the duties on any given day.

Standing there on the edge of the parade square that morning, we were already aware of what was about to happen. Each one of us would be on duty sometime during the holidays. All that remained was for the sergeant major to give us the date and time we had to report.

The moment someone caught a glimpse of the sergeant major's big frame coming down the pathway, all the chatter ceased, as each man stood properly at ease, looking straight to his front. It was well known that the sergeant major always had a couple of extra duties ready to hand out to anyone stupid enough to try his patience.

The sergeant major was unusually brief that morning. Rather than read out the name, he simply told us to each check the new duty roster once the parade was over. The morning parades normally took a few minutes, but rather than dismiss the company, the sergeant major seemed to hesitate for a moment. Each man stood perfectly still, waiting for the command to fall-out. His next words caught us all by surprise.

"Gentlemen, it has come to the attention of the company commander and I that a certain rumour has been floating around the battalion and I intend to put a stop to it right now." He paused a long moment to scan the faces before him. It seemed as if he was trying to find the right words. When he finally spoke, his normally loud and aggressive tone was strangely absent. His voice remained calm and restrained as he delivered his message. "The best way to combat a rumour is with the facts, so here it is. The rumour is true. This battalion will be going on duty with the U.N. this coming spring. In February we will begin training for a six-month tour of duty with the United Nations Force in Cyprus."

On the ride home that afternoon I briefly considered waiting until after Christmas to break the news to Brigitte, but I quickly put that idea aside. She had already made friends with some of the other military wives, so it was only a matter of time before she heard about Cyprus. It was best to tell her right now, so we could sit down and discuss the entire matter.

Every evening I had looked forward to going home, but today I hesitated. As I slowly prodded up each flight of stair, my mind was filled with all manner of thoughts.

I was torn between feelings of guilt and selfishness. On one hand I felt a deep sense of guilt about leaving my wife and children to fend for themselves, but at the same time I couldn't help but feel enthusiasm and excitement about the prospect of going to Cyprus.

I kept reminding myself that the decision to go to Cyprus was out of my hands. I was, after all, a soldier, and like every other soldier in the battalion I had been ordered to go.

* * *

In the weeks leading up to our deployment, I didn't find the endless exercises or the daily training particularly difficult. The job of patrolling and manning an observation post in Cyprus would be completely new to me, but I felt confident in my ability to do the job. The needles parade, dental checks, and even the medical officer's prodding and poking every bodily orifice was bothersome and annoying, but none of these procedures were the source of my insomnia.

I knew Brigitte was worried, but she never once complained. I, on the other hand, spent many sleepless nights thinking about what lay ahead for all of us. I knew Brigitte was a true survivor, but that didn't lessen the concern I felt about leaving her alone with two small children in a country where she barely spoke the language. Unlike today, the military of the sixties and seventies did not have social workers on staff, nor was there a family resource centre offering assistance with child care.

Other than having each soldier sign over a percentage of his pay to his wife, the military generally took a "hands-off" approach when it came to dealing with families. After the battalion deployed, there would be a small group of roughly thirty soldiers left in London. Their job was to maintain and operate the base until the unit returned. Should a women run into serious problems she did have the option of calling the base, but more often than not she was left to her own resources.

In hindsight I realized it was better not to know what lay ahead for all of us during the months to come. Yes, we would return from Cyprus after our six-month tour ended, in October, but our separation was far from over. Who could have foreseen that after just thirty-six hours at home, our entire battalion would depart on yet another lengthy operation? It would be December before any of us saw our families again.

Sometimes these things are best left to the unknown.

PART ONE

The Cyprus Years

BACKGROUND

In 1959 the Mediterranean island of Cyprus gained its independence from Great Britain. However, the Greek and Turkish communities on the island could not coexist peacefully, and sporadic fighting soon broke out. By early 1963, with both Greece and Turkey threatening intervention, this minor dispute was quickly becoming an international conflict.

By 1964 the United Nations Force in Cyprus (UNFICYP), which included a Canadian battalion, was in place to keep the peace.

Despite the speedy intervention of the U.N. force the conflict continued and led to the partition of Cyprus into Turkish and Greek republics, with the soldiers of UNFICYP manning the famous "Green Line" separating the two warring factions.

For the first six years of the mission the Canadian contingent was headquartered in Kryenia and was responsible for manning positions across the northern sector of the island. At the beginning of 1970 the Canadian contingent was moved from the relative quiet of the north into the much more volatile sector of the Green Line, which ran through the very heart of the city of Nicosia.

On July 15, 1974, officers in the Greek Cypriot National Guard staged a coup d'état against the president of Cyprus, Archbishop Makarios. Their aim was to unite Cyprus with the Greek motherland.

Turkey reacted five days later by launching an amphibious invasion of Cyprus with forty thousand troops. After successful landings near the coastal towns of Famagusta and Kryenia, they quickly secured each beachhead and immediately began moving inland toward the city of Nicosia. Their final objective was to be the Nicosia International Airport, at the western edge of the capital city.

Elements of the Canadian Airborne Regiment were deployed to the airport, which had now been defined as "A U.N. Protected Zone." As the United Nations' chief of staff and the Canadian contingent commander, Colonel Clay Beattie warned both sides that his soldiers were not only staying in position, but they were prepared to defend the airport by whatever means necessary.

The Turkish invading force certainly had the means to overwhelm the much smaller and lightly equipped U.N. force, but chose to stop just short of their main objective. An uneasy truce settled over the area. The Canadian contingent continued to occupy the airport, while the invasion force took up positions surrounding the property on three sides.

In addition to preventing the Nicosia airport from falling into Turkish hands, the action defined a new style of peacekeeping: active intervention between opposing sides rather than passively occupying ground between them.

CHAPTER 1

Meat for the Sausage Machine

APRIL 1970

Small eddies of snow drifted over my well-shined boots as I stood rigidly to attention at the edge of the parade square. From the corner of my eye I could see the commanding officer (CO) and his entourage slowly making their way toward me. I desperately wanted to move around and try to get some feeling back into my legs and arms, but I knew full well that any movement would only serve to bring down the full wrath of the ever-watchful sergeant major. Even through the layers of my combat shirt and coat, I could feel the cold metal of my rifle as it pressed against my side. In spite of the leather gloves, the fingers of my right hand had become stiff and numb from holding onto the pistol grip. All I could do undetected was slowly wiggle my fingers inside the glove in an effort to restore circulation.

I wasn't worried about the mock briefing I was about to give. I had gone over it so many times I could practically say it in my sleep. My only fear was that the numbness in my arms and upper body would cause me to drop the rifle as I tried to salute. Thankfully, when the CO stopped three paces in front of me all my moving parts still worked.

Once the formal salute was out of the way I could move about freely as the CO questioned me about my observation post (OP) duties and responsibilities. "And where exactly is your area of responsibility?" the colonel asked.

"My task is to watch this section of the 'Green Line' from that road junction to the west, to that corner to the east." As I spoke the words I could not help but feel rather silly as I pointed off to the imaginary road network to the left and right.

"What about communications with headquarters and the other positions?"

"Every hour on the hour we carry out an all stations radio check, and if that fails we can contact the headquarters using the field telephone," I said, pointing at the empty space behind me.

After a few more questions, the colonel seemed satisfied, as he quickly departed for the next mock observation post just thirty metres further down the parade square.

Once the CO and his entourage finished and disappeared into the headquarters building we were finally dismissed and could head for the warmth of the barracks.

Had it not been such a cold spring day I may have actually found this exercise rather funny, but after yet another bitterly cold March morning standing on the side of the parade square, I just felt thoroughly ridiculous.

The first battalion of the Royal Canadian Regiment was just thirty days away from departing for a six-month tour of duty with the United Nations, on the island of Cyprus. I may have only been a junior corporal, with absolutely no U.N. experience, but even I could see the absurdity of standing in a March snowdrift practising for a summer tour of duty on a tropical island in the eastern Mediterranean. The average daily temperature in Nicosia, Cyprus, when we arrived in April was expected to be twenty-five degrees Celsius and would only continue to rise as we got further into the summer.

By the end of March 1970 the winter finally began to show signs of losing its grip. When the last mounds of snow melted away in early April, our preparations were almost complete. All that remained were a few of the more important, but generally unpleasant tasks that had to be completed before departure.

When you are growing up poor in Toronto's Cabbagetown, seeing a dentist is not something very high on your priority list. On the few occasions when the school forced us to go to the dental clinic the entire experience had proved painful, in every sense of the word. The school would send us up to a large brownstone building on College Street, which I quickly learned was a school of dentistry.

As a twelve year old fidgeting nervously in the chair, it was difficult to tell who was more frightened, me or the dental student standing over me with a sharp pointy instrument shaking in his hand. The older man standing in the back was obviously the teacher, but usually his first indication that the student had done something wrong was the scream of the helpless victim sitting in the chair.

The fact that the dentists in the military were fully qualified gave me little comfort. The level of skill may have evolved somewhat, but personally I found the experience was as painful as ever. I may not have known or understood the mechanics of dentistry, but judging from the speed with which patients were being pumped through the dental office each day, the number of extractions far exceeded the number of teeth being filled.

After five years in the military and twice annual visits, many of my back teeth had already been sacrificed to time and efficiency, but what remained were at least in relatively decent shape. That is not to say I wasn't still anxious and a little nervous every time I entered a dental office. There was always the chance another cavity would be found and my overworked dentist would once again be faced with the decision to spend ninety minutes fixing it or thirty minutes yanking it out.

It may have been a cool April morning, but the dry heat of the over-crowded waiting room only served to add to my anxiety. By the time my name was called that morning I was already swearing profusely, but after some initial sticking, scraping, and probing, the dentist finally declared me fit for duty.

After drawing our weapons from the armoury one early morning our company loitered on the grass behind the building, waiting for the sergeant major to arrive. The mood was light as we all stood around joking and laughing. Today promised to be an easy day on weapons training on the twenty-five-yard range.

Even after the sergeant major arrived and we formed up in three ranks, the horseplay continued. We all knew that the sergeant major was not the most patient man and he soon took control of the company in his usual fashion. "Shut the hell up and pay attention!" After a moment of complete silence, waiting to ensure he had our full attention, he finally spoke. "Well, gents, it seems that someone has screwed up the range booking and we will have to wait until later in the week." *Damn*, I thought, *now we will have to spend another morning standing around the parade square pretending to man an observation post.* Judging by the amount of cursing and grumbling throughout the group, most were probably thinking the same thing. "If you ladies are finished whining, I'll go on." The sergeant major grinned sarcastically. "You won't get to shoot at targets today, but that doesn't mean someone can't shoot at you." We were all more than a little puzzled, as he stood silently waiting for his words to sink in. At last he continued with a huge grin of his face. "When I fall you out I want you to return your weapons to the lock-up and fall back out here for needles parade."

Slowly we moved in through the big hanger doors in the drill hall. None of us were too anxious to be first, but that didn't much matter because barely had we cleared the door before the duty sergeant began yelling for us to strip to the waist. Again, we all took our time unbuttoning our shirts while pretending to look in vain for an empty clothes hook on the cinder block wall. The sergeant began yelling impatiently for us to hurry up, as the last man gingerly fell in to the rear rank.

I had managed to delay long enough to get a spot in the back of the group, but quickly discovered that all my efforts not to be the first one stabbed by the waiting medics were wasted. "Right, when I call your name, form up in a single file facing me!" the sergeant shouted. We should have known. Military parades, whether it is for needles or to issue equipment, or even get paid, were all done alphabetically. For someone with the name "Burke," this was good, most of the time. On the twice monthly pay parades, when each man picked up and signed for his pay, it could be a very long day in line if your name was Zink and you had eight hundred men standing in front of you.

When one thinks of getting a needle, the experience normally involves simply rolling up your sleeve for the smiling doctor or nurse, who gently rubs the area clean with an alcohol swab, inserts the needle, and then removes it while telling you what a good and brave soul you are. Military needles parades are nothing like that.

The medics were lined up about a metre apart and facing each other. Rather than a simple single hypodermic, each one held a needle gun, capable of firing a shot of serum into our waiting arms. Our job was to walk through the gauntlet of needles, with both arms by our sides. The trick was to keep moving slowly forward, always looking straight ahead as each medic, in turn, stuck his gun against your dangling arm and fired.

Getting through the needles parade was only half the battle. Having been shot full of all manner of liquids for everything from yellow fever, to typhoid, to polio, and God knows what else, we now faced the inevitable after effects of all of these drugs coursing through our bodies.

Having had most of the shots before going to Germany, I was well aware that within a couple of hours all of my limbs would begin to stiffen up, to the point where it was difficult and painful to even swing my arms. Soon after that you begin to feel quite lethargic and want nothing more than to lie down and curl up in a ball. Death or at least unconsciousness would be a welcome relief at this point.

We may have seen ourselves as sick, pathetic creatures who wanted nothing more than to be left alone, but that was not about to happen. The army and its doctors had decided, in their wisdom, that leaving us alone to die was not the right answer. Quite the opposite, their solution to bring us back from this near-death experience was to take us to the gym for a hard physical workout.

We presented a less-than-inspiring picture as our entire company of corpse-like soldiers went through a series of exercises, including jogging, sit ups, push ups, and knee bends, all the while trying to keep down what little food we had left in our stomachs. As the physical training instructor told us with a look of disgust, "You fucking people look like death warmed over."

Of course the army was right. The exercises were designed to get these magic liquids flowing through our bloodstream and get the stiffness out of our joints. By the next morning, we would all feel much better, in spite of ourselves.

By early April 1970, the activity surrounding the imminent departure for Cyprus was reaching a fever pitch. Mornings were packed with everything from practical exercises to lectures on weapons, vehicles, and radio equipment.

Afternoons were devoted to administration. One-hundred-and-one details on each person had to be checked and then checked again. The paperwork alone was daunting. Forms for security clearance took at most a few hours, but for former immigrants like me, it took days of gathering information on everything from the birthdays of each family member, to the dates and locations of every job I had ever held, and, most difficult of all, finding the flight number of the aircraft I had arrived from Ireland on some thirteen years earlier.

To deal with the sheer volume of paperwork required on each individual, the army had long ago invented a process they called The Departure Assistance Group. The soldiers in the battalion preferred to use a much more descriptive term. We simply called it The Sausage Machine.

The term itself was an apt description of what actually happened.

The training building was set up with a series of desks lining the entire length of the hallway. The clerk at each desk had a specific function, from checking identification cards, to ordering dog tags, sorting out next of kin forms, to confirming that each person had an up-to-date will completed.

As the term "sausage machine" would imply, each soldier, armed with a blank clearance form, would enter the building through the front door. The soldier being processed was not unlike a piece of raw meat being fed into the front of the machine. He would report to each desk, where he would be processed through one of many administrative steps, getting his clearance form stamped and signed by the clerk before moving on down the line. By the time the soldier exited through the back door of the training building some hours later, he was like a well packaged piece of meat ready to be shipped out.

CHAPTER 2

Knowing Enough to Be Dangerous

It had been a long, tiring flight, but after a full seventeen hours we could finally step out into the fresh air of a hot and hazy Cyprus evening. It had been cool enough to wear our winter combat jacket when we departed Trenton on the first leg of our journey. Even during our brief stopover for refuelling, in Germany we were only too happy to have our coats and gloves to protect us from the cold spring rain.

It may have been well past seven o'clock, but the sun still shined brightly on the hot tarmac of Nicosia Airport. I could feel the small beads of sweat slowly streaming down my back. Like everyone around me, I would have loved nothing more than to peel off my thickly lined jacket, but that was not to be. So we stood there grumbling in the sweltering heat, waiting for someone to finally give us the word. One individual had actually been so bold as to fall in with his jacket partly undone. It took only a minute for the sergeant to chastise the offender and tell him to rebutton his coat to the neck.

As the sergeant major so often said, "Uniformity is the key, gentlemen. I'll decide what you wear and I'll let you know when you are hot or cold." After thirty minutes standing in the unaccustomed heat, he finally relented and we were allowed to remove our combat jackets and stuff them into our kit bags. You could hear an audible sigh of relief throughout the ranks as we finally felt the breeze touching our overheated bodies.

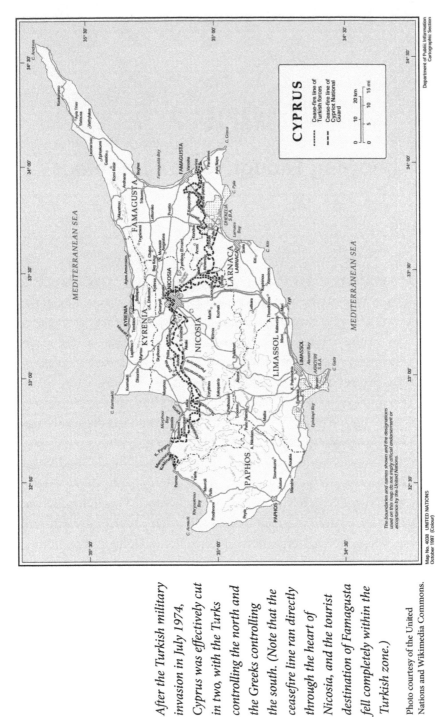

After the Turkish military invasion in July 1974, Cyprus was effectively cut in two, with the Turks controlling the north and the Greeks controlling the south. (Note that the ceasefire line ran directly through the heart of Nicosia, and the tourist destination of Famagusta fell completely within the Turkish zone.)

Photo courtesy of the United Nations and Wikimedia Commons.

"Pay attention!" the sergeant major screamed over the noise of a C130 Hercules aircraft taxiing down the runway behind us. "When I call your name, fall out to the right."

Lloyd Wells, my Newfie friend and roommate for the next six months, stood next to me. When he looked at me and shook his head I knew we were both thinking the same thing. The roll had been called just before we boarded the plane in Germany. Why were they calling it now? We had come off the plane and moved about ninety metres. How could anything have possibility changed? My mind was somewhere else and when my name was called I completely missed it. "Corporal Burke!" The sergeant major yelled for the second time. "Well now, isn't it nice of you to finally join us." His voice was steeped in sarcasm, but thankfully he let it go and called the next name.

After calling the first fifteen names on the Alfa Company roll he stopped. It took a few minutes to register, but based on the grumbling whispers in our little group of fifteen I knew I was once again a victim of having a name near the beginning of an alphabetical list.

By the time our bus transport appeared on the tarmac it was well past dark. I still had the faintest glimmer of hope that I might be wrong about the fate of our little group. We were all tired after the prolonged flight and looking forward to a little rest before assuming our new duties on the Green Line, but as soon as the sergeant major opened his mouth, we knew it was not to be. "You fifteen stand fast," he said, looking in our direction. "The rest of you board the buses."

Once the bus convoy pulled away, our forlorn little group just stood there waiting for the axe to fall.

The company sergeant major had departed with the buses, leaving us under the command of one very pissed-off master corporal. We were standing there simply because our names were the first fifteen on the nominal roll. Master Corporal Jack Lynch was there because of some smart remark he had made within earshot of the sergeant major. His outburst had initially cost him five extra duties, but when that failed to shut him up, the punishment had immediately doubled.

Master Jack, as we all called him, was one of those soldiers who seemed to attract trouble at every turn. He and I had spoken many times and there was no doubt he was one extremely intelligent individual. The majority of the time it was his sharp intellect that seemed to be the root of his problems. As the saying goes, "He did not suffer fools gladly." When statements were made or orders given that Jack deemed to be incorrect or downright stupid, he just could not keep his thoughts to himself.

After a less than enthusiastic briefing by Master Jack, we were quickly loaded aboard a waiting truck for the short drive to the company headquarters, which straddled the Green Line in the western suburbs of Nicosia.

The aircraft that had brought us to the island was already being refuelled and inspected. In just a few hours it would depart with the unit we were replacing. After six months on the island of Cyprus, the soldiers of the Black Watch Regiment of Canada would be leaving and our battalion would be assuming command.

The last fifteen soldiers from the Black Watch were still manning all the Alfa Company observation posts and impatiently waiting for us to arrive and relieve them.

As I made my way along the narrow road I swung the flashlight beam back and forth, looking for the dirt track leading off into the darkness. "It has to be here somewhere," I mumbled to myself. The duty corporal had been kind of vague in the directions he had given. This was his last shift before going home and he was only interested in turning things over to Master Corporal Lynch so he could make a quick exit. When I tried to question his hasty directions, he just dismissed me with a wave of his hand. "Just keeping going down the road and watch for a dirt track running off to your right. Don't worry, you can't miss it."

With every step further into the darkness, I was losing what little confidence I had. I couldn't help but smile when I remembered that well-known phrase the duty corporal had used. "Don't worry, you can't miss it." Why was it when someone said "you can't miss it," you invariably did? Just as I was about to give up and start backtracking, I saw the dark outline of a path snaking off to the west. After following the path for a couple of hundred metres of nothing but complete blackness, I finally topped a small rise and there before me I could see the distant flood lights illuminating the Green Line. I was still about 275 metres from the OP I had been assigned to take over, but I could already see the faint outline of a soldier looking in my direction. Once I reached the end of the dirt track and stepped out of the shadows and onto the main road, the soldier in the distance sprung into action.

Now that I realized I was heading in the right direction, I knew I could relax a little. When the duty corporal back at the platoon headquarters finished his briefing, I still had a number of unresolved questions swirling around in my head. "Not to worry," he said with obvious impatience, "the man you're replacing will explain everything you need to know."

As I continued to move cautiously along the unfamiliar road, I couldn't help but become a little concerned as I watched this soldier galloping toward me. Surely this couldn't be the guy I'd be replacing? Unfortunately it was.

When the soldier and I were just metres apart, he finally slowed down. His entire face was stretched in a huge grin as he stopped to greet me. "Here is your weapon." He thrust the submachine gun (SMG) into my hands and took but a second to catch his breath. "You'll find a duty book telling you everything you need to know in the OP." I wanted to ask him all kinds of questions, but as he spoke he continued to move away from me. Almost like an afterthought, he yelled over his shoulder. "Don't forget the radio check and frequency change at midnight." I stood there in a daze as his figure got smaller and smaller in the distance. "What is the new radio frequency?" I shouted after him through the darkness. "Look in the duty book!" he screamed back just before disappearing into the night.

I stood there for a few moments surveying my surroundings. Here I was, standing alone on the Green Line, in downtown Nicosia, and I had absolutely no idea what I was supposed to do. The only thing that was clear to me was the fact that I would be out here alone for at least the next three hours and I had gleaned only enough information about my job to be a danger to myself.

I did know that I was now standing on what was considered to be the most active and volatile section of the Green Line. From our many intelligence briefings back in Canada, I knew that particular stretch of road had a higher number of shootings and other incidents than any other part of the entire island. In this heavily built-up area of the city, the Green Line was nothing more than a two-lane street, with Turkish and Greek positions facing each other across the narrow divide. All that separated the opposing groups was a small outpost, with a U.N. soldier patrolling the road between them.

My position was call sign 21 Bravo, and as I stood at the intersection next to my outpost, the floodlit street allowed me to clearly see call sign 21 Alfa, which was about eight hundred metres to the west. Although I couldn't see it, I knew our other platoon OP, call sign 21 Charlie, was positioned on the roof of a wool factory somewhere off to the south. I had briefly considered heading down to speak to my counterpart on 21 Alfa, but looking at my watch I suddenly realized I had less than fifteen minutes to the next radio check.

The observation post was nothing more than a wood frame and corrugated tin hut with a small U.N. flag and radio antenna protruding from the roof. The entire structure was only slightly larger than a phone booth. The back wall contained a narrow shelf with just enough room to hold a laminated map, a duty log book, and the all-important radio.

A Canadian soldier mans an outpost on the outskirts of Nicosia, 1970.

Photo courtesy of the Royal Canadian Regiment Museum, London, Ontario.

After surveying my tiny domain I was beginning to feel a little more confident. It had only taken me a few minutes to scan the log book and find the four-digit number I would need to change the radio frequency at midnight. *So far so good*, I thought to myself. Perhaps I could get through this first night without screwing up. That's when I spotted the radio and immediately knew I had a problem.

In the weeks leading up to our departure, we had done a good deal of refresher training on all the equipment we would use on the mission. When it came to communications, at least four lessons had been devoted to the 25 Radio Set, which was the standard radio used throughout the military. The set-up and operation of the 25 Set could not have been easier. The large rectangular battery fitted into the recess at the bottom. Once you flicked the switch on top to the "on" position, all that remained was to rotate the illuminated dials to the four-digit code and the radio would automatically calibrate to the correct frequency.

The ten minutes I had remaining until the midnight frequency change would have been more than enough time, if only I had a 25 Set to do the job. It took a moment to register, but at least I knew what type of radio it was. I just kept staring at it, almost willing it to change.

The 510 Radio Set may not have been an antique, but it was certainly older than me. I did remember seeing it during basic training six years earlier, but never again since. The 510 Set was not a bad piece of equipment and worked quite well once it was in operation. The problem was that the process of setting it up could be difficult and time consuming. Unlike the newer radio sets that calibrated the frequency automatically, all of the calibrations on the 510 had to be done manually.

I could clearly see the Turk and Greek positions some forty metres on either side of me, but I had not seen any signs of life since I arrived. As I started to work through my radio problem I was sure my cursing and swearing must have alerted the sentries.

I knew it was extremely asinine to take out my anger and frustration on an inanimate object, but I have to admit I felt better after I picked up the radio and slammed it back down on the shelf. I just found it incredible that in all those hours of communication training back home, no one had thought to mention that we would be using a radio left over from the

Korean War. My little temper tantrum aside, another glance at my watch told me I better calm down and get to work. It had been six years since I had gotten a lesson on the 510 Radio Set, but from the deep recesses of my mind, the main teaching points were slowly coming back to me.

The small rubber earphone gave me some trouble, but after a little wrestling I finally managed to screw the cable jack into the recess. With one hand holding the rubber piece to my ear, I slowly adjusted the frequency dial with my other hand. It took a moment but finally I heard the low-pitched tone I was listening for. I continued to adjust the calibration dial slowly, as the tone increased and then slowly decreased. What I was looking for was the "Zero Beat," the point where the tone reaches the highest point in the apex and then begins to decrease. Thankfully the night was generally quiet as I cupped the rubber piece around my ear and strained to hear the low-pitched tone. After two or three attempts, I finally reached what I thought was the zero beat. The only sound I could hear was my own heavy breathing as I carefully withdrew my hand and sat waiting in the dark. It was less than three minutes to midnight and now all I could do was sit, staring at the radio, hoping to hear a human voice coming through the static. The minutes ticked by and still I heard nothing. At four minutes past the hour the radio suddenly sprung to life. "All stations, this is call sign 2, radio check, over." It took a number of repeated calls before all the stations on the company network finally responded. Judging by the lateness of the call and the hesitation in most of the voices, it was obvious that the majority of us, including the duty corporal at the headquarters, were having similar difficulties adjusting to our new and unfamiliar duties.

Up to now I hadn't paid much attention to my new surroundings. Once the radio had fallen silent all the other night sounds seemed to be amplified. The Green Line itself was illuminated with floodlights, but all the houses, buildings, and fields on the fringes were steeped in darkness. I couldn't see much, but all around me I could hear the many noises of a city at night.

Somewhere not too far away I heard the bark of a dog. In the distance a truck motor roared to life and slowly the noise faded as the truck moved further away. Even the ordinary sound of a toilet flushing in a nearby house seemed oddly loud.

The Greek and Turk positions were just metres away but both were completely quiet. If not for their national flag flying over each position, I would have been hard pressed to distinguish one faction from the other. Each had commandeered a house on their side of the Green Line. What had once been someone's home now took on the look of an armed fortress. Even in the dark I could see a scattering of bullet holes peppering the walls of each house. All of the window glass had been long ago removed and now a sandbag wall filled the frame. In the middle of each frame a sandbag had been removed to allow a rifle or machine to be fired through the small open parapet.

I knew I wasn't alone when I heard a muffled couch coming from the Turk position. I slowly made my way toward the edge of the road to get a closer look. As I stood there straining to see through the gloom, I could almost feel that I was being watched. Just as I was about to turn around, I caught a glimpse of something out of the corner of my eye. The sudden tiny amber glow of flame quickly faded, but I knew it could only be one thing. I waited patiently, staring at the same spot, and after a moment I saw the shadowy figure take another drag on his cigarette. Considering I was standing on a floodlit street, I am sure he could see me clearly, but thankfully he remained silent behind his barricade.

I fully intended to try and make contact with these Greek and Turk soldiers and hopefully gain some better insight into what these people and this conflict were all about. But that was something for later when I had some "on the ground" experience and gained more confidence in my ability to do the job effectively.

Right now my only hope was that this first night would end without incident. I knew I didn't have a clue what I was doing out here, but the sentries on either side of me didn't need to know they were dealing with a complete novice.

By the end of my second hour on duty I had circled the intersection in front of my OP for about the fiftieth time and still couldn't stop shaking. I knew it was too late now, but that didn't stop me from cursing my decision to leave my combat jacket with my kit bag, back at the platoon headquarters. Somewhere in the past I remember reading about climate change in a desert environment. Just a few hours ago I had been standing on the tarmac of Nicosia Airport, watching and feeling the slow waves of heat rising from the asphalt runway, and now here I was, shivering under the clear night sky, with nothing more than thin nylon shirt to stave off the cold.

I had to stay within earshot of the radio, so all I could really do was keep moving in a small circle. I had briefly considered calling Master Corporal Lynch, but thought better of it. Jack was performing the first of many extra duties and had been in a foul mood ever since we left the airport. The hasty briefing he received from the outgoing duty corporal only served to make matters worse. A couple of the stations had been late in responding to the one o'clock radio check, and judging by Jack's barking voice when they finally answered, his mood had not improved. He and I normally got along quite well, but I was not about to ask him to deliver a coat.

Shortly before three the night sky was lit by the glow of trace ammunition streaking across the horizon. I watched and counted each long burst of machine-gun fire. It took a moment for the sound to reach me. The noise made by automatic weapons fire at night had always reminded me of something being torn or ripped apart. Judging by the time it took for the low muffled sound to reach me, I knew the source must have been many kilometres away. I waited a full five minutes for someone to come on the air and report the shooting, but the radio remained silent. Surely someone closer must have heard it. I quickly scanned the map and jotted some notes in the margin. After a few more seconds of self-doubt, I took a deep breath and depressed the send button on the handset. "Call sign 2 this is 21 Bravo Shot rep, over." Even though a shooting report had a relatively simple format, I still kept going over my notes as I waited for headquarters to answer. It took two attempts before I got a very curt response.

"Call sign 21 Bravo wait out." Knowing Master Corporal Lynch as I did, I am sure he was swearing at me as he fumbled around trying to find the correct form. "Call sign 21 Bravo send your message." During the practice exercises back in London, I could send one of these reports in a split second, without the benefit of written notes. Now that it was real, I took a full minute just to study the map and the info I had scribbled in the margin. Again I took a deep breath before hitting the send button. Even the sound of my own voice sounded foreign to me as I spoke in a very slow and precise manner.

"Call sign 2 this is 21 Bravo, Shot rep. Three machine-gun bursts of approximately fifty rounds were seen being fired from an area approximately sixteen kilometres northwest of my position. Area of impact unknown, damage unknown, over." Again I waited patiently for him to come back. I knew the report was sketchy with a lot of unknowns, but I could only report what I saw. I fully expected to be asked for more detail, so his hasty reply was a little surprising.

"21 Bravo this is 2, message acknowledged, out."

I sat there just staring at the radio, afraid to move in case he came back on seeking some clarification, but after a few minutes of unbroken static, I resumed my little circular patrol route around the OP. Each time I reached the centre of the intersection, I stopped and scanned the length of the road, looking and hoping to see some sign of my relief.

When my replacement finally arrived at four o'clock I was dog tired and shivering from head to toe. Naturally my replacement had numerous questions on this, his very first shift. Remembering how unsure I had been just four hours earlier, I stood there and tried to be as thorough as possible.

As I made my way back to the platoon headquarters I felt a sudden surge of confidence. Maybe I wasn't as clueless as I thought. I chuckled to myself as I trod down the winding path. The brisk walk was giving me some new sense of energy as I tried doing some mental arithmetic. My first OP duty was complete and now there were only one hundred and thirty nine more shifts to go.

CHAPTER 3

Life on the Green Line

I have to admit to feeling a little depressed when I first laid eyes on it in the grey pre-dawn light. If it looked this bad at four o'clock in the morning, how much worse would it look in the light of day? All I could do was stand there and shrug my shoulders. It may not have been much to look at, but at least it had a roof and four walls. Like it or not, it would have to do.

Bullet holes peppered the entire front wall of the one-storey building. The window frame at the top of the main door had a large piece of cardboard taped over the opening where the glass used to be. After some initial fumbling, I finally managed to find the light switch. The single bulb dangling from the high ceiling only provided enough light to see part way down the narrow hallway. As I made my way along the corridor I could hear snoring coming from most of the rooms. I was having some difficulty seeing through the gloom, but based upon the smell I knew the toilet had to be off to my right behind one of the closed doors. A small pool of grey light shining through the window on the back wall was all I needed to find what I was looking for — the last room on the right.

This little cinderblock school house, just metres away from the Green Line, would be home for me and roughly half of our twenty-four-man platoon for the next six months.

At least the one large window in our room still had all its glass intact. I didn't want to turn on the overhead light and disturb my roommate, curled up on the bed behind the door. Once I found my kit bag sitting on top of the other bed, next to the window, I quickly set to work unpacking. Checking out the entire room would have to wait until later. Right now I was only interested in finding my sleeping bag and crashing for the next few hours.

Our platoon headquarters, along with the remainder of our troops, would be housed just a few metres up the road in what used to be the Public Works Department (PWD) for the city of Nicosia. With the outbreak of civil war in the early sixties the entire complex had been abandoned by the locals and was quickly taken over by the U.N. The PWD encompassed a large parcel of land surrounded on three sides by a two-metre stone wall. A single-storey red-brick building stretched across the front of the compound. The work yard behind the building looked like a vast wasteland of dilapidated sheds and workshops. Most of the garages and maintenance bays no longer had doors. Everything from bulldozers to front end loaders and maintenance trucks sat abandoned throughout the yard. Years of unrelenting summer heat followed by winter rains had turned most of the machines to rusted piles of junk.

We were barely into the first month of our tour and already the average daily temperature was an absolutely stifling thirty-eight degrees Celsius. All of the OP shifts has started out being three hours long, but we soon discovered that standing on the Green Line in mid-afternoon could be downright dangerous. OP 21 Charlie was always the worse duty of all, but working there for the noon to three shift brought its own particular brand of torture. This observation post was considered one of the most important positions on the entire Green Line. From its location on top of a six-storey factory one had an unobstructed view over the entire city centre. The position may have been strategically important, but for the observer on duty it could be three hours of torture just standing there, completely exposed to the elements.

They say it is a soldier's lot to complain, but if the truth be told, we really didn't have that much to bitch about. Sure it was hot, but what would you expect the weather to be like on a tropical island in the middle of summer? It may have been too hot to eat in the mess hall, but there was certainly nothing wrong with the food. I remember the envy I felt seeing these same cooks on winter exercise back in Canada. We would line up to get our food and then have to head back out into the winter cold. They could stay there all day in the warmth of the kitchen tent. Now I just felt sorry seeing them standing there dripping sweat in the sauna-like kitchen and trying to cook over those huge M37 burner stoves.

Our little room in the school house may have been plain and austere, but it was better than sleeping outdoors. Keeping the doors and windows open at both ends of the building did allow an easy entry for the lizards, mice, and other rodents, but at least we had a little breeze to combat the oppressive heat. On more than one occasion I awoke to a salamander scurrying across my chest, or received a fright when a mouse jumped out as I opened a drawer. It happened so often it almost became commonplace. It wasn't the rodents that bothered me as much as the spiders and snakes. Every time I went to bed I would first grab the end of the sleeping bag and shake it violently to ensure that when I got in I was alone. Before getting dressed I would perform the same shaking ritual with my boots.

When it came to the soldiers in our platoon, I felt truly fortunate. After returning from Germany just three months earlier I had been posted into Alfa Company, where I knew only a handful of the soldiers. The pre-deployment training may have been rather unrealistic, but at least the shared experience gave us an opportunity to learn each other's strengths and weaknesses. By the time we boarded the aircraft for Cyprus, we were one tight, cohesive group.

Certainly there would be a number of arguments and disagreements over the months ahead. Sometimes tempers would flare and fists would fly, but that was rare. Considering we lived in such close quarters, with no place else to go, the majority of us got along amazingly well.

Two of our section commanders were older sergeants approaching the end of their careers. It was obvious by their demeanour that they knew how to do just enough to get by. Like most of the soldiers, it had only taken me a couple of shifts to figure them out. If I showed up on time and didn't do anything completely stupid, they just left me alone. Our third section commander was a completely different story. I always had difficulty trying to figure out Master Corporal Lynch. I sometimes think his strange behaviour was just an odd little game he liked to play, so we were always on our guard. Prior to going on any shift, we were required to appear at the platoon office for inspection. If Jack was the duty NCO you never knew what to expect. Sometimes he would barely acknowledge your presence. He would simply glance up from whatever it was he was doing and tell you to carry on. Other times he would circle around you as you stood to attention. It could be three o'clock in the morning, but a wrinkle in your pant leg or a fleck of dirt on your boots would be enough to send you running back to the quarters for repairs.

On one occasion, in the middle of the night, after I had been inspected twice and given a lecture on paying attention to detail, I was finally allowed to depart for duty. Roughly an hour into my shift, Jack suddenly appeared out of the darkness. Unfortunately for me, his unannounced arrival caught me breaking one of the rules. In the instructions it was very clearly stated that we were to continually patrol our area of responsibility. When Jack came around the corner, there I was sitting on the stone wall across from the OP. My weapon and my hat lay unattended beside me while I smoked a cigarette. I grabbed my submachine gun and jammed my hat back on my head, but it was far too late. I had been caught red handed. I started to blubber some lame excuse but he just waved his arms and smiled. "Relax, take a seat," was all he said before plopping himself down on the wall. He pulled a small flask from his pocket and poured the contents into a cup.

"I just wanted to get out of the office for a while. So how are things going?" We sat there together talking casually and sharing his flask of coffee for about thirty minutes. "Well, I better head back to the office," he finally said as he jumped down from the wall, crushed his cigarette butt, and headed off into the night. I would never call us close friends, but we did get to know each other over the years. In all that time the only thing I did know about him for sure was that he was completely unpredictable.

Soon after leaving Cyprus, Jack and I went our separate ways and it would be more than twenty years before I saw him again. When we ran into each other again in the summer of 1993, Jack had been long retired. As I grabbed his hand to shake it I should have noticed, but I was too busy babbling on about the old days. When I finally stopped to take a breath there was only silence. Gone were the sharp retort and quick wit he had become famous for over the years. He just stared at me and smiled. He had absolutely no idea who I was. As his wife later told me, Jack was in the latter stages of dementia. He died in a Toronto hospital a year or so later.

Strangely enough, one of the things that drew us all together into a tight-knit group was our shared dislike for the two people running our platoon.

In our six months on the island I don't believe I ever heard anyone utter a positive word about our platoon warrant officer. He just seemed to exude an air of arrogance toward everyone around him. I learned very early on that he was not one for small talk.

On the few morning parades he held his manner was always short and to the point. He never asked if there were any questions. Once he finished speaking, he would simply tell one of the NCOs to take over and he would turn and leave. He and I crossed paths one early morning as I made my way toward the office.

"Good morning, warrant," was all I said, as we passed on the roadway.

"Who the fuck made you the weather man," he said, scowling, and kept walking.

Because the Public Works Department was such a large and secure facility, much of the material used to repair and maintain the observation posts was stored there. The pioneer platoon staff who did the repair work would show up periodically to pick up or drop off whatever was necessary to do the job. One afternoon, about a month into the tour, two of the pioneers showed up with a load of gravel. Our platoon warrant met them at the front gate and announced his intention to search their truck before they would be allowed to leave. According to the warrant, some tools had gone missing, and these guys were his chief suspects. Naturally they didn't take well to being called thieves and a loud argument ensued. After about ten minutes of shouting the driver looked like he was giving up and he jumped back into his truck. The warrant's smile of victory was quickly erased as the hydraulic lift slowly started to rise and the gravel started to pour from the back of the dump truck. Once the massive pile of gravel was neatly deposited in the middle of the entrance, the truck pulled away. Those of us who had witnessed the confrontation had a hard time suppressing our laughter, but that soon changed. A couple of hours later we didn't find it nearly as funny as we laboured to fill wheelbarrow upon wheelbarrow and slowly lug the gravel to the back of the building.

For the next five months, neither side gave an inch. The warrant wouldn't allow a vehicle into the compound without a search and the pioneers would simply drop off every delivery at the front gate. The only ones suffering were the off-duty soldiers who had to manhandle the lumber, gravel, paint, or bags of cement into the compound.

Our platoon warrant officer may have been an extremely obtuse individual, but at least with him you always knew where you stood. The young lieutenant running our platoon gave all the illusion of being a friendly, approachable officer, but we soon learned that appearances can be deceiving.

One particularly hot afternoon I had been sent out to the back compound to rearrange some recently delivered stores. I was just an hour away from going on duty and didn't want to ruin my shirt with sweat. With my shirt and hat placed neatly nearby, I set to work stacking the corrugated iron sheets and lumber. Within minutes the thin green T-shirt I wore was already soaked with perspiration. I was so intent on my work and hadn't heard our platoon commander come up behind me.

"How are you doing there, Corporal Burke?"

"Good, sir," I quickly answered. He just smiled and continued up the path and disappeared around the building. Only a few minutes later I heard the duty NCO calling my name as he came around the corner. He almost sounded apologetic as he spoke.

"You are improperly dressed, Burke. Consider yourself on extra duties." I just stood there, open mouthed with the sweat dripping off me. "You can thank our illustrious leader for that," he said with a half-hearted smile.

His underhanded approach was bad enough, but as the tour went on, his behaviour toward the soldiers under his command only became more bizarre. Perhaps four or five times each week, usually during the hours of darkness, our young platoon commander would sneak out of his room, jump on his bike, and head out on an inspection of the outposts. Even the duty NCO was not told of his departure for fear he would warn those of us on duty. He didn't actually visit us on the Green Line, but rather took a route that would take him around and behind our positions. Once he got within sight of the Line, he would leave the bicycle and move through the darkness on foot until he could get a clear view of each position and its occupant. Using a wall or a bush he would remain under cover, just watching to see if anyone was breaking the rules. Only after he returned at the end of his shift would the poor unfortunate soldier find out his fate from the duty NCO. Sitting down or smoking or talking to the locals would normally get you from three to five extra duties. Naturally, with a first name like Thomas, our sneaky lieutenant soon became known as "Peeping Tom."

Making small talk with the Turkish or Greek soldiers was definitely forbidden. I believed the rule was in place in case one side saw you speaking to the other and assumed you were being biased. Like most of the guys, I had started out being very tentative around them, but after a while, when most of us got to know each other by sight, it became quite difficult to ignore someone who was just trying to say hello or good morning.

The Green Line was considered "neutral ground" that neither side was allowed to enter, at least as long as they were in uniform. Soldiers on duty could not leave their side of the line, but that didn't prevent them from shouting obscenities at each other on a regular basis. I know the Greek and Turk soldiers actually lived in their positions and were forced to remain at these isolated locations, sometimes for weeks or months at a time. I couldn't blame them for becoming bored, but sometimes their frustration boiled over, and on several occasions this would escalate into shots being fired. We had the difficult job of trying to maintain some level of peace on our little corner of the war. The trick was to step in quickly and try to defuse the situation before the firing started. It felt a little like being an NHL referee caught in the middle of a fight. Of course it is much more nerve wracking when the opponents have guns instead of hockey sticks.

The majority of incidents would start from one side complaining about something the other side had done. Unfortunately for me, the first incident I had to deal with was actually caused by me trying to do my job.

One of the key points put forth by the U.N. when the ceasefire agreement was signed dealt with the defensive positions built up by either side.

Although it did allow some minor repairs, it forbade any improvements to their current fortifications. Obviously the idea was that if neither side could strengthen or improve their positions, the fortifications themselves would eventually deteriorate to the point where they would have to be abandoned. In theory it sounded simple and straightforward, but for the soldiers who had to enforce it, things could become a bit complicated when you tried to differentiate between repairs and improvements.

I was nearing the end of a long shift, but thankfully the sun was starting to peek over the horizon. By now I had at least learned to dress appropriately for those cool Cyprus nights. I still had roughly an hour to go, but as soon as the first grey light hit the Green Line, I was already scanning the road for my little friend with my morning coffee.

Bubble-Up Charlie was a true entrepreneur. He may have only been ten years old but he recognized a need and he was making a small fortune filling it. Each morning, just after first light, he would appear with steaming cups of instant coffee, precariously balanced on a large tray. At one hundred Cypriot mils, or about twenty cents Canadian, the price

Soldiers from Delta Company on the daily foot patrol through downtown Nicosia.

Photo courtesy of the Royal Canadian Regiment Museum, London, Ontario.

was quite reasonable. If you wanted powdered cream and sugar, the price jumped to 150 mils. Strangely enough Charlie never seemed to have change, so most of us just gave him a 250 mil bill and told him to keep the change. Considering you could buy a jar of instant coffee for less than a thousand mils, or one Cypriot pound, our little friend was raking in a huge profit. He may have been doing well in the morning, but during the hot summer afternoons he really made a killing. He would usually make three or four runs along the Green Line selling cold drinks. You could choose either a rather strange but tasty beverage called banana cola, or you could have the drink that gave Charlie his name: Bubble-Up Cola.

After handing over my money, I sat down on the low brick wall adjacent to the OP and wanted nothing more than to enjoy my morning coffee. I knew Peeping Tom never came sneaking around at this hour, but I still searched through the dawn light looking for his prying eyes. The Kyrenia Mountains, to the far northeast, were still not visible in the morning haze. Already the humidity was started to rise. It was going to be another exceptionally hot day.

Even though I was only a short distance away and looking directly at the Turkish position, it still took a few moments to register. "Damn it," I muttered to myself. "Don't these people realize my shift was almost over?" The new row of sandbags stretching across the top of their machine-gun pit was unmistakeable.

After gulping down the last of my coffee, I slowly made my way toward the Turkish position. By now it was full daylight and I could clearly see the sleepy sentry moving around behind the sandbag wall. He may have looked dozy, but he still had rifle tucked under his arm. I stopped well out in front of the position and waited until he looked in my direction. The guy looked like he was only half awake and I had no intention of surprising a man holding a loaded weapon. "Good morning," I said as I slowly continued forward. "Can I speak with your commander?" He moved his rifle into the ready position, but thankfully the barrel remained pointed at the ground. We stood there staring at each other, but still he said nothing. "Commander, commander," I kept repeating, as I pointed toward my shoulder, as if to indicate where an officer wore his rank. I have no idea if he understood, but after a moment he turned around and disappeared into the house. I just stood there silently waiting, not knowing if my lame attempts at communication had been understood.

When the sentry reappeared, he was accompanied by a young lieutenant who looked rather annoyed. He stood there looking quite impatient as I began trying to explain myself in pidgin English. "They are new and must be removed," I said, pointing at the offending sandbags. I was about to try explaining further, when he cut me off.

"Excuse me," he said in perfect English, "but what the hell are you talking about?" A grin of satisfaction filled his face when he realized he had caught me off guard.

"Those twenty sandbags," I said, trying to recover. "They constitute an improvement to the position and will have to be removed."

For a long moment he looked at the wall, as if he was seeing it for the first time. Finally he spoke. "That's not an improvement. It's just routine repairs." His smile told me he was beginning to enjoy our little confrontation.

"Four or five bags could be considered routine, but not twenty," I said, trying to sound as officious as possible. After a few moments of consideration, he nodded like he had arrived at a decision.

"Five sandbags are okay?" I wasn't actually sure, but I had said it and could hardly change it now.

By the time my relief arrived, fifteen of the twenty sandbags were already removed, leaving a gaping hole near the top on the wall. Each time I returned for duty, five more bags had been added. Within the month, the entire wall had been replaced, five bags at a time.

I saw the young Turkish lieutenant a few times after that, and on each encounter he would wave and say hello. I have to admit to being initially upset over the sandbag issue, but once he told me all he had been through, it was hard to hold a grudge. It turned out that his good command of English was the result of living in the U.S. for a few years. He had been in his second year of studies at Boston University when he made the fatal mistake of returning home for a holiday. After being detained at Istanbul Airport, his passport was taken from him and soon after that he was drafted into the army. When I first met him, he had already been stuck on this small outpost for months, with no end in sight. How could I fault him for wanting to make some improvements to his otherwise bleak existence?

The ever-increasing heat of July and August only served to heighten the level of tension all along the Green Line. We hadn't seen a single drop of rain since May, and everywhere you looked the terrain was brown and parched. By early afternoon the hot, dry winds would blow in off the Mediterranean Sea and whip up the sandy soil into clouds of dust hanging over the entire city. During the early summer a U.N. tanker truck would slowly make its way down the Green Line each day. A perforated hose stretched across the rear of the vehicle would spray a fine mist of water along the road to combat the dust, but by midsummer the rationing of water put an end to the spraying program.

With the unrelenting heat and lack of water, our schoolhouse barracks quickly became almost uninhabitable by noon each day. A sweating, dust-caked soldier coming off duty in the afternoon would have to wait until the water came back on at sundown to get cleaned up. The odour of unwashed bodies and toilets sitting stagnant and un-flushed permeated the entire building.

Early in the summer a few of us came up with the bright idea of building our own indoor swimming pool. It was a relatively simple plan, really. After picking out one of the many abandoned garages behind the platoon headquarters, we removed the metal door and built a cinderblock wall across the front. After filling in the cracks in the cement floor we now had a completely enclosed structure. With water only being available at night, it took us a full four days to fill our pool to one metre deep. With the dark grey walls and no lights inside our converted garage the water looked as black as oil. It took some time to get used to the cold water, but once the word spread about our little pool there always seemed to be several people lined up waiting their turn. Unfortunately our little work crew had forgotten one key engineering requirement during construction: drainage. After a day or two of unwashed bodies entering the stagnant water, a large film of greasy slime covered the surface. When the medical officer came to investigate he took one look and immediately shut down our little bacteria factory.

The excessive heat did come with one significant benefit. By noon each summer day, an uneasy quiet would settle over the entire Green

Line. As the temperature rose, the number of incidents would drop. The U.N. soldiers may have been stuck in the open, but by twelve o'clock the Turk and Greek soldiers were well undercover and hidden from the baking sun. With the approach of early evening, each side would slowly stir to life and the battle of wills would begin anew.

During those first few weeks on the island, I had felt a good deal of apprehension every time I'd gone on duty. Now, better than half way through the six-month tour, those feelings had all but disappeared. I had gained a good deal of confidence in my ability to do the job, but, like most of the soldiers I spoke to in our company, I still had a heightened sense of unease every time I entered the Green Line.

We all believed it wouldn't take much for this standoff to erupt into a full-blown war, with us caught in the middle. It didn't take a military genius to see just how thin the balance of power was between the two sides. The Greeks' army certainly outnumbered their opponents on the island, but the Turkish Air Force was among the very best equipped in the world, and from their homeland they were less than twenty minutes flying time from downtown Nicosia.

That heightened sense of unease was probably a good thing. It certainly kept us alert and watchful. All we could really do was deal with minor incidents as they occurred and hope our actions were helping to maintain the status quo.

Considering the constant heat, primitive living conditions, and pressure on the job, it is quite amazing that the majority of our soldiers held up so well. There were a number of soldiers given heavy fines or even jail time for drunkenness and fighting, but when alcohol is cheap and soldiers are packed together, they will always find ways of blowing off steam. Although I saw many a drunken soldier in the canteen or around the quarters, in my six months I never saw one on the Green Line.

Unfortunately, there were a couple of incidents that can only be described as exceedingly strange. Had anyone asked me to choose two people who would fail under pressure, their names would have never made the list.

One of the warrant officers in Delta Company disappeared one day, late in the tour. After many hours of searching, he was finally found wandering alone downtown. He was completely sober but appeared to be in a daze, not knowing where he was. When the military police tried to put him in a Jeep he insisted that he could not leave because he was "waiting to catch the train." There are no trains on the entire island of Cyprus. After a short stay in the British military hospital he was shipped home to Canada. By the time we arrived home, he had already started the process for a medical release from the military.

Personally I found the second incident much more disturbing because I watched it unfold.

Mike Desmond was the oldest corporal in our platoon. By all appearances he was an extremely conscientious, well-adjusted soldier. Whenever he went on duty, his turn-out was meticulous. With his tall, thin frame, highly shined boots, and perfectly pressed uniform, he could have been the poster boy for U.N. soldiers. He and I had only done a few duties together, but I always found him to be an affable, easygoing individual.

Each morning after breakfast he could be seen scraping leftovers into a bag and taking it back to the quarters for what he called his pets. Long before we moved in, the Public Works Department compound had been overrun with stray cats. Every morning you could see ten or more of these strays just loitering around Mike's door, waiting to be fed. Our platoon warrant had told him to get rid of the cats, but regardless of how many times they were scared away, they always returned to Mike's room at feeding time. After a while, the warrant just stopped trying, and slowly but surely the herd multiplied.

One memorable night, near the end of the tour, I was once again scheduled for duty on OP 21 Bravo. When I arrived to relieve Mike I saw him standing near the low wall with his back to me. With his body blocking the flood light it was difficult to see, but he appeared to be arranging something on the flat surface of the wall. When I called out to him he just waved his arm but continued to work away.

When I got to him, he finally stopped and turned. I am not ashamed to admit that what I saw absolutely frightened the hell out of me. For a fleeting second I felt like running, but Mike just stood there with a twisted grin on his face. His arms were covered in blood. Large gobs of blood were dripping off the bayonet he held firmly in his right hand. "I've always wondered what made these things tick," he said, stepping away from the wall to reveal his handiwork. Laid out neatly along the top surface were the remains of at least two cats. Two heads sat staring blankly ahead. Everything from tails to internal organs was arranged in order along the wall. I cannot honestly remember what, if anything, I said. I just could not take my eyes away from the carnage. After a moment, he took a rag from the OP and slowly wiped the blood from his bayonet and placed it back in the scabbard. He tried wiping the blood from his arms but only managed to spread it around.

Mike saw no problem with his manic behaviour. In fact, he was only too willing to explain the importance of his little experiment to anyone who would listen. Once the word reached the company commander, Mike was quickly removed from all duties involving loaded weapons. As unbelievable as it sounds now, no one in a position of authority saw fit to send him home or ever to the hospital for a psychological evaluation.

I did three more shifts on OP 21 Bravo before departing, but regardless of how tired I was I could never bring myself to sit on that wall. The rains of October did manage to wash most of the evidence away, but large dark bloodstains remained imbedded in the cement.

Mike was promoted to master corporal shortly after we arrived home and for years afterward I would see him going about his daily business. He always looked like a man without a care in the world.

The trick to maintaining some level of sanity was to try and get away from the rigours of work whenever possible. Finding sufficient time could be a real problem, considering that approximately one third of the platoon was on duty at any given time. For those waiting to go on duty, there was a strict rule that prohibited the consumption of alcohol for four hours before their shift began. Show up with the smell of booze on your breath and you could be assured of a steady diet of extra duties for a very long time. Showing up drunk for duty would not only guarantee you a lengthy stay behind bars, but the unending hatred of all the soldiers who had to cover your shifts while you languished in the guardroom.

There were a good number of bars on the Greek side of the downtown, but for those of us doing daily and nightly observation post duties, it was difficult to work around that four-hour ban on alcohol. It is not easy to sit there in a crowded, noise-filled bar watching others enjoy themselves. I have no doubt that the two hundred or more soldiers that comprised Headquarters and Support Companies worked very hard at their day jobs, but I must admit to whining in envy of their unrestricted freedom at night.

As the summer wore on, we could at least look forward to our one seven-day break at the leave centre in Famagusta. Judging by the sheer volume of tourists crowding all the hotels in this coastal town, you would find it hard to believe we were in a war zone. After leaving Nicosia we had to pass through a large Turkish enclave in the centre of the island. We continued southeast for a few more hours before once again emerging back into Greek territory, near the coast. After checking into the Florida Hotel, my leave mates and I were off to the nearest bar. It only took a few steps across the street to find the first of many bars and cafes lining the narrow beachfront strip. The endless line of hotels, restaurants, and bars hugging the shore line were all teeming with life.

If not for the extreme heat and palm trees lining the street, I could have sworn we were in some English seaside resort. The Greeks may have owned everything in the city, but the tourist population was almost exclusively British. Even the chalkboard menus in the cafes and restaurants only advertised such Brit delicacies like bangers and mash or chips and eggs.

My time in Famagusta was far too short, but the opportunity to do nothing but eat, sleep, and drink far too many brandy sours was a welcome reprieve from the stresses of the job.

I made a promise to myself that somehow or other I would get back there, but little did I know that the Famagusta I would return to four years later would be nothing more than an abandoned ghost town. The wide, flat beaches would make an ideal landing area for the Turkish invasion force that would land on the island in July of 1974. By the time we returned to Cyprus, the town was firmly under the control of the Turkish military and all of the Greek population had fled inland.

Nine years later, while on my third tour, I would manage to catch a glimpse of the town, but only from a hilltop some distance away. Through my binoculars I could just make out the faint outline of the many hotels lining the beach. Most of the higher buildings appeared to have gaping holes caused by shell fire. The homes and businesses sitting back from the main road were barely visible through the weeds and underbrush that had sprung up all around them. Other than a single military truck moving down the highway and the odd stray dog, there were no signs of life anywhere. Famagusta was dead and gone.

Back in Nicosia there was a daily run to Five Mile Beach near the town of Kyrenia, but unless you had at least a twelve-hour gap between duties, it was difficult to squeeze in. The two-and-a-half ton truck departed at ten o'clock each morning and after a difficult and lengthy drive through the Kyrenia Mountains, you would arrive at the U.N. beach on the northeast coast of the island. The beach itself was quite nice, but the three hours spent bouncing around on those wooden benches in the back of the truck hardly made the trip worthwhile.

Famagusta Beach before the 1974 invasion. After the invasion the entire city became a ghost town.

Photo courtesy of the Royal Canadian Regiment Museum, London, Ontario.

I only managed to get there twice in our six-month tour, and despite the bone jarring ride in the "Deuce and a Half" truck, I found it refreshing just to get away from the heat and dust of the city. Lying there in the warm sand, breathing in the fresh sea air, I could truly relax and forget about the Green Line, at least for a few hours.

Just fifty metres or so out from the beach sat Snake Island. Calling it an island was a bit of a misnomer, considering it was more a rocky outcrop and only a few hundred metres in circumference. It may have looked small and easy to swim around, but the waters surrounding it contained a dangerous undertow. Unfortunately, these strong currents were to be the cause of our only fatality during the tour. On July 31, 1970, Private Ted Hall drowned while attempting to swim around the tiny island. Ted was in another company and, although I hadn't seen much of him since arriving in Cyprus, he and I had worked together a few times back in Canada. Ted was a quiet, unassuming kind of guy, but a good soldier who did his job without complaint.

CHAPTER 4

Returning Home to Chaos

It may have only been early autumn, but when they opened the aircraft door at London Airport the blast of cold night air caught us all by surprise. It was mid October, and after an exhausting seventeen hours in the air we were finally home.

The fifteen-minute bus ride back to Wolseley Barracks allowed just enough time for our flight commander to explain the debriefing procedures. Once our rifles were turned in to the weapons store, we would be given a short medical briefing, after which we could pick up our kit bags and finally go home.

As soon as the first man entered the drill hall, the entire building erupted into a wall of noise. Anxious wives shouted and waved trying to get the attention of their husbands. A few of the smaller children ran forward trying to find and hug their long-lost fathers. Flashbulbs popped and television camera light filled the hall. Babies cried, not knowing what all the noise and excitement was about. Even as I tried to hug my wife, a microphone was shoved into my face as some woman from the local television station peppered us with asinine questions. "How does it feel to be home?" My two-year-old daughter held firmly to my leg and tried to turn away from the outstretched microphone. "How does it feel to have your daddy home?" My ten-month-old son only screamed in protest when I tried to take him from his mother's arms. The look of fright in his eyes told me he wanted absolutely nothing to do with this man in the strange uniform.

"Right, gentlemen," the sergeant major shouted through the bedlam. "Quickly now, form up in three ranks and we can get this briefing over with."

Even after the noise died down the sergeant major still waited a few moments before speaking. The crowd was just a few metres away, but still the media people pressed forward, trying to pick up on what was being said.

With a clear plastic container and a brown paper bag held in his outstretched hands he began to speak. His loud, concise instructions were delivered with all the subtlety of a ten-pound sledgehammer.

"The doctors need to see if any of you people have picked up and disgusting little bugs while you were away. In order to do this, you will need a specimen jar." He waved the container back and forth so all of us could see. "I want you to take this home tonight and shit in it. Let there be no misunderstanding, gentlemen, I do not want your dog's shit, nor do I want your cat's shit. All I want is your shit!" He paused a moment to let his message sink in. "Tomorrow morning at nine you will report to the medical infirmary and drop off your little package, inside the paper bag."

As I left the drill hall, I couldn't help but wonder if the sergeant major's message would make it into the news the following day. Fortunately for all concerned, it did not.

To my great relief, all of my worry and concern about leaving Brigitte alone in a strange country proved to be completely unnecessary. I know it can't have been easy, but in our six months apart she never once complained. It was only after I had been back for a few days that I learned that shortly after I left my two-year-old daughter had broken her arm. When I asked Brigitte why I hadn't been told, her answer was simple. "They wouldn't let you come home over a broken arm, so why tell you when you would only worry?"

There was no doubt that we were all very happy to be home, but our joy was tempered by the knowledge that our homecoming could be short lived. The Canadian newspapers we received in Cyprus were usually about a week old, but in the days leading up to our departure only one story filled the front page of every publication. We arrived home on October 15, 1970, just three days after the Quebec government had officially requested the use of an armed military force in the province. The FLQ Crisis had begun.

I thought that surely they would leave us alone. After all, we had just gotten home from six months in Cyprus. My optimism was dashed when I watched the news the following day. Any doubt about our battalion's involvement was put to rest when the prime minister put the War Measures Act into effect.

When we reported to the barracks the morning after our homecoming, the mood was subdued. Under any other circumstances, standing there in line with a hundred or more men, all holding a smelly little "medical specimen," would have seemed hilariously funny. All the jokes were replaced by serious conversation about the impending situation. It was no longer a matter of if we would deploy, the only question was how soon it would happen. Like all the soldiers in our company, my afternoon was spent turning in my tropical kit and filling my kit bag with all the warm clothing necessary for a long winter deployment to Quebec.

The mood of the soldiers remained sombre as we boarded the bus in Wolseley Barracks that Sunday morning. "Look at the bright side," somebody joked, "at least we got two days off."

The regimental sergeant major (RSM) did not look at all happy as he stood there counting the soldiers. By the look of things the battalion was missing at least twenty or more soldiers. The RSM could rant and rave as much as he wished, but all of us knew just what had happened.

In the 1970s the leave policy could become a bit complicated. Every man in the battalion was entitled to thirty calendar days of annual leave. If you were leaving the province of Ontario, travelling days were added, depending on just how far one had to go. Going to either British Columbia or Newfoundland would give you the maximum allowance of eight days travelling time. When you returned from leave, the pass would have to be handed in with a stamp from a post office at your destination in order to prove you had actually been there. The policy was probably in effect for about ten minutes before the first soldier figured out the obvious flaw in the system. The Holiday Inn, St. John's, Newfoundland, became one of the more common addresses used, but it really didn't matter. Once you had the leave pass in your hand, you simply passed it to a Newfie who was actually going home and could easily get the pass stamped for you.

In the days leading up to our departure from Cyprus, when the leave passes were drawn up, who could have guessed that the War Measures Act would change everything. Once the government declared a state of war, the RCMP quickly fanned out all across Newfoundland. Their job was to find and order these elusive soldiers back to their home base. Imagine their surprise when they discovered that most of these soldiers had never left London. Many a charge was laid and heavy fines paid over the days and weeks that followed, but within a few days of arriving in Hull, Quebec, the battalion was back to full strength.

After the tropical heat of Cyprus, the biting cold of the Gatineau Hills in Quebec was truly a shock to the system. We had only settled in to our hastily arranged quarters in the Hull Armoury when the first call came in. It was believed that members of the FLQ cell who had abducted James Cross and Pierre Laporte were hiding somewhere in the vastness of the Gatineau Hills and our job was to find them. Three times our company deployed into the heavy underbrush in one continuous extended line, but after a lengthy search we came up with nothing. After the last futile search, one of the guys did joke that he had seen a lone man scurrying through the woods in what looked like a ragged and torn Montreal Canadiens hockey shirt. Someone else told him not to worry. It was probably just a draft dodger still hiding out from the Korean War.

When we weren't searching for our elusive enemy, our ten-man section had the unenviable task of providing a protection detail for various politicians.

Guarding them in their homes could be rather dull and boring, as we spent days and nights prodding around outside, just watching and waiting for intruders that never came.

One Member of Parliament whose name I don't wish to remember lived in a high-rise apartment building in downtown Ottawa. When he arrived home at six o'clock in the evening, he would close the apartment door behind him, leaving me and one other soldier to stand guard in the hallway until he re-emerged for work the next morning. My companion and I would sit outside that door for twelve to fourteen hours straight, without being offered so much as a glass of water.

On the first morning he came out for work, I immediately followed him down to his car in the underground parking lot. My task was to guard and escort him to his office in the west block of the Parliament buildings. It certainly wasn't easy squeezing into the backseat of his small sedan, wearing and carrying all that kit. Had anyone tried to attack us while we travelled through the city, I would have had a difficult time reacting with all that bulky equipment on my web belt and the heavy steel helmet on my head. Trying to swing my long-barrelled rifle around in such close quarters would be next to impossible.

I had just settled into the backseat when the MP turned and spoke to me for the first time. "Would you mind sitting on the floor?" he asked. It took me a moment to register the question and respond. There were a few MPs who found our presence embarrassing. A couple I had met actually thought they could take care of themselves if attacked and were far too gung-ho to need a soldier escort.

Just a few days earlier I had to perform the truly demeaning task of escorting a minister's wife while she did her grocery shopping. If he thought my presence in his car was a source of embarrassment, it didn't compare to the conspicuous feeling I had walking into a crowded supermarket. I can think of nothing more awkward or silly looking than the sight of a fully armed soldier walking behind a housewife as she slowly moved down each aisle, filling her shopping cart.

This guy is either embarrassed to be seen with me or he thinks I am nothing better than a misbehaving dog, I thought to myself. Regardless of what he was thinking, I was not about to sit on the floor. For just a moment I imagined how satisfying it would be to jam the barrel of my rifle straight up his ass.

"No, sir," I finally said, smiling. "I think I'll just stay right here." Judging by his total silence throughout the car trip, my decision did not sit well with him.

After dropping off my surly MP, I made my way to the pickup point in front of the Lord Elgin Hotel and awaited my ride back to Hull.

Standing there on the busy sidewalk with full equipment and a rifle slung over my shoulder, I could not help but feel a great sense of unease. Most of the passing pedestrians were quite friendly. Some waved and said good morning. One or two even stopped and offered me a coffee, but I just found the whole scene sadly depressing.

It was that same feeling I had when first we arrived in Cyprus. At least there I could find solace in the knowledge that this was not my fight. The struggle for Cyprus would go on, but at some point I could go home to a safe and peaceful country. Elgin Street may not have been the Green Line, but there I was, standing with a loaded weapon in the very heart of Canada's capital, just steps away from Parliament Hill. It may not have been a full-blown war, but when you have armed soldiers in the streets of downtown Ottawa, you know you have a serious problem that simply cannot be ignored.

It would be December before we finally left Quebec, but it would take much longer than that before my feelings of unease would finally disappear and some sense of normality returned.

One of the more unpleasant side effects of the FLQ Crisis was the damage done to a number of soldiers and their families. I can't put a precise figure on it, but I do know there was a significant number of separations and divorces in the battalion in the weeks and months after our return. There may have been a variety of factors involved, but the couples I knew personally all voiced the same basic reason for their decision. Six months of separation was difficult enough, but adding three more months in Quebec was just too much for many to deal with.

CHAPTER 5

The End of a Stalemate

JUNE 1974

I should have known he was lying when his lips started to move. When the company commander called me to his office in early June, I already had some idea what it was about. My new platoon warrant officer, Raymond O'Quinn, had warned me just days earlier that they were considering sending me out to Shilo, Manitoba, for the summer. Under normal circumstances, working out west as a course instructor for three months would not have been a problem, but it was what was to happen after I came home that had me truly concerned.

My friends and I all agreed that 1970 had not been a very good year. Between our Cyprus tour and the FLQ Crisis, we had spent a total of nine months away from home. All of that should have been a distant memory, but I could not help but curse my bad luck. The instructor task in Shilo, Manitoba, would probably take up the entire summer and end just in time to start the work up training before the battalion was due to depart for another tour of Cyprus. All told, it looked like I would be on the road again for nine months.

Those first few months of 1974 had started out very well for me. Not only had I been promoted to master corporal, but I had gone back to the job I enjoyed most: pioneer platoon. After a prolonged stint as a section commander in a rifle company, I would once again get to work with explosives, mine warfare, and bridging equipment. It was the opportunity to participate in a variety of tasks, with all types of equipment, which made the pioneer platoon such an interesting place to work.

Now, standing nervously in the hall, waiting to see the company commander, I could not help thinking that my good fortune was about to take a turn for the worse.

Major Leslie was his normal friendly self. As I stood at attention before his desk, he continued to make some small talk about work, the weather, and even asked about my family. *This can't be good*, I thought to myself. My belief had always been that when people make small talk in situations like this, the news is usually bad. If the news is good, people generally don't beat around the bush. I just stood there answering his mundane questions and hoping he would get to the point.

After my fourth or fifth curt response to his questions, he finally got down to business. "Right," he said, opening his notebook and scanning down the page. "The battalion has been tasked with providing four instructors for the University Officers' Training Program this coming summer. You will be employed as a section commander and instructor for this officer basic training, in Shilo, Manitoba, commencing on June 21." When I asked him when it would end, it took him a few seconds of find the date in his notebook. "It looks like the course ends on August 30, just before the Labour Day weekend." He looked up from his book. "Any other questions?" he asked, still smiling. By now I had resigned myself to my fate. Once the pre-deployment training started in September leave is not normally authorized, but I had to at least try. "Any chance I could get some annual leave in September before we deploy to Cyprus?"

The major's smile got even wider and for a second I thought he was actually taunting me. "Oh," he said "you didn't know. You're not going to Cyprus." It took a moment for that to sink in, as I continued to stare ahead blankly. "The situation in Cyprus had become quite stable, so the Department of National Defence has decided to cut back our commitment from a full battalion to roughly two reinforced companies." I just stood there not knowing how to respond. "We have more than enough soldiers in the battalion who have never done a U.N. tour, so you won't be required. Do a good job in Shilo and we will see about getting you some leave when you return."

When I finally left his office I couldn't stop grinning for the rest of the day.

If the North American continent were a man needing a prostate exam the doctor would surely start in Shilo, Manitoba. Aside from the military there was absolutely nothing there. Once the base outlets closed at six each evening, the only place to even get a cup of coffee was thirty kilometres away in the town of Brandon. Our quarters sat adjacent to the parade square where we could literally see the waves of summer heat rising from the asphalt. Whenever the wind blew in off the prairie we were faced with a dilemma — we could cool our room down by opening all the windows, but the breeze from the west also carried the noxious odour of the huge pig farm just outside the camp gate.

Thankfully the job I had been sent to do was both interesting and busy. Each morning at six I would arrive at the students' quarters and take them on a five-kilometre run. After a hasty breakfast, they would line up by their beds for morning inspection. By eight the first of perhaps seven lessons and drill periods would begin. In the regular force this course took over five months to complete, but because our students were all militia officer cadets attending university, everything had to be crammed into their seventy-five-day summer break. If we were to turn these cadets into fully qualified second lieutenants by August 30, there was barely a moment to spare.

After the final field exercise in mid August, the whirlwind of activity finally started to slow down. My section of twenty had lost two for medical reasons and three more as training failures, but it had been an interesting summer and we were all looking forward to the end of training and a chance to finally get some leave.

Unfortunately for the four of us who had come from the battalion in London, the news was not so good. When our company commander called at the beginning of August, we already had a pretty good idea of what he was going to tell us. All you had to do was read a newspaper or turn of a television and see that the Cyprus situation was deteriorating rapidly.

The Turks had invaded the island, and in just forty days every available soldier in the battalion would be departing for Cyprus.

After returning from Cyprus in 1970, I had just three days at home before heading for Quebec. This time at least I managed to scrape together a full week of leave before commencing our pre-deployment training.

CHAPTER 6

The Man in the Tree

OCTOBER 1974

When forty thousand Turkish soldiers invaded the island of Cyprus in July 1974, the United Nations' reaction was swift and immediate. What has started out as a routine six-month tour for the Canadian Airborne Regiment quickly turned from peacekeeping to active intervention. As the Turkish invasion force moved toward Nicosia Airport, the Canadian commander announced that his soldiers were there to defend the property by whatever means necessary. The lightly armed Canadians stood their ground as the Turkish force finally halted within sight of the airport runways.

By the time we arrived on the island in October, the situation had stabilized somewhat. There were still a number of skirmishes between Greek and Turk forces and the Greeks had conceded much of their territory. The Turkish military now controlled much of the island. It seemed like it would only be a matter of time before they executed a final push to take the capital city of Nicosia and the all-important international airport.

As our Boeing 707 aircraft made its rapid descent, all I could see was the crystal blue waters of the Mediterranean below us. We had all heard the distinct sound of the landing gear locking into position, and as every pair of eyes peered anxiously out the windows, it appeared like the waves and the aircraft's underbelly were about to make contact. I was beginning to have some regret about the box lunch I had eaten earlier, as our bumpy ride continued. The sudden thud as the aircraft struck the runway caught most of us by surprise, but any sense of relief quickly vanished, as we were immediately sucked back in our seats by the force of the pilot applying the brakes. When the plane finally came to a stop there was a momentary silence throughout the cabin. Doug Tanner sat smiling in the seat next to me. "Welcome to white knuckle airlines," he said, still holding firmly to both armrests. We craned our necks and stared out the port side window. Huge waves crashed against the shoreline, just a couple of hundred metres away. Further out to sea a number of warships sat at anchor. A massive aircraft carrier dominated the skyline. It was too far away to distinguish any real detail, but someone said it was the flagship for a French naval fleet operating in the eastern Mediterranean.

The commanding voice of the pilot finally broke the tension. "Welcome to Larnaca, Cyprus, gentlemen."

Compared to Nicosia International Airport, where we had landed on my first tour four years earlier, the Larnaca Airfield looked rather small. Landing at the main airport in Nicosia was no longer an option. It had been closed to all forms of air traffic since the July invasion. A large Turkish force of tanks and infantry still surrounded the area, with only a reinforced Canadian infantry company standing between them and the airport.

Once we had disembarked, it was easy to see why our landing had been so rough and abrupt. The runway jutted out along a spit of land paralleling the shoreline. I will readily admit that everything I know about flying and landing an aircraft could be written on the head of a pin, but even I could see by the length of the runway that a pilot would have to get down quickly, at the very start of the tarmac, in order to maximize the amount of distance available for a safe landing.

As we made our way inland from the coast, signs of change were everywhere. The small pockets of Turkish-controlled territory that had existed back in 1970 were now greatly expanded. At first glance the land itself looked relatively unchanged, but as we got closer to Nicosia areas of devastation began to appear. The scorch-marked and bullet-riddled building, with a burned out hulk of a tank sitting nearby, was our first real evidence that we were entering a war zone. On the outskirts of the city we came upon what remained of a two-storey structure. The building sat atop a small rise and looked down onto one of the main road junctions leading into the city. Judging by the soccer pitch and playground out front, it must have been a school. Now it was nothing more than a burned out shell surrounded by bomb craters and the remains of numerous fighting vehicles. Later I learned that this strategically important position had been held by a Greek Cypriot Battalion, but after a week of fierce fighting the Turks had finally overrun the position. Casualties on both sides were counted in the hundreds.

The last part of our journey took us through the southern half of the city, still controlled by the Greeks. Just as we reached the barrier dividing the Turk and Greek sectors, the bus made a final turn past a U.N. checkpoint and came to a stop. We had arrived at what would be our barracks for the next six months.

For decades the Ledra Palace had been considered by most to be the finest hotel in the eastern Mediterranean. Look in any tourist brochure and you could read where it had managed to hold on to a five-star rating for more than a decade. But that all ended when the hotel became the very epicentre of the fight for control of Nicosia just two months earlier. The sandbagged windows and bullet-riddled walls were evidence of the heavy fighting that had taken place all around the hotel. The marble columns at the main entrance and sweeping driveway leading to the front door were now completely blocked off by a wall of sandbags. With a temporary truce in place, the narrow street immediately in front of the hotel driveway had become the dividing line between the two factions. At either end of this ninety-metre gap, the two sides faced each other from behind their hastily built fortifications. This former five-star hotel sat directly in the middle of the demilitarized zone and formed part of the newly adjusted Green Line.

The hotel's interior still showed some signs of its former opulence. The thick red carpet lining the hallway was beginning to show the effects of heavy boot traffic. The rod iron railing on the grand staircase was chipped and faded and long overdue for a thorough cleaning. The

Wearing a beard as a member of pioneer platoon could become quite uncomfortable in the heat and dust of a Cyprus summer.

Collection of the author.

Denny Dwyer and I just looked at each other and smiled. At breakfast we had already been warned about our upcoming task.

Our platoon office was situated on the other side of the parking lot, tucked in behind the hotel. This small enclave of buildings had been a Greek army headquarters before the war, but now because of its location inside the protected zone, it had been taken over by the Canadian contingent and renamed Wolseley Barracks.

The young engineer captain who was now our boss seemed friendly enough. After returning our salute he told us to take a seat. Raymond O'Quinn stood smiling near the side of the officer's desk.

The captain didn't waste any time getting to the point. "As you may have heard, our contingent has been assigned the task of minefield clearance for a good portion of the island. The three-man team has already been named, but because of the sheer number of minefields they will have to deal with, you two have been assigned to assist them for the next few weeks."

A hundred thoughts filled my head as we walked back across the parking lot. I have to admit to feeling a little nervous, but mostly I felt a sense of excitement at the prospect of finally putting all of that training to some practical use. After years of learning everything there was to know about mine warfare, the training was over and we were about to experience the real thing.

The three members of the actual mine-clearing team would do the bulk of the work throughout the island. They would have the difficult job of tackling the larger and more complex of the minefields. Their team would be made up of the most capable and experienced soldiers in our platoon. Sergeant Louie Warran, Master Corporal Scotty Grant, and Master Corporal Don Travis were without doubt the most knowledgeable soldiers in pioneer platoon. Over the next six months they would be faced with the daunting task of finding and marking the numerous Turk and Greek minefields scattered all over the island.

Mine and Denny Dwyer's job would be similar to the main team, only on a much smaller scale. He and I would be working for a British engineering officer and over the next several weeks our little group would be tasked with finding and marking the minefields and danger areas to the north and west of the city.

Denny Dwyer was part of the engineer group that had been recently amalgamated into our new platoon. Other than a brief introduction, we had never spoken to each other until that morning. As we made our way back across the parking lot, his first words did little to instill confidence in me. "I really wish I had paid more attention during those mine warfare lectures." His remarks left me dumbfounded. I searched his bland facial expression, trying to determine how I should respond. It took a few moments, but finally a small smile near the corner of his mouth told me I was being had.

As I was to learn over the next few days, Denny possessed a rather dry sense of humour and enjoyed nothing better than getting a reaction from those around him. I was to work with many engineers over the years, and he would be among the most knowledgeable I had ever met.

We started the new task the very next morning. I can't speak for Denny, but I know I was more than a little nervous as we waited in the parking lot. We had been standing there watching the traffic flow for just a few minutes before we saw our ride slowly negotiating the speed bumps and passing through the barrier gate. As the Land Rover Jeep made its way toward us, we both stood tentatively waiting to meet our new boss.

After introducing himself and his driver, the British officer sat us down for a detailed briefing.

Although landmines are certainly designed to kill the enemy or disable his vehicles, this is not their primary goal. The first few soldiers in an advancing column may become casualties, but any competent commander will surely stop once he knows the terrain ahead is sewn with mines. The primary purpose of any minefield is to first deny the use of ground and thereby channel an enemy into terrain of your choosing.

In many cases, particularly from the Greek side, these minefields had been laid in great haste, as a means of slowing down the relentless advance of the Turkish invasion force. Little attention had been paid to the marking of this deadly ground, and consequently the civilian casualties were beginning to mount. Already there had been reports of at least three fatalities in one particularly vulnerable group. The hilly interior of the island was populated by many small herds of goats and sheep. Two old men and one young boy had already died after wandering into a minefield while tending their flock. A U.N. vehicle on patrol near the northern city of Kyrenia had struck a land mine, but fortunately only one man had suffered minor injuries. With six separate national contingents, totalling over two thousand peacekeepers spread over the entire island, it would only be a matter of time before a U.N. peacekeeper was killed.

With a temporary truce now in place, our job was to find these minefields near the southern and western approaches to the city and erect a barbwire fence around the perimeter.

Although our British boss was one of the best map readers I had ever seen, there were a number of times over the next two months where we would find ourselves actually inside the minefield while still searching for the boundary lines.

Once we had defined the danger area, the work itself was not particularly difficult. We would simply drive in six-foot metal pickets about forty-five metres apart and string barbwire between the posts. Next we would place red triangular signs all along the fence line. The average civilian may not have understood the word "MINES" printed boldly in black, but the skull and crossbones stencilled across the top should have made it obvious that this was an area to be avoided.

One of the little tricks we discovered early on was that we could often tell we were close to a minefield simply by the smell. The bloated carcasses of dead animals would litter the area. The explosive charge contained in an anti-personnel mine was more than enough to hurl even a large animal well up in the air.

The American M16 mine, otherwise known as the "Bouncing Betty," was a particularly nasty device used by both sides. Once the mine was buried, the three tiny prongs protruding above the ground were difficult to see. The downward pressure from an animal's hoof or a human foot was enough to set the device in motion. This mine did not just explode, but rather, as the nickname would imply, the entire device was propelled straight up and only detonated when it was roughly a metre above the ground. The millisecond it took for all this to happen left the target with no time to react. Anyone or anything within the three-metre circumference of the blast would be instantly shredded by the metal shrapnel.

Often we would find pieces of the animal spread over a large area. Denny and I would always keep a scarf handy to shield our mouth and nose from the pungent odour. Even worse than the smell were the swarms of flies that would surround us every time we stood still. As soon as we finished a job and got back on the road we would have the driver speed up. It might be a while before we could have a shower or change clothes, but with the windows down and the wind whistling through the truck, we could at least feel some small degree of cleanliness.

Our job may have been tough at times, but paled in comparison to what the main mine clearance team was dealing with on a daily basis.

One day in November, Don Travis and Scotty Grant had come across the bodies of two small children lying half buried in a minefield. Normally neither side would allow the team to actually enter a minefield to remove a corpse, but in this case, because they were children, the team was asked to retrieve the bodies.

Lying side by side, the two team members carefully checked the ground before them. Using a short, spiked prodder, each team member would cautiously stab the ground as they continued to crawl forward in unison. The bodies were just thirty metres inside the minefield, but the job of prodding and clearing a path still took many hours. Once they reached the bodies, they then had to use their bare hands to search around and under each tiny corpse before they could be safely moved. The bodies of these children had been left to decompose in the hot sun for two months. As Don Travis told me later, this was the most difficult job of all. "I must have washed twenty times a day, but even after a week, I still could not get the smell of those children from my hands."

It may sound callous, but in spite of the carnage we encountered, we still managed to maintain some sense of humour. When we pulled up to a new site and commenced work we were all business, but once the task was complete and we were back on the road, the conversation turned to other things. A psychologist today would probably come up with some fancy diagnosis and tell us we were "compartmentalizing our emotions." I can't speak for the others, but for me the jokes and banter were just our way of relieving some of the tensions of the job.

The officer turned out to be one of the more down-to-earth Brits I ever met. Unlike many of the arrogant and aloof British officers I met in Germany, he never talked down to us. When it came to a discussion about how a particular task should be handled, he would not hesitate to ask our opinions. Even including Canadian officers, I found his leadership style refreshingly rare.

Our Brit driver would take the brunt of our jokes mostly about his skill behind the wheel. When I suggested one day that the British were responsible for teaching the Cypriots how to drive on the "wrong" side of the road, my remarks led to a hilarious commentary on everything England had done for "we colonials." Once we turned off the main road and moved toward our next task, the banter would cease as we got back down to the serious business at hand.

On a cool day in early December, the atmosphere in the truck was anything but light as we headed south on the main road out of the city. At about the ten-kilometre mark, the major pointed to the turn just ahead. As we continued along the narrow road, nobody spoke. Before leaving the hotel parking lot, the major had warned us that this morning's task was different.

Even before the vehicle came to a stop, we could see the dead body dangling from a tree just forty metres from the relative safety of the road. The man's body was wedged between the low-hanging branches, and his shredded shirt and pants blew in the wind. Thankfully we could not see his face, but judging by the grey hair on the back of his head, he was an old man. What remained of his dog lay scattered in pieces below him.

"Was it the shepherd or his dog that triggered the mine?" I wondered out loud.

"Does it really matter?" the officer said as we all continued to stare.

Using the road as the boundary line, Denny and I were able to erect the fence very quickly. After placing the last of the mine signs along the wire, we both stopped for one final look at the old man before jumping back in the Land Rover. With no room to turn around, our driver began the careful process of backing up to the road junction. All the time we could see the hanging body through the windshield. This time there were no jokes about his driving skills.

News of the man in the tree spread quickly, and in the days and weeks that followed there was a continual flow of civilians and even some U.N. soldiers trekking to the spot to get a look. I know he was long past caring, but each time we approached, I hoped some strong wind would come along and finally knock him to the ground where he could lie in peace, away from all the gawking eyes.

Much later in the tour, long after I had moved on to other jobs, I happened to overhear a conversation which caught my attention. I hadn't thought about him for a long time, but the very mention of the man in the tree brought back the vivid picture of his remains. Apparently his body had disappeared. Whether it had been moved or simply fell hidden in the rocks and underbrush below nobody knew. I was just happy in the knowledge that this man would no longer be subject to the ghoulish stares of strangers.

When I last drove by there in early spring, the area looked peaceful. The odour of dead flesh had disappeared, taking the swarms of flies with it. A man had died a sudden and violent death on the piece of ground. Now all that remained were some small ribbons of clothing still trapped and fluttering in the tree branches above.

CHAPTER 7

The Crack and Thump of Christmas

Each morning as Denny and I stood waiting for the major to arrive, we would watch the event unfold. It had become a routine you could actually set your watch by.

At precisely eight o'clock in the morning, the first limo with its armed escort would arrive at the U.N. checkpoint. The machine-gun mounted vehicles surrounding the limo would peel off and take up positions on either side of the road. Only the limo would proceed past the checkpoint and slowly turn to enter Wolseley Barracks. Within three to four minutes the entire procedure would be repeated as a second limo and armed escort arrived.

Both of the black stretch limousines were identical, but the small flag and pennant fluttering on the hood told us that the Turkish and Greek peace negotiators had arrived.

Those first few days and weeks the mood seemed very hopeful. Each morning and afternoon the spokesperson from each side would be met by a sea of reporters and television cameras, all pressing forward trying to get the latest information. The English language Cypriot newspaper was filled with stories of how well things were proceeding.

By the end of November, the crowd of reporters had slowed to a trickle. Newspaper stories about the negotiations first moved from the front to the back page and then disappeared from the papers altogether. Even the official U.N. reports we read were beginning to sound repetitious. The words may have been altered slightly, but the weekly bulletin always contained the same basic message: "The negotiations are an ongoing process, but we remain hopeful as the parties continue to work through their differences."

As Christmas approached the weather began to take a turn for the worse. From the window in my room I could see the snowcaps beginning to form near the peaks of the Troudous Mountains Range, off to the south. Nicosia sat in the lowlands, near the centre of the island where it never snowed, but we did have to contend with a steady diet of rain throughout the winter.

Don and I had just arrived back from another long and wet day in the field. All we wanted to do was get out of our wet clothes and get some dinner. As usual, the box lunch we took with us each day was long gone by mid-morning, and after many hours of lugging equipment and building fences we were starving.

Just as we alighted from the Land Rover, platoon warrant Raymond O'Quinn shouted to us from across the parking lot. The platoon commander was already seated as we entered the office. He got to the point in his usual brisk fashion. Our task of marking mine fields was ending at Christmas.

I would have thought I would feel some sense of relief now that our job was over. Instead the surprise announcement gave me a strong feeling of letdown. My initial apprehension about the dangers of the task had disappeared within the first week on the job. By early November I had actually looked forward to the challenges each new day would bring. The job certainly had its hazards, but I believed that the risks we faced were easily offset by all the good we were doing. I was keenly aware that our achievements could never by objectively measured. Did our minefield fences save lives? We could never truly know. All we could really do was take comfort in the knowledge that we were doing all we could to minimize the harm.

"Peace on earth, my ass," was all I could think of to say, as I once again lay awake listening to the steady thud of bullets striking the wall outside.

It was Christmas Eve and for the third night in a row the Turk and Greek positions all over the city had opened fire.

The first time it happened, I remember lying there in bed, half asleep, trying to figure just what was causing the crack and thump sounds coming from outside. After cautiously crossing the darkened room and peering through the narrow wooden slats on the window, I knew what it was. The sights and sound of weapons training was still clear in my mind. The distinctive crack make when machine guns and rifles open fire was unmistakable. The split second between the crack and thumping sound of bullets striking the building told me these weapons were being fired from very nearby. Long lines of phosphorous tracer ammunition illuminated the night sky all across the city. The steady stream of small arms fire from the nearby Turk and Greek positions all seemed to be aimed directly at the hotel. Small ripples of stone dust appeared all across the front walls as machine-gun bullets continued to pepper the building. The dots of red light from the phosphorous tracer rounds looked almost majestic as they arched over the hotel roof and disappeared.

I could hear the shouts of the sergeant major coming from the hallway. "Stay away from the windows," he commanded. Like most people, I just ignored him. I just crouched there staring through the window as the fascinating light show engulfed the entire city.

When I finally answered the steady knocking on my door, I found the hallway crowded with soldiers in all manner of dress. A few had managed to pull on a pair of pants, but most stood around in their underwear. After an hour of indecision, we were finally sent back to our rooms, with strict instructions to keep the lights out and remain away from the windows.

The good news was that it did not appear that the war had begun anew. Based on the random nature of the fire, it didn't seem that the Turks and Greeks were even firing at each other. Most of the weapons were being fired into the air, but the chalky white surface of our hotel was just too big a target to ignore.

The discussions we had about who had opened fire first seemed to be evenly split for both sides. We could argue at length, but when it came right down to it, we simply didn't care who started it. As the unwilling occupants of the target zone, we were well aware that a Turkish or Greek bullet could kill us equally as well. The more pressing question we all asked was why this was happening. Officially we were told that it was just a few undisciplined soldiers from both sides, but unofficially most believed that it had a great deal to do with the stalled peace talks.

The second night, when the weapons opened up around midnight, I hardly gave it a second thought. By the time the first few rounds impacted the building, I had already pulled my mattress and blanket off the bed, placing it near the far wall, well away from the window. Within a few minutes, I was fast asleep, completely oblivious to all the weapons being fired around me.

The conversation at breakfast was dominated by what we were now calling "the fireworks show," but after three nights in a row, it had almost become the new norm. Like most of the people in rooms facing the front of the hotel, I would automatically place my mattress on the floor and set up my little fortress before going to bed each night.

Thankfully the nightly fireworks finally ended just after the New Year. Whether it was unruly soldiers or a means of jump starting the peace negotiations, we were never told. Each day the limos continued to appear in the morning and disappear in the afternoon, with no apparent change in the status quo. By now most of us had ceased to care and were just grateful to finally get off the floor and sleep in a bed.

A Christmas spent away from home and family is never pleasant, but at least I was not alone. Whenever I felt a little down, I would always remember the Christmas of 1966. It had only been eight years, so the memory of sitting alone in my cell at Number One Field Detention Barracks in Germany was still vividly clear. I was just halfway through my fourteen-day sentence for fighting and wouldn't be released until New Year's Eve. I may have had to sleep on the floor of this dilapidated and bullet-riddled hotel but that was still infinitely better than sitting alone on my wooden bed, in an eight by ten cell on Christmas Eve.

Christmas Eve had been a light day's work for most of our platoon. Now that our mine marking job was at an end, Denny and I had spent the majority of the afternoon cleaning up and returning our equipment.

When I got to the mess in the early evening the atmosphere was rather sombre. Most of the guys were crowded around the bar talking about work. There seemed to be an unspoken understanding that all things associated with families and Christmas should be avoided. By eight o'clock the crowd had increased, but still the conversation remained quiet and subdued. Just when I thought that this would turn into another uneventful night, things began to take a dramatic change for the worse.

Sometime in late November, back in London, the drill hall had been the scene of the kids' annual Christmas party. In years past this had always been a much anticipated event. Hundreds of soldiers and their families would fill the huge hall. Everywhere you looked there were tables of cakes and candies. The highlight of the afternoon was the arrival of the guest of honour. As Santa came through the door handing out candy canes, the entire building would erupt with the sound of screaming children.

This year's party was no different, but with all the fathers away in Cyprus, it was decided that one activity would be added. A movie camera was set up in a corner of the drill hall where wives and children could record a message to daddy.

The person who brought the projector into the mess that Christmas Eve night probably thought he was doing a good thing. Now I am sure he realizes it was a big mistake.

I knew most of the mess members very well. We had some tough customers among us. Most could do things that would make the average civilian cringe. It would take an awful lot for most to let down their hard shell and allow you to see the person inside. But almost as soon as the first family appeared on camera, some of these hard cases began to crack.

When you see a child up there crying on the screen, asking for their daddy to come home, how could you not be moved? Some of the wives tried to look cheerful, while others almost looked angry and upset that they had been left alone to deal with these screaming children.

At some point I heard someone suggesting that maybe the projector should be turned off, but it just kept going, as the images of family after family rolled across the screen. Even in the semi-darkness of the room you could see the tightly locked faces of those watching. It felt a little like

watching a train wreck. You wanted to stop looking, but you couldn't tear
your eyes away.

It started with someone ordering a shot of liquor and slamming
it back with a beer chaser. Soon the beer was forgotten and everyone
seemed to be downing shots of the hard stuff. Maybe it was an accident
or done on purpose, but a broken glass and spilled drink started the fight.
When someone tried to break it up, his efforts were met with a right
hook to the side of his head. In less than a minute there were four separate fights going on in different areas of the barroom. The flying chair
may not have broken the glass door, but the banging noise was enough to
alert the duty sergeant, who came running down the hall. Through all the
mayhem, the images of children continued to fill the screen.

Maybe it was because it was Christmas, but rather than march all of
the participants to the jail just across the parking lot, the good sergeant
ordered everyone back to their rooms. Nobody said a word as they made
a hasty exit. Even in their drunken state, I think they all realized just how
fortunate they were. Any thoughts the rest of us had about remaining
were quickly quashed by the sergeant's booming voice. "Gentlemen, the
bar is now closed and anyone still here when I come back in ten minutes
will be spending the night in the crowbar hotel!"

In the days that followed, there could have been no doubt that the
company commander and even the commanding officer knew about the
incident. Even without the duty sergeant's report, the number of black
eyes and bruised faces were ample evidence of a brawl. There may have
been some extra duties handed out, but I never actually heard of anyone
being brought up on charges. Had I been asked at the time, I would have
strongly suggested that charges be laid; not against any of the soldiers
involved in the brawl, but the idiot whose idea it was to show the film in
the first place.

My new job may not have been very glamorous, but I welcomed the chance
to once again get out of the city and see a different part of the island. As
our little work party headed down the highway, I sat quietly in the back
corner of the truck, carefully going over my notes on "beehives." It had

been a very long time since I last used this particular explosive device and I wanted to make sure I had the correct safety distances required.

The beehive was a shaped explosive charge we employed as a rapid method of boring holes in the ground. As the name would imply, the device looked a lot like an oversized beehive. The cylindrical case was about the size of an office waste basket and contained roughly ten pounds of high explosive packed tightly inside its metal shell. When placed on the ground, the three legs attached to the bottom of the case ensured that the beehive was always exactly ten inches above the intended target area. The bottom of the casing was shaped like an inverted cone, similar to what was found at the base of most wine bottles.

To detonate the device, you simply placed a length of safety fuse and an attached detonator in the recess on top of the beehive. Once the fuse burned down to the detonator, it would set off a chain reaction. The detonator would set off the main explosive charge inside the beehive. Almost instantaneously, the heat created from the high explosive would shoot downward, turning the inverted cone into a solid bolt of molten metal, which would be propelled straight down into the ground. Even in the rocky terrain of Cyprus, the tremendous downward force could easily create a bore hole about three metres deep.

Even though it had been a long time since I last used a beehive, I could foresee no problem with the actual set-up of the device. I did, however, have a good deal of concern about setting off such a large explosion within forty-five metres of a large building.

Five Platoon, Bravo Company, was responsible for manning the isolated observation posts, at Louroujina and Pyroi, some fifty kilometres from Nicosia. The soldiers of Five Platoon had worked hard to make improvements to their primitive surroundings, but because of their isolated location, they still lacked some of the more basic necessities. All of their water had to be brought in a trailer truck once a week. A small generator could be fired up each night to provide lighting for the kitchen and living spaces. Some of the outdoor toilets were fast approaching the end of their usefulness and the kitchen roof was leaking badly.

Our little work party of pioneers and engineers had been sent out from Nicosia to try and fix some of the more pressing problems. The fact that we lived in relative comfort at the Ledra Palace while the soldiers of Five Platoon were stuck in these primitive conditions for six months was not lost on us. At least I could empathize with their plight. The sparse living conditions and limited water supply I had experienced during my first Cyprus tour was nothing compared to what they were dealing with each day. The guys at Louroujina and Pyroi had a very tough job, so anything we could do to help make life a tiny bit better would be appreciated.

It may not have been glamorous, but when nature calls, my job that day would prove of paramount importance. I was to blow deep holes in the ground and prepare the site for the new outdoor toilets.

As I set up the first of many beehive canisters, I was still concerned about the building sitting so close by. This particular explosive produced an extremely loud cracking sound when detonated. My fear was that the subsequent shock wave could actually damage or even knock down any nearby structure. All I could do was ensure all the windows and doors were fully open and hope that this would dissipate the shock wave. These guys had it hard enough; they didn't need someone like me coming out here to destroy their sleeping quarters.

As I watched anxiously from a safe distance, I felt the slight rumble in the ground just a fraction of a second before hearing the tremendous crack. Clouds of dirt and debris had enveloped the building and seemed to take forever to clear. As I walked back to the site, I was relieved to see the building still standing. Other than a broken pane of glass and some loose rock landing on the roof, there was no damage. By day's end I had gone through eight beehives, with the final damage tally being just a few broken windows and a picture or two blown off the walls.

That night we were treated to an excellent dinner, followed by a few beers in the makeshift canteen. Our small work party, along with the fifteen or so soldiers not on duty, filled the long table running down the centre of the room. The clouds of cigarette smoke and fumes from the propane heaters made it difficult to see through watery eyes, but a few trips out into the night air quickly cured the problem. As I stood there breathing in the cold night air, I couldn't help but be amazed by the view. Now that we were far from the lights of Nicosia, every star was visible in

A U.N. peacekeeper stands watch on the plains outside Nicosia. Note the Kyrenia Mountains in the background.

Photo courtesy of the Royal Canadian Regiment Museum, London, Ontario.

the clear night sky. The moon looked even larger as it hung low over the silhouette of the Kyrenia Mountains in the northeast.

The conversations we had that night in the canteen were about nothing in particular and by ten o'clock most had headed off through the darkness using a flashlight to find their bed.

By noon the following day, the kitchen roof was nearing completion. It had taken the whole morning to rip out the old roof and replace the damaged pieces with sheets of corrugated metal.

Corporal Sonny Graham was the man in charge of this project. Some of us in the work party may have outranked him, but that didn't matter.

When it came to carpentry or most forms of construction, Sonny was far and away the most knowledgeable man for the job. As the morning wore on, Sonny continued to move back and forth across the apex of the roof, giving instructions in his usual calm and quiet manner. Once all the overlapping sheets were in place, all that remained was to hammer them together with roofing nails.

We had been working since seven o'clock that morning, so the smell of hamburger patties cooking below told us that lunch wasn't far off. It may have been caused by our rushing to eat or simply a lack of attentiveness on Sonny's part, but that is when the accident happened.

Sonny was pointing at something and just about to speak when he took one pace forward and set his foot on the seam between two sheets of corrugated metal. The instant he stepped on the loose seam, both sheets separated and he went plunging through into the kitchen and landed squarely on the cooking grill below. The big iron grill was easily able to support his weight, but except for the ones stuck to the bottom of his boots, most of the semi-cooked hamburger patties went flying in all directions.

The cook may have been momentarily startled, but recovered quickly. Looking up at Sonny standing on his grill, he tapped him on the leg with his spatula. "Seeing as you are not on the menu, would you mind getting off my grill?" Sonny just stood there in stunned silence and only jumped off after feeling the sizzling heat on the rubber soles of his combat boots.

Lunch was definitely ruined, but thankfully Sonny was not hurt. He may have hoped to forget the entire embarrassing matter, but we were not about to let that happen. Each time the story was retold it just seemed to get funnier. When Sonny tried trading in his boots because of the half melted soles, even our normally grumpy quartermaster could not hold back the tears of laughter.

CHAPTER 8

Welcome to Broken Down Airways

I felt a momentary wave of dizziness as I sat bolt upright in bed. At first I thought it was the banging noise of gunfire that jolted me awake, but this sound was coming from the hall outside my room. "Everybody out in the hallway," the impatient voice yelled as he continued to hammer on my door. By the time I got outside, the duty sergeant was already banging on the next door. Once again the hallway was full of half-dressed soldiers, all looking dazed and confused.

It was already getting close to dawn, and with the exception of what sounded like heavy truck traffic, it had been a relatively quiet night. Even after we got dressed and reported to the downstairs lobby, the area around the hotel remained disturbingly quiet. From our vantage point, it may have seemed to be just another average day in Nicosia, but, as we were soon to learn, the situation was anything but normal.

The Turkish army was on the move and, according to the latest intelligence briefing, they were moving toward Nicosia International Airport.

Our company commander's briefing that morning was quite clear. During the initial invasion back in July, General Beatty, the Canadian chief of staff for all U.N. forces in Cyprus, had declared the airport a "U.N. Protected Area," and that decision was still in effect. Two Canadian Airborne soldiers had been killed defending the airport back in July and now the soldiers of the First Battalion of the Royal Canadian Regiment were busily preparing for a renewal of the battle.

Nicosia International Airport had changed little since the July invasion. From a distance, the massive terminal building looked like it was ready to receive passengers. Only when you got close would you notice the sandbag wall surrounding the main doors. The huge plate-glass windows on either side of the entranceway were covered in layers of dirt, making it impossible to see inside. Each of the six-metre-tall panes of glass was dissected with wide strips of masking tape to protect against flying glass, should the building be fired upon. A long line of luggage carts looked oddly out of place just inside the main lobby. The large sign on the far wall had arrows to help point you to the arrivals and departures area. Most of the open areas were now lined with bunk beds for the hundred or so soldiers who called this home. Using tables and chairs from the nearby restaurant, a makeshift mess hall had been set up near the ticket counter. In spite of all the things the guys had done to make the place feel "homey," it was still looked like a giant draughty barn. When you walked down the centre hall, you could hear the sound of your footsteps resounding off the marble floor.

The once busy coffee shop and newspaper stand sat open and abandoned. Further down the corridor sat the now famous Barclays Bank, with its big doors secured with a chain and padlock. Through the window I could see some overturned furniture and various pieces of paper scattered about. It all looked peaceful and quiet now, but seven months earlier it had been the scene of utter chaos.

Back in July when word of the invasion first reached the employees of the Greek-owned bank, most just went about their normal business. The Turkish landing force was still kilometres away in Kyrenia and Famagusta. Everyone knew that the Greek forces on the island vastly outnumbered the Turks, so it could only be a matter of time before these invaders were pushed back into the sea. By the end of day two, the sound of artillery fire could be heard coming from west of the city. When a Turkish armoured column was spotted just a few kilometres from the airport, the real panic began. The bank staff, along with every airport employee, literally dropped everything and made a run for the safety of the city. When soldiers of the Canadian Airborne Regiment arrived minutes later they found the doors of the bank wide open and

In July 1974, Nicosia International Airport was taken over by the Canadian contingent and declared "A U.N. Protected Zone." Note the aircraft ramp being used as a stairway to the lookout post.

Photo courtesy of the Royal Canadian Regiment Museum, London, Ontario.

stacks of money still sitting on shelves inside the open vault. Within a matter of hours, the Canadian contingent had taken control of the entire airport, and the Turks had stopped just beyond the outer fringes of the airport property. Some months later, when the military police turned the money back over to the bank's representative, every penny was accounted for.

All things considered, the main terminal had stood up well to the long months of abuse. The question was whether it could survive another round in the battle to control the strategically important airport.

The terminal may have weathered the storm, but the rest of the airport was a sea of devastation. Most of the outer buildings and hangars had either fallen down or been cannibalized for anything usable. The rusting hulks of five or six jumbo jets sat on the two main runways. You could still see the long lines of black rubber where these massive passenger planes had been towed across the tarmac and positioned to block the landing of any Turkish military aircraft. Even with the rust starting to spread across the fuselage, the faded lettering told us that most of these passenger jets belonged to Middle East Airlines.

A British Airways jet still sat just forty-five metres away from the front of the terminal, its flattened tires and bent nose wheel making it impossible to tow away. A line of bullet holes was stitched neatly across the portside windows. The stairway ramp remained in place against the door frame, but the tilting body of the aircraft had created a large gap between the exit ramp and the open hatchway. From our position on the ground we could clearly see the first few rows of seats inside. Considering the passengers and crew must have disembarked in great haste, the aircraft interior looked oddly neat and tidy. Someone with far too much time on their hands had taped a cardboard sign just below the nose cone. Under different circumstances, it may have been funny, but now it just seemed rather sad. The words "British Airways" had been scratched out and over top was written, "The departure of Broken Down Airways will be slightly delayed."

By mid morning, our forty-man platoon of pioneers and engineers was already busy reinforcing and repairing the numerous trenches and bunkers surrounding the airport terminal. The asphalt runways made it impossible to dig down, so all we could do was build a series of sandbag walls to protect the soldiers covering the southern approaches to the airport. Most of the barbwire and concertina fences built seven months earlier were still in place. All we had to do now was add additional rolls of wire to the already formidable barrier.

The largest weapon we possessed on the island was the 106 recoilless rifle. This three-metre-long, 400-pound anti-tank gun was no doubt a formidable piece of weaponry. A well-trained crew could fire a high explosive shell out to a distance of one thousand metres and destroy most heavy battle tanks, including the Soviet-built T55 and T62 used by the Turks.

Unfortunately, it had three major drawbacks. It had to be loaded manually and even the most experienced crew could take at least twenty seconds to get an accurate shot away. The gun had to remain stationary during firing, and although it may not sound like a lot, sitting still for twenty seconds in the heat of a battle could seem like an eternity. Probably the single biggest drawback to the 106 recoilless rifle was what was referred to as "the weapon signature." When the firing knob was depressed, the force of the shell exploding down the barrel would produce a large cloud of flame and smoke, which could be easily seen by the enemy. This "weapon signature" made the gun crew instantly visible and extremely vulnerable to enemy fire. Of course, nobody knew for sure, but most experts believed that the life expectancy of a gun crew could probably be measured in minutes.

The T55 and T62 tanks of the Turkish armoured regiment have no such drawbacks. Their gun-stabilizing mechanism allowed them to fire on the move. Even if the 106 gun crew managed to knock out the first tank, the others were already aiming their gun turrets toward that big puff of smoke off in the distance.

By late afternoon, all of our defensive stores had been used up. The men of the anti-tank platoon were busy checking the sights and preparing their guns for action. All six weapon systems were deployed facing east to cover what was considered the most likely approach. A few of the smaller eighty-four-millimetre anti-tank guns had been scraped together to bolster the position, but with a maximum effective range of four hundred metres, they were of limited use. The remainder of the company, armed only with rifles and general purpose machine guns (GPMG), was spread out facing north and west.

By nightfall we were ready.

I was absolutely dog tired as I made my way down the corridor looking for a quiet place to spread my sleeping bag and get some rest. It was only nine o'clock but I had managed to draw the midnight shift on sentry duty. The terminal was normally well lit, and on any other night it stood out like a beacon shining down on the city. Tonight was different. The company commander had ordered all lighting to be minimized. With all the overhead lights now extinguished, the few remaining lamps looked like pinpricks of light in the otherwise total blackness of the building. Every so often you could see the narrow beam of a flashlight as someone moved along the darkened hallway. The only outside illumination came from a pair of spotlights positioned on the roof, above the control tower. Both lights were there to ensure the blue and white flag of the United Nations could be clearly seen by the Greek and Turk positions surrounding the airport.

After a little searching I finally found a quiet spot near the end of the ticket counter. As I blew up my air mattress and organized my kit, I couldn't help but notice the large directional sign that hung on the wall above me. Based on our current situation, I could only hope the words "Departure Area" had not taken on some new, more ominous meaning. For a moment, I actually considered moving, but after reminding myself I was just being silly, I settled down and fell into a deep sleep.

At first I thought I was imaging it, but when I heard my name called for the third time I knew I wasn't dreaming. The beam from the waving flashlight blinded me as I struggled to sit up and try and figure out what was going on. I recognized the voice, but couldn't quite comprehend why he was there or what he was saying. Why would Raymond being waking me up for sentry duty? I slowly pulled the sleeping bag down over my feet and stood up. Warrant Officer O'Quinn finally stopped talking when he realized I wasn't listening. He just stood there looking impatient as I scratched myself and squinted to read the time on my watch. "It's only eleven o'clock. I don't start my shift for another hour," I complained.

Thankfully, Raymond maintained his temper, in spite of my continued whining. "Get dressed and come with me," was all he said.

As we walked down the lounge full of sleeping soldiers, I again asked Raymond what was going on. "I just volunteered you for a special job. You will be working with three other soldiers from the company, but you are in charge," he whispered. By the time he and I reached the company commander's office, I was wide awake. Raymond had given me the gist of my task. It was now up to the major to fill in the details.

Our tiny section of four sat and listened intently as the company commander began to explain.

The U.N. position, known as Checkpoint Foxtrot, sat about two kilometres down the main road leading into the airport complex. This key position was manned by a Finnish platoon, whose job it was to control the southern approach road to the airport. Any vehicle approaching the checkpoint must first pass through a traffic circle, roughly one hundred metres north of the position. All vehicle traffic from the two major highways coming from the east and west converged here and then fed off onto separate arteries leading either north to the city centre or south onto the airport road.

As the company commander explained, although it was considered unlikely, there was always a possibility that a Turkish armoured column could attempt to infiltrate the airport from the south. The Finnish platoon manning Checkpoint Foxtrot had nothing heavier than a .30 calibre machine gun to stop them.

There was a momentary silence and the major stared directly at me to see if the information was sinking in. I knew that this was not the time for questions, so I just nodded my head and waited for him to continue.

Now his words became much more formal. "Master Corporal Burke, I want you to take these three men and set up an anti-tank position on the slope adjacent to Checkpoint Foxtrot. When you arrive on location, you will be met by the Finnish platoon commander, who will assist you in sighting your weapons." I wanted to ask the obvious question, but the major continued to speak. "I want to make one point perfectly clear. The platoon commander is in charge and you and your men will only fire if given a direct order by him." When his words became less formal, I knew he was about the deliver the bad news. "Unfortunately, all of our 106 Recoilless Rifles and 84 millimetre anti-tank guns are already positioned along the eastern side of the airport and can't be spared. You will have twelve M72 anti-tank weapons to do the job." He paused and waited for my questions. I believe he could see the doubt in my eyes, but I could think of nothing concrete to say.

The 66 millimetre M72 light anti-tank weapon is a fine piece of kit, if it is used as the designer intended. For the want of a better term, this rocket launcher was actually a disposable weapon, designed to be used once and then discarded. In the closed position, the tube was just thirty inches long and came with a high explosive rocket already inside. Because of its light weight, each man in an infantry platoon could easily carry at least two of these anti-tank weapons slung over his shoulder.

To fire the M72 all the soldier had to do remove the pin holding the front and rear cover in place. Once the detent lock on top was depressed, the soldier could pull to extend the tube, like a telescope. Placing the launcher on his shoulder, he could then cock the weapon, look through the sights and fire when ready. The average soldier could complete these steps and fire the weapon in roughly twenty seconds.

I had fired the M72 many times and generally I could hit what I was aiming at. The weapon system was relatively easy to set up and fire, but to successfully engage a target you had to first understand two of its key characteristics. According to the users' manual, the M72 had a maximum range of approximately 250 metres, but we all knew from experience that this was a bit of a stretch. If you truly wanted to hit what you were aiming at, your target needed to be within 150 metres before you engaged. The type of target was also critically important. The rocket was most effective against lightly armoured vehicles and trucks, but didn't have the heavy punch necessary to take on a main battle tank. Hitting the tracks would certainly immobilize the tank, but did nothing to stop the immediate return fire from its powerful main gun.

The cold night wind whistled through the canvas, making it difficult to hear as our truck sped down the road to our destination. Checkpoint Foxtrot was only a few kilometres away, so I had to talk quickly. When we rolled into the Finnish position, I wanted them to see a group of professional soldiers ready to do a job. I knew my tiny sections of three were all well experienced soldiers, but still I wanted to make sure they remembered the drills. "Don't forget to snap the tube so it's fully opened and locked, otherwise you could have a misfire!" I yelled through the noise. Even in the darkness, I could see each man nod to confirm he understood.

We had been lucky with the weather for most of the day, but by early evening the rain had returned. It was more of a slow drizzle, but with the forward movement of the truck and the sound of drops hitting the canvas, it sounded like a downpour. It was going to be a long, cold night sitting in the Finnish position.

The bright lights of Checkpoint Foxtrot were a stark contrast to the airport terminal we had just left. The wide beam of two large spotlights shined down on the road below. Both beams were meant to illuminate the traffic circle below, but with the rain and overcast skies, we could barely see more than a few metres of the roadway in front of us.

Thankfully the young Finnish platoon commander was waiting for us when we arrived and he and I quickly set about the task of finding the best position.

I have worked with many soldiers from Finland over the years and always found them to be very competent and professional, but generally speaking they were not a particularly friendly or outgoing group. Although the vast majority spoke English, they were not ones to make any kind of small talk. If asked a question they would answer, but conversations were usually short and to the point. They just went about their job in a quiet and efficient manner. You may be able to elicit the odd smile from one of them, but laughter was extremely rare.

"Miserable night," I said as he and I went about the business of finding a suitable location to position each of my men. His reply was more of a grunt of agreement as we continued to prod through the darkness. At least we didn't have to do any digging. A line of prepared trenches stretched along the high ground, just off to the west and well away from the lights of the checkpoint. My only concern was to ensure that the four of us were sufficiently spread out so that if we were fired upon one tank round could not take out the entire group. Our new boss seemed to understand and just stood back as I assigned each man to a position and once again explained the rules of engagement. I knew I was being repetitive, but I wanted to make absolutely sure they understand their responsibilities. "You will only fire if you get a direct order from me." We were all nervous, but I made every effort to speak calmly and slowly to each man individually. "The Finnish lieutenant is in charge," I said, pointing in his direction. "He will give me the order and I in turn will give you a fire order." As I delivered the instructions, I leaned forward to make sure I could see the men's faces through the rain and gloom.

From my position in the middle I could not see the men on either side of me, but every so often I could hear the reassuring sound of somebody moving about, trying to stay warm. At least the rain gear was keeping us semi-dry. The first part of the night had seemed to go quickly, but now alone in the dark the night seemed endless. I knew looking at my watch every few minutes didn't help, but each minute of quiet would bring us closer to dawn. Every so often my senses would be aroused by the sound of vehicle engines from the traffic circle below. Sometimes I could catch a faint glow of headlights as a vehicle slowly manoeuvred around the circle. After a moment I could relax knowing that yet another car was heading in or out of the city. Once or twice I heard the distinct noise of a diesel engine truck as it changed gears to negotiate the tight turn. I listened intently to see if the noise increased to indicate the truck was turning toward us. Each time they turned away and I could stop staring as the sound slowly disappeared in the distance. The Finnish platoon commander had vanished in the darkness soon after we moved into position. I could only hope he was within yelling distance if I needed him. Around three o'clock he suddenly came strolling out of the darkness. He sat down beside me to deliver some rather unsettling news. There had been some radio reports that confirmed that a long line of convoy lights had been spotted coming out of the hills to the east of the airport. Judging from the engine noise and the number of lights, it was thought to be at least a squadron of heavy tanks. Our positions to the south of the airport remained unnervingly quiet.

At dawn the sun remained hidden behind the banks of heavy cloud, but slowly the darkness gave way to the grey light of morning. It was somewhat reassuring to be able to see the soldiers on either side of me. The rain had finally stopped and slowly I could start to see the road network below.

It was just after seven o'clock when Raymond O'Quinn arrived with some good news. We were being pulled back to the airport. It looked like the crisis was at an end. Turkish forces had come within sight of the eastern boundary to the airport and halted. Whether it was the Canadian Peacekeepers standing their ground or a U.N. Security Council resolution that forced them to stop, we didn't know. It may have been a combination of many things, but at least for the moment it was over.

Within two days we were once again back in the Ledra Palace. There were frequent breaches of the uneasy peace in the days and weeks that followed. I remember reading a newspaper report a week or two after things settled back down. I could only shake my head in frustration as I read the report about how the situation was returning to normal. How could anybody think there was anything even remotely normal about this troubled island?

CHAPTER 9

One Egg Per Man, Per Day, Perhaps

Sergeant Major Ed Laporte was not a man to be trifled with. He was not one to waste time on small talk. Like most of those who had reached his exalted rank, he tended to be blunt and direct. He was a Korean War veteran and had served in the regiment for decades, so when he spoke, you listened. He may have been feared by some, but he was definitely respected by all.

As I stood outside his office door that morning, waiting for him to arrive, I felt a little uneasy. The unusually warm March weather may have been the cause of some of my discomfort, but mainly I was concerned because I had no idea why I was there.

Earlier that morning as I left the mess hall, I had been cornered by our engineer platoon commander, Captain Dempsey. I still felt a slight sense of embarrassment after our last encounter. He kept using words like "great" and "terrific" to describe the job me and my three-man section had done working for the Finns at the airport. I couldn't help but be embarrassed by the praise, considering we had done nothing more than sit in a hole all night and waited for an enemy that never came.

Now as he approached me outside the kitchen, I could only hope it wasn't to talk about the airport again. Thankfully it was not.

After returning my salute, his smile disappeared as he got down to business. "Apparently Sergeant Major Laporte is not happy with the engineer corporal he has working for him and I am sending you over there to replace him." I still didn't know what job I was to do, but after checking his watch, his swift departure left no time for questions. "Report to Sergeant Major Laporte's office and he will brief you," was all he said as he quickly walked away.

As soon as I spotted the sergeant major coming through the entrance to Wolseley Barracks, I came to rigid attention. Just as I opened my mouth to report, he cut me off. "I know why you are here, master corporal. Follow me."

After carefully setting his drill cane on the desk and removing his beret, he finally spoke.

"For two months now, I have been after those engineers to build me some trenches around the perimeter of Wolseley Barracks. All they have managed to do so far is bury me in paperwork. As of today, you are taking over the job." He paused a moment for emphasis. "I don't want to see another blueprint drawing or a soil analysis or even a stores list. What I want to see are holes in the ground!" I had some questions, but I was not about to open my mouth until I was sure he was finished. After sitting down his voice seemed to become calmer. "I will give you today to look over the site and gather any stores and equipment you need, but starting tomorrow morning, I expect to hear the sound of digging shovels." Again he took a moment to just stare at me. "Do you have any questions?" Given some time to think, I could probably have come up with a whole list of questions, but at that moment I could only think of two things to ask. My first question was met with a blunt reply. I had exactly thirty days to complete the task. I held the most pressing questions for last because I knew his answer would dictate whether or not the task could be completed successfully and on-time. How many soldiers would I have for a work party and where were they coming from? He actually smiled as he gave me his one-word answer: "Prisoners."

Just days after our confrontation with the Turks, the airport had once again become the focal point of activity. This time, however, it was a completely internal problem. Apparently one of the Canadian cooks working at the airport had been caught with marijuana. It had only been one cigarette, but when the military police searched his bed space, they came across a very incriminating diary. The book not only talked about a rather large pot party at the airport, but it listed the names of all those who had participated. The guardroom at Wolseley Barracks had only enough jail cells to accommodate six or seven prisoners at one time. Each of the twenty or more soldiers named in the diary had to be questioned. The guardroom became a revolving door, as each soldier was brought in and held for questioning. After two or three days, one batch would be returned to their company for duty, while the next group moved into the cells.

Considering the seriousness of the charge, each man had to be offered the choice between appearing before the commanding officer for a summary trial or being tried by court martial. Only two or three choose the latter and were sent back to Canada to await trial. The remainder were dealt with by the CO and in most cases they received fourteen to twenty-one days in jail. The cook whose diary had started it all was returned to Canada. Officially we were told he had chosen trial by court martial, but according to the rumour mill he had been sent home for his own protection. Had he been kept in the battalion I have no doubt he would have met with some type of accident. By the time the unit returned to London, in late April, he was long gone, never to be heard from again.

Each morning after breakfast I would report to the guardroom and "sign out" whatever poor unfortunates happened to be in jail that day. The military police sergeant would hand me a very officious-looking document outlining my responsibilities for the prisoners in my custody that day.

They were not allowed to speak unless I spoke to them. They could have one ten-minute break at mid morning and afternoon. They could have as much water as they wished, but no food. At noon I would march them back to the guardroom, where they would be given a twenty-minute lunch break.

Naturally, at first we all found it rather awkward. I knew most of these guys and generally speaking they were good soldiers who had obviously made a stupid mistake. It would take a few hours to get used to the situation, but I soon realized that although they were not happy with their current predicament, at least for a few hours they could get out of their cells and away from all the questions. Needless to say, most of these prisoners knew as much about trench construction as I did. After a few minutes explaining what had to be done that day, I could just step back and watch. Sometimes an hour or more would go by in complete silence. The only sound would come from pickaxes breaking through the soil or steel pickets being hammered into the ground.

Any thought I had about giving these guys a break was quickly ended on the very first morning. The machine-gun trench we were working on sat just in front of the entrance to Wolseley Barracks. Everyone from the commanding officer to the regimental sergeant major and the entire headquarters staff had to pass by as they travelled between their office and the hotel. When a couple of the prisoners had asked for a smoke during the break, I had given each of them a cigarette without a second thought. They had barely taken a puff before I heard the bellowing scream from behind me. I hardly had time to turn around as the big frame of the RSM bore down on me. "Why are those people smoking, master corporal?" He was just inches away from me as he pulled his drill cane from under his arm and used it to point at the two offenders. For a brief moment I thought he was going to hit me with the outstretched cane. I opened my mouth to speak, but his tirade was far from over. What had started out as a random act of kindness now felt like the crime of the century for which I was about to be hauled away and summarily executed by firing squad. At last he stopped shouting and walked away, but not before one final threat to place me behind bars should this ever happen again. Later that day, I was informed by the duty sergeant that I had been "awarded" five extra duties for my horrendous crime.

Most of the trenches were relatively easy to dig, due mainly to the sandy soil. However, once the hole was sufficiently deep, the work became tediously slow. Sheets of corrugated steel had to be quickly but carefully put in place to prevent the walls from caving in. Two men would hold the corrugated sheet flush to the wall, while another hammered in the steel pickets needed to hold it in place. Problems arose when the vibration from the sledgehammer striking the picket would cause the wall to collapse.

They say that doing the same thing over and over again and expecting different results is the very definition of insanity. Each time the wall collapsed the trench became increasingly wider. A normal slit trench is supposed to be roughly twenty-four inches wide, but after the fourth cave-in the gap was more like forty inches. It took a suggestion from one of the smarter inmate workers, but when we discarded the corrugated sheets and used a wall of sandbags to line the interior, my sanity finally returned.

As I stood there surveying the work on the second to last day, I could not have been happier. It was almost over. I truly hated the job I had been given, but soon I could get back to working in a more normal environment, where people could smoke and laugh without fear of retribution.

In spite of the many mishaps and frequent interruptions the work remained on schedule. With just two days remaining before the end of the thirty-day deadline, we were just finishing up the last machine-gun position when we hit another snag.

This final machine-gun position sat just off the road behind the hotel and roughly 180 metres from the Greek army position, at the very edge of the United Nations enclave. From their position they could easily see everything we were doing.

The Greek soldiers manning the position seemed friendly enough. Each morning they would wave and shout hello as we arrived to start work. All day long we could see them moving about behind their sandbag wall. Once or twice they even invited us over for coffee, knowing full well we could not accept.

I carefully moved around the work site trying to view the trench from every angle. We were about to place a thousand pounds of dirt onto the roof, so I wanted to make absolutely sure the frame was strong enough to receive it. Once I was satisfied that the roof beams and walls could support the weight only one key step remained.

This entire structure had been designed with the sole purpose of firing a machine gun. If the weapon could not be positioned to cover the entire arc of fire, the trench would be little more than a well-reinforced hole in the ground.

After carefully setting the tripod in position at the centre of the U-shaped trench, I mounted the .30 calibre machine gun in the bracket. It took only a moment to confirm that the muzzle and barrel were protruding through the weapon's slit and I could easily traverse the barrel left and right, to cover all the ground in the arc of fire.

I was just about done when I heard the first yell coming from the Greek position. I may not have understood the language, but the meaning was clear. Our Greek sentry was not happy with what I was doing. I had been so busy checking the elevation and depression of the weapon, I had hardly noticed, but once I looked through the sight, I realized the weapon was pointed directly at him.

I could understand his concern. Whether loaded or unloaded, nobody likes having a weapon pointed at them. I tried swivelling the barrel off to the left, but it was too late. Already the Greek officer commanding the position was headed in my direction. The problem was no longer the shouting or even the machine gun placement, but rather the Greek officer entering the U.N. enclave. I don't think he even realized what he was doing. He was about forty-five metres from me when it dawned on him that perhaps this was not a good idea. He continued to yell, but at least he had the good sense to stop moving forward. Both of us were looking across the parking lot toward the Turkish position at the front of the hotel. The Turk sentry had heard all the commotion and was now standing on top of his sandbag wall trying to see what was going on. He and I could see each other clearly, but thankfully the vehicles in the parking lot were obscuring his view of the Greek officer still standing in the middle of the road.

The momentary stalemate was broken by the arrival of the military police sergeant. Without saying a word, he and I began walking toward the intruder. As if on cue, as soon as we stopped, the Greek officer began pointing at the offending weapon. "No good, no good," the officer repeated while going through the motions of holding and aiming an imaginary weapon. His meaning was clear and we both nodded our heads in agreement.

With that out of the way, the sergeant pointed at the ground and began waving his arms across his body. "You cannot be here. No good, no good," he said, parroting the officer's words.

At last both parties seemed satisfied with the outcome. The young officer had even shaken hands with us before disappearing behind his sandbag wall. "Thank god that's over," I said while the sergeant and I made our way back toward the position.

Any sense of relief I felt quickly dissipated when I saw the stern expressions of the sergeant major and the engineering officer waiting to meet us. After briefing them on all that had happened, I was ordered to remove the gun immediately and stop all work on the position until further notice.

To me it seemed like a long time, but after a full week of waiting I was called before the engineer officer to hear the news. The Greeks had sent a formal written protest to the U.N. headquarters and after some lengthy negotiations my crew and I could get back to work and finish the position, but I was not, under any circumstances, to have a machine gun or any type of weapons anywhere near the trench. When I reminded the captain that I hadn't finished sighting the weapon and reinforcing the area around the gun slit, I was abruptly cut off. "You have your orders, master corporal. Just get the roof done as soon as possible. This discussion is now closed."

The roof took less than a day to complete. The finished project may have been a week overdue, but at least the sergeant major seemed generally pleased with the work. In the weeks that followed, I found myself stopping to look every time I passed. I was relieved to see the roof was holding up under the weight of eighteen inches of dirt. It was difficult to tell for sure, but when I looked from the front, there appeared to be a very slight tilt in the weapon's firing slit.

When I returned nine years later, I was curious to see if the position had withstood the test of time and the elements. I was surprised to find little had changed. The weeds and underbrush had grown wild on the roof and around the edges, making the whole position almost blend into the surrounding landscape. A new layer of sandbags propped up the front wall on either side of the still sagging gun slit. I once again had a fleeting thought about whether or not a machine gun would fit, but just as quickly I dismissed the notion. I had satisfied my curiosity and realized I no longer cared.

The Dhekelia military base sat on the southern coastline of the island and had been occupied by units of the British army since the Second World War. Even after the conflict ended in 1945, the Brits had continued to maintain a strong presence because of its strategic importance in the eastern Mediterranean. Unfortunately for the unwilling Brits, the island's proximity to the Palestinian coastline also made it the ideal location to detain Jewish refugees from Hitler's Europe. These refugees were the fortunate ones who had somehow managed to survive through five years of war and then find passage to what they were calling "The Promised Land."

As I stood at the entrance to the rifle range, it was hard to believe that this long, empty strip had been once part of a huge expanse of land used to house the thousands of refugees who had been caught trying to enter Palestine. Their dreams would have to wait until 1948 when the United Nations General Assembly finally past the resolution which created the state of Israel.

I thought it ironic that although this piece of land had not been used as an internment camp for more than a quarter century, the refugee problem still existed. The occupants had changed from Jews to Greek Cypriots, but just a few kilometres to the east of the British base, yet another refugee camp had sprung up to house the displaced civilians from this latest installment in the ongoing battle for control of Cyprus.

It was a gorgeous spring afternoon in what promised to be an excellent week of range work. The winter rains had ended and spring had arrived early. The mild March temperatures finally allowed us to dispense with our heavy combat jackets. The oppressive heat of summer was still a couple of months away and, best of all, we had only forty days remaining in our six-month tour of duty.

Our small cadre of eight NCOs had been sent down from Nicosia to set up and run the ranges for the battalion. Each day for the next two weeks one of our companies would arrive to complete the annual weapons' qualification on the rifle, pistol, and submachine gun.

The range sat in a small valley, running east to west along the coast. Standing on the raised firing point we could clearly see the sparkling blue waters of the Mediterranean just a few hundred metres to the south. The high rolling cliffs at the western end of the range gave us a natural barrier to prevent any stray bullets leaving the range. The base of the cliff, immediately behind the targets, contained many huge crevices where the earth had caved-in from years of bullets impacting against the sandy soil.

The safety staff on the British army ranges in Dhekelia. Even in Cyprus every soldier in the battalion must qualify annually on the rifle and submachine gun. Sergeant Ron Eddy (far left, kneeling) organized the setup of the range. The author (far right, standing) was part of the safety staff.

Collection of the author.

The first morning of firing everything was right on schedule. By seven o'clock we had already finished our breakfast and the twenty-man relay was just taking their positions on the one-hundred-metre firing line.

The lieutenant running the range was a highly experienced safety officer. Those of us on the range staff probably had a combined total of over a hundred years of range work, but that was in Canada. Firing on the ranges in Cyprus presented some rather unique problems.

Normally any firing range would require red flags to be flown to indicate danger and warn everyone in the surrounding area that live fire was taking place. This was one of the basic requirements for practically any range in the world, except in Cyprus. When we arrived that first morning red flags were flying at the front and back of the range, but before firing could commence both flags would have to be pulled down. When it was first mentioned at the safety briefing we all thought it was a joke, but once we stopped to consider the situation, we understood the need for caution. The Turkish national flag and the standard range flag were basically the same in dimension and colour, with the small white crescent moon on the Turkish flag being the only real difference. From a distance an onlooker could easily mix up the two red flags and possibly assume the sound of weapons fire was coming from the Turks.

After all the red flags were taken down and stowed away, there remained just one more unusual and potentially dangerous situation to deal with.

After a long pause, the range officer finally gave the order to load. The order to fire should have followed immediately, but once again he paused and took a deep breath. We all understood the source of his hesitation.

We could count at least ten civilians scattered across the hills in front of us. All of them were women busily picking wild mushrooms along the face of the steep cliff. Our British liaison officer had told us that this was quite common. The Brits had long ago given up trying to clear these women from harm's way, and after years of unsuccessful attempts they had finally reached a compromise. The pickers could stay, as long as they remained close to the summit. "Don't worry, these mushroom pickers will stay at least sixty metres up on the face of the cliff." His words offered little comfort to our already nervous range officer.

When he finally gave the command, his voice sounded nervous and hesitant. "Relay, 100 yards at your target in front. In your own time, fire!"

We may have been concerned, but our uninvited guests hardly paused in their work as the bullets began to fly down range. All morning long we watched as small jets of dirt sprayed outward from the impact of bullets striking the cliff face. It took a few hours and probably a thousand rounds of fire before we finally relaxed. By mid-week our odd situation had become almost a regular routine. Each morning after breakfast and again after lunch, the range officer would stand on the firing mound and scan the entire area with his binoculars. Once he confirmed that none of the pickers had wondered down the cliff, he would order the red flags taken down and we would commence firing without further delay.

By the time a new group of firers arrived from Nicosia each morning, our eight-man staff would have the range set up and ready to go. At 6:30 a.m. the staff would already be busy setting up everything on the range. When the new relay stepped off the trucks, they would find a well-organized range.

The arrival of the company quartermaster with lunch each day was always a welcome sight. The firing relays could have an early breakfast before leaving Nicosia and supper after they returned, but the staff had to remain on the British base throughout the two week period. Lunch would be our only opportunity to eat what we considered a decent meal each day.

I had spent close to five years living on British rations in Germany, and six years later I found little had changed. There may have been some slight improvement in the quality of the food, but they still insisted on frying almost everything. Anyone that said that breakfast was the most important meal of the day obviously never ate in a British mess hall. In the morning I would stand and watch as the cook cracked open each egg and deposited the contents in a deep fryer. Once it bobbed to the top, he would remove the finished product and put it on a plate right next to the equally fried sausage and tomato slices. Stabbing your fork into the egg yolk usually produced a small gush of grease and fat to shoot into the air. The running joke each morning was that if you stayed real quiet while eating this meal, you could actually hear the sound of your arteries hardening.

I have no doubt that we were all a little spoiled by the generous portions we normally received in Canadian mess halls, but considering the small servings we received at each meal, coupled with the length of time we spent on the range each day, it was not surprising that we were always hungry. The phrase "one egg per man, per day, perhaps" may have been a joke, but it was not that far from the truth. Each night around ten o'clock we would head for the soldiers' canteen, or as the Brits called it, the NAAFI (Navy Army Air Force Institute). After a beer and a couple of meat pies to fill the half-empty hole we would head for our bunks to get a little sleep before the daily cycle started again.

The food may have been bad, but we certainly were not starving. If the truth were told, it had been an excellent couple of weeks on the range and other than the two minor glitches on day one, things had gone smoothly. We whined about the food simply because there was little else to complain about.

It would take one of those small life lessons on our last range day to show us how truly petty and insignificant our complaints really were.

The last firing relay had already departed for Nicosia as we went about the task of cleaning up and closing down the range. As usual there were many loaves of bread and cans of juice left over from lunch. Normally we would take them back to the quarters for a late night snack, but because we were heading home to the Ledra Palace, we simply threw them in the back of the truck. The plan was to take the excess food and drop it at the garbage dump.

I can't remember who brought it up, but when someone mentioned dropping the food off at the refugee camp, we all instantly agreed.

The camp sat just off the main highway, and as we approached we could see a group of around ten children playing soccer just inside the fence. We were all aware that the camp was a restricted area, so rather than face the hassle of trying to gain entry we decided to simply pass the bread and juice over the fence to the waiting kids. Almost as soon as we backed the truck up, the kids began to press up against the fence. Standing on the tailgate it was easy to reach over and drop the food into their outstretched arms.

Most of them appeared to be boys, but I did spot a pretty young girl desperately trying to fight her way to the front of the pack. She was a scrawny little thing who couldn't have been more than ten years old, but somehow she managed to squirm her way through the much bigger boys. I held the bread just over the fence, waiting for her reach up and retrieve it. Her fingers were just inches away when she suddenly disappeared. Some unseen hand and grabbed her dress and flung her backwards onto the ground. I stood there still holding the loaf. She tried to get up and come forward, but it was too late. The noise and excitement had drawn a crowd of adults who had little difficulty pushing and throwing children aside as they fought their way forward. For a moment it looked like the fence would collapse from the weight of grown men and women pressing against it. The fence posts began to sway back and forth as people started to climb over the top. We were left with little alternative other than to drop all the food and drive away before we were stampeded by the ever increasing crowd.

No one spoke as we headed down the highway. It was almost like there were no words to describe what we had just witnessed. Later on when I thought about it, I still could not comprehend how normal human beings could devolve into an uncivilized mob so quickly. It took me quite a while to realize that my lack of understanding probably stemmed from the fact that I could not possibly comprehend what they were going through. Perhaps when you had lost everything and were suffering the pains of hunger the instinct to survive far outweighed all other needs?

CHAPTER 10

The Slow and Rocky Road Home

After the aborted attempt to take control of the airport, the situation settled down to an uneasy quiet. A large Turkish tank force still occupied the vast stretches of territory to the west and north of the airport. It seemed like both sides were taking a long, deep breath before deciding what to do next. Breaches of the peace continued to be reported on a daily basis, but these incidents were all of a minor nature. Many of the other national contingents had suffered casualties, but with less than a month remaining, some of us were beginning to think we could escape this war zone without losing a soldier. The possibility was hinted at among our group, but we never discussed it out loud for fear of changing our luck.

It was just after midnight on the first day of April when I once again heard the familiar thud of bullets striking the front wall of the hotel. When I peeked through the wooden window shutters I could see the dotted lines of machine-gun fire crisscrossing the city. At first the sound was muffled in the distance, but quickly grew louder as the Turk and Greek positions near the hotel joined in. The firing at Christmas had been sporadic, but tonight I was witnessing a much more intense and sustained display of firepower.

Other than the steady thud of bullets impacting the wall, the hotel seemed oddly quiet. No one was banging on doors warning us to stay away from the windows. The hallway remained empty.

After a few minutes I felt my way through the dark and slowly set about the task of pulling my mattress off the bed and onto the floor. Every so often the sound would momentarily die down and I would doze off, only to be jolted awake, as the noise of fire would once again intensify.

As I walked into the mess hall the next morning, it felt good just to see and hear people again. There were more than a few good-natured jokes and complaints about the lack of sleep, but most of us were just happy that the long night was finally over.

It was about mid morning when I first heard the rumour. One of the guys mentioned that an officer had been injured by fire during the night. No one seemed to have any concrete information, so we soon forgot about it and got back to work. Our section was doing some much needed maintenance on our vehicles. As we continued our work in the parking lot, it became difficult to ignore the increasing flow of traffic entering the hotel. At first it was the military police arriving in force. Minutes later we watched as the commanding officer and his entourage came into the parking lot. They were not running, but they were definitely in a hurry to enter the hotel.

Just before noon the engineering officer called us together to give us the news. Captain Ian Patten had been found dead in his room. No one knew the exact details of when it occurred, but sometime during the night he had been struck and killed by small arms fire.

In the days following his death there was much speculation about how and why it happened. Opinions on which side fired the fatal shoot were divided. To the best of my knowledge, neither the Greeks nor Turks ever admitted responsibility. It would be many months before we heard the board of inquiry finding. His death was ruled an accident.

I didn't know much about Captain Patten, having only seen him around the hotel on the odd occasion. As the humanitarian officer his job mostly entailed working with various government agencies and civilians groups throughout the island. I do remember his broad smile as we passed each other in parking lot one morning. His cheerful "good morning" as he returned my salute was the only time we ever spoke.

After the memorial service the body of Captain Patten was shipped home to his wife and family for burial.

Captain Patten died on the first day of April 1975. After that the firing just stopped. The nights that followed were eerily quiet. Slowly things began to return to normal.

With barely three weeks remaining in our tour of duty and just ten days after the death of Captain Patten, we had our second fatality. Private Stephen Kohlman had died as the result of a vehicle accident while travelling between his platoon headquarters at Louroujina and the observation post at Pyroi.

Standing there at the memorial service I still had a clear memory of our brief encounter two months earlier. After a hard day's work, followed by an excellent meal, we had all gathered around the table in the tiny canteen. The conversation was about nothing in particular. We talked about home, hockey, and our jobs. I had to listen to some good-natured ribbing about living in luxury at the Ledra Palace. I responded by complaining about the poor maid service and how they kept forgetting to place a chocolate mint on my pillow at night. The back-and-forth banter continued, but by ten o'clock the crowd had thinned out and we all headed off in the dark to find our beds. Stephen Kohlman would always be remembered as a quiet, easy-going, young guy and a good soldier.

The day we had been all thinking about had finally arrived. We were going home. The buses to take us to Larnaca airport were standing ready, just across the parking lot. All things considered, we should have been a happy group, standing there waiting to depart, but the mood in the ranks was anything but light. Our hundred-man flight party had been standing for over an hour, waiting anxiously to board the buses. The barrack box containing the majority of our equipment had been shipped days earlier, leaving us with just our rifle and kit bag to take on the plane.

We had been rushed out of the hotel and shouted at to fall in quickly. With all the hurry, we all assumed that once the sergeant major called the roll, we could simply stow our kit in the luggage racks beneath the bus and get on board. But still we stood there waiting. "Typical army routine, hurry up and wait," someone grumbled from the rear. We all shook our heads in agreement. One of the older soldiers was bold enough to ask the sergeant major what the holdup was, but was instantly told to keep quiet and wait.

When the Land Rover Jeep pulled into the parking lot, most of us hardly noticed. What we didn't know was that this Jeep contained just one final surprise before we left the island.

"Right, gentlemen, open your kit bag, place it on the ground in front of you, and take a pace to the rear!" The sergeant major's command needed no explanation. When we saw the German Shepherd being led from the Land Rover, we all knew what was to happen next.

It had been weeks since the last members of the infamous airport pot party had been dealt with by the military justice system. Most of the soldiers in the battalion may have considered it a dead issue, but to those in a position of authority, it was far from over.

The drug-sniffing dog and his handler slowly made their way down the long line of kit bags. The dog stopped a few times and took an extra whiff, but each time it quickly moved on. Just before reaching the end of the line, the dog suddenly stopped and stuck its snout in a bag. Judging by the wagging tail and excited behaviour, it had obviously found something of interest. The dog handler looked equally pleased as he patted the animal and fed it some sort of treat. By now the sergeant major and a military policeman (MP) were converging on the culprit. The owner made a move toward the bag but was told to step back. His efforts to speak were instantly cut off by the glare of the sergeant major.

Within moments half the contents of the kit bags were strewn about the ground, but still the military policeman continued to dig. I thought it odd that the owner looked anything but nervous. In fact, he was actually smiling as the search went on. He tried saying something as he pointed at the bag, but once again his words were cut off. It looked like the MP finally hit pay dirt when he withdrew a small black shaving case from the bottom of the kit bag. After dumping the contents on the ground he found a small plastic vial and passed it to the sergeant major. The suspect was at last allowed to speak. He was obviously angry, but still chose his words carefully. "It's a prescription, sir. I got it from the medical officer just yesterday. You can check with the medic if you don't believe me, sir," he went on sarcastically. For a moment I thought the sergeant major was about to apologize but he simply smiled and handed the painkillers back to the soldier.

Our initial anger about the long holdup was quickly forgotten in the excitement of finally departing the city and starting the long trip home. Nothing illicit had been found, so like most, I believed the worst was finally over.

Before reaching London, our Boeing 707 would have to first stop in Ottawa to drop off the twenty or so members of the engineer regiment returning to their home base in Petewawa. Because the plane was being refuelled, all of us would have to get off and wait in a holding area just inside the terminal. From where we stood we had a clear view of the engineer group as they made their way through the arrivals area. Any hope we may have had that our alleged drug problem was left behind on the island of Cyprus was quickly dashed when we saw Canadian customs go to work on our engineer friends.

We watched in silence as each man was told to empty the contents of his kit bag on the counter. Not only did they search through every item in the bag, but each soldier had to turn out the many pockets in his uniform, as well as open each compartment in his wallet. I saw one engineer's face turn red in embarrassment when he accidently dropped a packet of condoms onto the counter. He moved to scoop them up but was told to wait while the customs official checked that there was nothing sinister left hidden in the wallet. One would think it would be extremely difficult to hide anything in something as small as a beret, but still some soldiers were told to remove their hats and stand there while the customs official felt around the brim searching for contraband.

We learned later that four of the engineers had been found with contraband. Although customs did not find any drugs, they did manage to find and confiscate a few cartons of cigarettes, two forty-ounce bottles of liquor, and several small pieces of gold and silver jewellery.

After witnessing all of that, a man would have to be a complete idiot to think he could get away with smuggling contraband. For the short flight between Ottawa and London the toilets in the aircraft were never empty. I can't say with certainty, but I do not believe that the illicit items being flushed down the toilet were drugs. Gold and silver were cheap to buy in the Middle East, but because Canadian import duties were so high, many of the guys had stashed away various bits of jewellery to take home to their wives. I often wonder what the airplane cleaning staff must have thought later when they came across this windfall of rings, necklaces, and bracelets filling the bottom of the waste disposal tank.

Our contingent had done some truly excellent work over the past six months. When we arrived on the island in October the situation had been very unstable. We had somehow managed to wedge ourselves between two hostile groups and helped to maintain the uneasy peace. Even when the Turks threatened the airport and a renewal of the war seemed imminent, our vastly outgunned soldiers had stood their ground and refused to blink. We may have been successful in maintaining the fragile peace, but the conscientious effort made by the majority of soldiers seemed to be completely overshadowed because of the actions of a few. Listening to the staff at higher headquarters or reading a newspaper would lead most outsiders to believe that we had a rampant drug problem throughout the battalion. We may have done some good work, but in the weeks and months to follow, all anyone seemed to remember was the so-called drug problem.

CHAPTER 11

Swan Song

OCTOBER 1983

As I sat in the adjutant's office waiting to see the commanding officer, I could not help but reflect on all of the changes that had happened in my military life in such a short time.

I had just returned from another five-year tour in Germany. During that time I had been promoted to warrant officer, and, after four straight years of night school, I had completed all the requirements for my grade thirteen diploma. My marks were high enough for me to receive an Ontario Scholar Award. Just weeks after graduation, I had been posted to the second battalion of the Royal Canadian Regiment in Gagetown New Brunswick.

I was just approaching the four-month period in my new job as the quartermaster for Lima Company when I received the call to report to the commanding officer. I assumed it was just a routine interview, but his opening remark caught me by complete surprise. "The regimental board has reviewed your file, and based upon job performance and your school grades we are offering you a commission to the rank of lieutenant."

After completing a battery of written examinations on mathematics and language skills, I was called before a board of four senior officers for one final interview. The questions and answers went on for two hours before they finally told me I had passed.

The good news was that because of my background and experience, I would not have to do the lengthy officer training course. Within the month I was sent to Chilliwack, British Columbia, for my six-week officer indoctrination course.

The bad news was that I was returning to my old company, in the same battalion, in Gagetown.

Perhaps in the civilian work world the transition from the factory floor to upper management could be accomplished with minimum fuss, but in the highly disciplined and tightly structured military world this transition was difficult. Normally someone in my situation would be posted immediately in order to get fresh start and make the necessary adjustment to a new position. Unfortunately for me, I did not have the luxury of time to adjust. My new job as the battalion transport officer meant I would remain right there in Lima Company. Every day I would have to deal with old friends who now saw me as something different. The daily greetings and friendly hellos were replaced by rigid salutes. What had once been casual conversations about work-related issues now became formal reports. They certainly were not doing anything wrong. We all knew that if a military organization was to operate effectively, this was the way it had to be.

My new peer group now consisted of the young officers in the battalion. The conversation in the mess on Friday night usually centred on their plans to head for the bars in Fredericton and pick up women. At the ripe old age of thirty-seven, with a wife and teenage children at home, I could add little to the conversation. I know it was meant as a joke, but having one or two of them refer to me as "dad" did little to alleviate my growing sense of alienation.

All of these thoughts filled my mind as I sat there waiting to see the colonel. It had only been fifteen minutes, but it felt much longer.

The commanding officer finally came breezing through the door and apologized for his lateness as he waved at me to follow him. Colonels never need to apologize to junior officers, but he was not your average commanding officer. Maybe it was because he had been promoted so late in his career, but he was obviously relishing this late opportunity to command a battalion. Rarely could he get from point A to point B without stopping and talking to everyone he met. He had the ability to listen to what was being said and make you believe that your words were important. Considering the large gap between our respective ranks, he and I seemed to get along very well.

The game of Trivial Pursuit had just come on the market and every Friday night I would look forward to playing the game in the mess. Someone had once told me that I was "a vast wasteland of useless information," which I took as a compliment. My winning record stood for five straight weeks and finally ended when the CO decided to join the game. I came close a number of times, but when the colonel was in the game, I never won again. I didn't know it at the time, but my efforts to beat him at trivia were futile. He was a card-carrying member of Mensa. To join this exclusive club you had to first take a supervised IQ test and only those who scored within the top 2 percent of the general population could gain entry.

As soon as we entered the office, the colonel closed the door and threw his hat on the desk. He was obviously running late, so he got right to the point.

"Terry, as you know, the battalion is short of officers and I need you to be my transport officer in Cyprus." I started to speak, but he raised his hand and continued. "I know you were slated to remain here as the rear party administrative officer and you have already completed two previous tours, but all that aside, I would like you to work for me in Cyprus."

I was well aware that in reality this entire conversation was completely unnecessary. He was the commanding officer and I was a lieutenant under his command. He could simply tell me I was going and that would be that. The colonel seemed truly pleased when I said I had no problem going, but as I left the office I couldn't help but feel a slight pang of guilt.

The truth was I was more than happy not to be stuck with the thankless job of administrative officer for the rear party. When the company commander first told me I was staying behind, I was elated, but once I actually discovered what my rear party duties would entail, my enthusiasm quickly disappeared. To do the job effectively I needed the skills of a family psychologist, coupled with the patience of a padre, along with a sound knowledge of financial planning. Needless to say, I possessed none of these particular skills. If the wife and family of a soldier working in

Cyprus experienced any one of myriad problems, I would be their point of contact. The problem could be as small as not getting regular mail from her husband or as big as not having the money to pay the rent. It really didn't matter; I was to be at their beck and call twenty-four hours a day.

In all honesty, before the CO had called me to his office that day, I had already made up my mind to request an interview. I had a checklist in my head and I was fully prepared to lay out all the reasons why he should take me to Cyprus.

As our Boeing 707 banked for final approach, I peered out the window at the vast expanse of water below. Nine years had passed since I last touched down on the island of Cyprus. The young officer in the seat beside me had been talking incessantly for the past hour. I couldn't begrudge him his obvious excitement on this his first U.N. tour of duty. He had finished his studies at the Royal Military College in Kingston and arrived in the battalion just six months earlier. He seemed so full of enthusiasm at the prospect of finally getting to do something worthwhile. He didn't actually say the words, but I could tell by his unending questions that this was a man who intended to leave his mark on this troubled island. He was going to change things for the better. Who was I to tell him differently? He didn't need to hear my thoughts.

Based on my limited exposure to him, he seemed to be an intelligent and sincere young lieutenant who could best learn from firsthand experience. As a junior platoon commander he would have little or no input when big decisions had to be made. His focus should always be on maintaining the peace in his tiny corner of the war. If he could do that successfully and get the twenty-four soldiers under his command home safely, he would have achieved the goal. I sat there just listening and nodding. I was not about to dampen his enthusiasm.

Our descent into Larnaca airport seemed much more gradual than I remembered. The runway had been extended, but the rocky shoreline of the Mediterranean still seemed perilously close. As soon as the aircraft doors opened the air was filled with the sound of heavy waves crashing against the shore. It was an unusually cool and wet day and each man had to be careful as he negotiated the slippery steps and scurried across the tarmac to the waiting bus.

I had been looking forward to seeing some old familiar terrain as our convoy drove north toward Nicosia, but the speed of the bus and the misty rain covering the windows made it difficult to see any details.

When we reached the traffic circle at the edge of the city the first bus in our convoy peeled off toward the downtown while we continued on to the next exit. The rain had let up enough to allow us a clear view as we approached Checkpoint Foxtrot. Using my coat sleeve to wipe the fog from the window, I could see the line of trenches my men and I had occupied that nerve-wracking night back in January of 1975. The long wait at the checkpoint gave me ample time to survey the entire position. The small guardhouse building in the centre of the road looked like it had a recent coat of blue and white paint and the rusty rows of barbwire had obviously been replaced by new rolls of concertina, but other than that I could see little change. A platoon from the Finnish contingent still manned the position. The trenches looked just as they had on that morning we left them.

Once we cleared the checkpoint, it was just a short drive up the road to what would be my home for the next six months — Camp Blue Beret.

The camp sat along a plateau overlooking the entire area. The barbwire boundary fence snaked along the edge of the ridge behind my quarters. My small room may have been cold and uninviting, but the view from behind the building would more than make up for that. Many a morning I would stand out back and watch the sun slowly rise in the eastern sky.

Just beyond the fence the land dropped away gradually to the north. Other than a few scrawny bushes and tufts of weeds, nothing seemed to grow in the brown sandy earth. Off in the distance I could see the ribbon of highway where it entered the suburbs of Nicosia. The international airport lay hidden in the low ground just a kilometre or so to the southwest. Getting a closer look at the old airport would have to wait until I settled into my new duties.

Just once, I thought to myself, *wouldn't it be nice to sit down and discuss my new job with my predecessor?* I knew it couldn't be helped, but that didn't make it any less frustrating. The officer I had replaced as transport officer was already in Larnaca and boarding the same aircraft that brought me here. Other than a brief glimpse as our buses passed on the highway, we would never see each other. I wasn't alone in my frustration. Right now there were new people throughout the contingent thinking the same thing, as we sat and tried to figure out our new duties based upon some hastily scribbled notes left by our processors.

My one good stroke of fortune was in having an exceptionally efficient sergeant to help me sort things out.

About a month before we left Gagetown, my warrant officer and second in command had come into my office to announce that he did not wish to go to Cyprus. He and I had been warrant officers together, which made the situation all the more awkward. To say I didn't like him would be putting it mildly. I could not stand the man and I knew the feeling was mutual. Rarely a day went by when he didn't inflict his particular brand of threats and abuse on the troops under his command. He only picked on the young soldiers he perceived to be weak and unable to defend themselves. The man was simply a bully who hid behind his rank.

Whether he went to Cyprus or stayed behind was not my decision to make. Only the colonel could decide, but I knew, as his immediate supervisor, my recommendation could help sway the decision in either direction. It would have been easy to recommend he stay in Gagetown. Life could be so much more pleasant without his constant disruptive rants. Still, I couldn't bring myself to do it. Like many of the soldiers in the battalion, I had already completed multiple overseas tours with NATO and the United Nations. Now this warrant officer, who had never once left Canada in his twenty years of service, was asking me to recommend he stay behind.

When his written request reached the CO's desk without any recommendation, the decision was brief and to the point. "Please inform the warrant that he has two choices: he can go to Cyprus or he can submit his release from the Canadian Forces." The next morning on company parade I could see a visible sigh of relief when I announced that he would be leaving and Sergeant Clifford would be taking over as the platoon second-in-command.

Had I been given the opportunity to pick and choose a senior non-commissioned officer (NCO) to work with, I could not have made a better choice than Wade Clifford. I may have taken on all the physical aspects of an officer, but I was still having some difficulty making the mental transition. I was well aware that most senior NCOs still looked upon me with some degree of suspicion. On more than one occasion since becoming an officer I had given a soldier a task to perform and then undermined his efforts by not allowing him the time to do the job in his own way. Rather than just simply telling him what to do, I was telling him how to do it. Even when a task was completed correctly, I couldn't help but think of how I would have done it differently. I may not have said it out loud, but I have no doubt they were picking up on my non-verbal signals. Within an hour of becoming my second-in-command, Sergeant Clifford was standing in the office doorway ready to confront me. "Sir, we have got to talk," was all he said before closing the door behind him.

It didn't happen overnight, but slowly over the next few weeks and months I finally began to understand that I was no longer a senior NCO. My job was not to stand over a soldier while he performed a task. My responsibility was to oversee the operation of transport platoon and make sure the organization was meeting its goals. Much of my time would be spent on administration. Writing reports and pumping out various bits of paperwork may not be glamorous, but at least it kept the soldiers free to focus on the job at hand.

It didn't take long for others to recognize Clifford's ability. Just a few weeks into the tour he was promoted to the rank of warrant officer.

Any success I had over the remainder of my career as an officer I would always attribute to the things I had learned from Warrant Officer Clifford during those six months we worked together in Cyprus. It may have been slow in coming, but by the time I left that island, the mental transition was complete. I no longer felt like a senior NCO dressed in an officer's uniform.

It would have been wonderful to arrive in Cyprus and spend a day or two just slowing working our way into our new duties. Unfortunately, the tight rotation schedule allowed little or no time for a smooth transition.

For the drivers in transport there was an added degree of concern for their safety during this hasty transition period. They may have been experienced drivers, but now they would have to drive on the opposite side of the road with literally no time to make the mental adjustment. Some of our drivers would have to step off an airplane after a seventeen-hour flight and be handed a vehicle to drive back to Nicosia. The situation may have been unavoidable, but the combination of being exhausted while driving a truck on the opposite side of an unfamiliar and very busy road could have been disastrous.

Thankfully we got through those first few hours with only one minor accident. The driver had managed to make it all the way from Larnaca to Nicosia without incident, but just as he was about to make his final turn he clipped the bumper on a civilian car. It had only been a momentary mental lapse, but rather than pulling out into the middle of the intersection to make the move, he turned hard right and found himself surrounded by oncoming traffic.

When the first week passed without any further accidents, I could finally allow myself to relax. The old familiar routine began to take shape.

Each morning I would wake at five o'clock to the dull clanging of my alarm clock. The winter rains had come early that year, so some mornings it took every ounce of willpower I had just to get out from under the blankets and put my feet on the cold cement floor. After throwing on some sweats and making a much-needed stop at the outdoor latrine, I would head up the road to meet the remainder of the company for morning physical training (PT). Other than the usual grunts and groans, the three-mile run normally started in silence. The first mile was always the worst. As a platoon commander I could consider myself lucky because I got to run up front. For the soldiers running near the rear of the company, things could quickly turn nasty. All the gas stored in the body overnight was now set free. When you multiply the problem by one hundred men, the smell became almost unbearable. Some mornings, especially if the canteen had been open late the night before, the methane cloud would seem to hang suspended in the air as it followed us around the three-mile running route.

After a shower, shave, and a quick breakfast, the real work day began at seven in the morning. Between driving, cleaning trucks, changing motor oil, and myriad other minor tasks, drivers rarely had a moment to spare. Twice each week all routine tasks would be put aside while the platoon fulfilled its primary function. Warrant Officer Clifford would take every available man and head for Larnaca Airport to meet the incoming supply flights. Their job was to meet the C-130 Hercules arriving from Canada by way of Lahr, Germany. If all went according to schedule they would have three hours to accomplish the task of unloading the aircraft. Whether it was caused by mechanical problems, bad weather, or any one of a number of other issues, the plane was frequently late. This was when the problems really began.

As soon as the pilot taxied off the runway, he would begin lowering the rear ramp. The moment the plane stopped, the drivers would immediately run up the open ramp and begin the difficult task of unloading the aircraft. Sometimes the pilot would come down from the cockpit and shout at the soldiers to hurry up. It didn't really matter what he said because nothing could be heard over the roar of the still-running engines.

Larnaca was the first of two stops for the C-130. The final leg of the flight would take them to Damascus, where they would offload cargo destined for the Canadian supply base in the Golan Heights. Just before reaching Syrian territory, the pilot must first ask permission to enter. The Syrians only allowed a small window of time for flights to enter their airspace, and failing to meet these strict timings would result in the aircraft being denied entry. If the pilot failed to turn around immediately, there was a good chance he would be fired upon. The big lumbering Hercules aircraft would have virtually no chance of survival against a Syrian missile.

The soldiers understood the gravity of the situation and were moving with all possible speed. Even before the unloading was complete, the plane would begin to move forward as the last pieces of cargo were flung off the back. Most of the pilots would give a quick thumbs up as they taxied back onto the runway for a hasty takeoff. Once they caught their breath, the drivers would begin organizing all the bits and pieces of cargo strewn about the tarmac.

* * *

The final few days of 1983 brought nothing but unrelenting rain. Christmas passed without any outbreaks of fire. Sitting outside my room in the darkness on a peaceful Christmas Eve I could almost forget we were living in a war zone. The lights of the city glowed brightly, and every so often I could see a narrow beam of headlights as a car sped down the highway. Except for the steady rain drumming against the roof, the night was completely quiet. You could allow your mind to play these little tricks on you in the darkness, but once the sun came up and you could see the barbwire fences around the minefields and the bombed out buildings there was no doubting where you were.

At first the paperwork involved in my job seemed overwhelming. Once the drivers in transport platoon got used to driving on the opposite side of the road our internal accident rate went down dramatically, but unfortunately the same could not be said for the numerous other drivers throughout the contingent. Thankfully the majority of accidents were minor, but rarely a week went by without at least two or three fender benders.

As the transport officer, I did have one small advantage over most of the other officers in the contingent. I had my own Jeep and could come and go as I pleased. Once I got a handle on all the paperwork, I tried to make time each afternoon to get out of the office and visit the other companies spread throughout the city.

The Ledra Palace hotel may have had a few more bullet holes in the walls, but basically the exterior looked the same as when I last saw it nine years earlier. The interior was quite another matter. What was left of the plush carpeting was held together with long strips of gun tape. The ornate railing that had once flanked the main staircase was long gone. With the guardrail gone, you could look straight down from the top floor landing to the basement, some eighteen metres below. A small sign on each floor warned people to walk in the middle of the stairway and stay away from the edges.

The Turkish and Greek positions surrounding the hotel now looked much more formidable. Each side had built concrete walls to replace the rusty sheet of corrugated iron and rotting sandbags. The two positions in front of the hotel had become one of the main crossing points for foot traffic between the Turkish and Greek sectors of the city. What had once been a hastily built fortification manned by a few soldiers was now a much larger system of bunkers and trenches.

Wolseley Barracks looked exactly the same; even the bunkers and machine gun trench I had a hand in building years earlier were still there. The officers' mess building near the front of the complex still hosted the peace negotiations, but the daily meetings had long ago been scaled back to once a week.

The airport complex was probably the most vivid reminder of just how little had changed over the years. The Turks had pulled back away from the airport boundary, but even though we could no longer see them, we knew they were still sitting and waiting in the hills, just a few kilometres away to the northwest.

The once majestic passenger jets still sat scattered about the tarmac. Nine years of decay had taken its toll. The combined effects of summer sun and winter rain had peeled away much of the paint. The British Airways jet still sat abandoned near the front of the terminal. I could still see some patches of blue and red paint on the frame, but the company name and logo had disappeared under a thick coat of rust.

The abandoned stretch of land between Checkpoint Foxtrot and the airport terminal had been taken over by packs of dogs. At one time they may have been docile house pets, but after years of running free they had become wild and unpredictable. As the packs grew and the food supply dwindled, these animals had become all the more vicious. Sometimes late at night we could hear them howling off in the distance. The dense underbrush on either side of the airport highway made them difficult to see in the daylight, but every so often you could spot them moving along the shoulders of the road, looking for food. The American M2 Jeep I drove had no doors or canvas superstructure, so whenever I went to the airport, I would check to ensure I was properly prepared to defend myself. It was only a wooden pick handle, but all of the vehicles carried one to fend off dog attacks. The pick handles we referred to as "puppy pounders" sat right next to the driver's seat and could be easily swung with one arm while still steering forward with the other. The worst thing you could possibly do was slow down or stop.

The old Green Line we had first manned back in 1970 was now deep inside the Turkish sector of the city. It had taken me a long time to get permission, but finally in the last month of our tour I was allowed to return briefly to some of our old haunts.

Standing on the small rise near a dirt track, I could see the former Green Line stretched out before me. The small metal observation huts we had used were long gone and the street had been paved. It seemed rather odd to see children playing and cars moving freely back and forth on what had once been such a hotly contested strip of land. Every house was occupied by a Turkish Cypriot family and I couldn't help but wonder what had happened to all those Greek families who had lived along this road those many years ago. Had they died trying to escape the invasion or had they simply abandoned their property and started a new life, somewhere else on the island?

I wasn't allowed to actually enter the public works department, but through the wire mesh fence I could see little had changed. The long red stone building spanning the front of the compound that had been the main quarters for our twenty-four-man platoon now looked crammed with an entire company of Turkish soldiers.

Thankfully I was able to end my rather depressing day with one bright spot. The small building where I had lived, just down the road from the PWD, was now teeming with life. Our once drab and dirty quarters had been converted back to its original use as a schoolhouse. All of the broken windows and ripped screens had been replaced and a fresh coat of whitewash made the place look cheerful and inviting. All of the barbwire surrounding the structure had been removed and the yard was full of happy, screaming children.

As I stood there watching the kids play, I couldn't help but remember that first time I saw this place in the grey light of dawn, on that very first day on the island fourteen years ago. My roommate Lloyd Wells and I had managed to scrounge up a roll of brown wrapping paper. The plan was to cover up the many holes and wallpaper the walls of our tiny room in an effort to make the place a little more liveable. We had only just begun when one of our section commanders stuck his head through the open door. When we told him what we were doing, he responded with words I will never forget. "I wouldn't do too much if I were you. I was at the company conference this morning and it looks like this war may soon be over." I had first heard rumours about our early departure before the plane even landed. Now the sergeant's confident words seemed to give credit to these rumours. Lloyd and I were just young and naïve enough to believe there was some truth to what he was saying. After the sergeant left, we decided that rather than paper the entire room, we would just plug the holes in the wall and wait for our inevitable departure back to Canada.

It had been fourteen years since I first set foot in Cyprus and I had long since stopped listening to idle rumours. Every new contingent seemed to bring it own fresh rumours about an early end to the trouble, but still it went endlessly on. After three tours spanning two decades, my time on the island was finally at an end.

I often wonder what that first contingent in 1964 would have thought if they had known that it would take more than thirty years before the last Canadian could leave Cyprus behind and finally go home for good.

AFTERMATH

THE UNITED NATIONS FORCE IN CYPRUS

Casualties and Statistics

Actions at the airport and other hot spots throughout Nicosia during the Turkish Invasion of 1974 came at a high cost for Canadian Peacekeepers. The Canadian Contingent suffered more than thirty casualties, including two dead: Private JL Perron and Private JJ Berger of the Canadian Airborne Regiment.

Canada kept an infantry battalion of varying size in Cyprus until the mid 1990s. Virtually every Canadian infantry battalion had completed multiple tours in Cyprus. The armoured and artillery regiments also took their turn.

The Canadian contingent varied in size during their twenty-nine years of involvement, from a high of 1,100 personnel in 1964 to fewer than five hundred in at the beginning of the 1990s. In all, about twenty-five thousand personnel served with the Canadian contingent.

A total of twenty-eight Canadian peacekeepers died in the service of peace in Cyprus.

Today a small memorial honouring their sacrifice stands at the site of the former Canadian Contingent Headquarters in Nicosia.

PART TWO

The Middle East Years

BACKGROUND

The United Nations Truce Supervisory Organization

In November 1947, the U.N. General Assembly endorsed a plan for the partition of Palestine, providing for the creation of an Arab and a Jewish State. The plan was quickly rejected by the Palestinian Arabs and the surrounding Arab States.

On May 14, 1948 the United Kingdom relinquished its mandate over Palestine and the State of Israel was proclaimed. Almost immediately the Palestinian Arabs and the surrounding Arab states declared war on the new State of Israel.

Fourteen days later the U.N. Security Council passed Resolution 50, calling for a cessation of hostilities. Within a few months the first group of military observers were in place to supervise the truce between Israel and its four neighbouring Arab counties.

These first military observers soon became the nucleus of a new organization called The United Nations Truce Supervisory Organization (UNTSO).

By August 1949, an Armistice Agreement had been signed by all the warring factions and UNTSO was assigned the function of overseeing the truce. UNTSO activity thus became spread over the five states of Israel, Egypt, Jordan, Lebanon, and the Syrian Arab Republic.

Following a succession of wars in 1956, 1967, 1973, and 1982, the function of the UNTSO military observers have changed from time to time, but they continue to remain in the area, acting as a go-between for all the hostile parties.

The United Nations Interim Force in Lebanon

In March 1978, the Israeli Defence Force crossed into Lebanon and attacked a number of Palestinian Commando positions. The U.N. Security Council quickly passed Resolution 425, which created the United Nations Interim Force in Lebanon (UNIFIL).

Israeli forces soon withdrew from the area, but when Palestinian forces began to renew their attacks across the border, the Israeli army once again invaded Lebanon and pushed north, all the way to Beirut.

In 1985 the Israelis withdrew to the south, but continued to maintain a strong presence inside Southern Lebanon. This narrow band of territory known as the "Israeli controlled area" stretches along the entire southern border between Israel and Lebanon.

The six national battalions that comprise the United Nations Interim Force in Lebanon continue to enforce the ceasefire all across South Lebanon, from the Israeli border north to the banks of the Litani River.

CHAPTER 12

Life in the Part-Time Army

The sign on the highway may have called it a city, but as I entered Brockville, Ontario, for the first time, it had all the feel of a small town. Driving along the main street, I could not get over just how picture perfect it seemed to be. When I arrived at my destination I took a few minutes to drink in the view. Standing there on the front lawn of the armoury I could see the waters of the St. Lawrence River as it made its way along the southern edge of the city. Somewhere out there in the middle of the river an imaginary line separated us from the United States.

From the outside, the armoury building was a very impressive site. The huge, fortress-like structure sat well back from the main street and covered half a city block. According to the chiselled cornerstone, the armoury had been built in 1910.

I must admit that it took me quite a while to adjust to my new role as the regular army advisor to the Brockville Rifles Regiment. Initially I had a good deal of suspicion toward these "part-time" soldiers, but soon realized that what they may have lacked in experience they more than made up for in their enthusiasm. The majority of these soldiers had full-time jobs or went to school and came to the armoury for training after spending a day in the classroom or at work. I soon realized that being in the militia took a special kind of commitment. The officers and soldiers were required to train for two nights each week and one weekend per month. When the average soldier was receiving roughly fifty dollars a month for their efforts, I knew the money was certainly not the incentive for showing up.

One training night in early February the commanding officer called all the unit officers and senior non-commissioned officers into the conference room to announce that the unit's budget had been expended for the year. The unit would not receive its new annual budget until sometime in April. The soldiers could still train, but there was no money to pay them. Any doubts I may have had about their dedication were soon put to rest as I watched these officers and soldiers continue to show up for seven straight weeks of training without receiving a penny in pay for their efforts. I often wonder how many regular force soldiers faced with a similar situation would have shown up and worked for nothing.

The work schedule was certainly not as intense as the regular force. Winters were spent on lectures and training in the armoury, with the occasional weekend exercise in the local area. Summers were spent in Meaford and Petawawa conducting training during the long school break.

I knew my time working with the militia would only last for three years, after which I fully expected to return to one of our three regular force battalions. When I finally received my posting message and read the details I just couldn't believe my good luck.

Some months earlier I had been interviewed by my boss in Ottawa. After some initial small talk we finally got down to the purpose of the meeting. Although the decision on where an officer will go on posting is normally based upon the needs of the military service, we were given this one opportunity to ask for a particular job or location. I handed him my list of three preferred locations and just sat back watching as he scanned the paper. Seconds ticked by as he continued to stare at the list. I had expected an immediate response to my unusual request, but his blank expression gave no hint of what he was thinking.

At last he spoke. "You do realize that there are only eight positions available to Canadians officers in the entire region?"

"I understand the difficulties, sir, but someone has to fill these positions, so why not me?" I tried to sound positive but I knew with every officer in the entire Canadian Forces eligible for these few positions, my chances of success were extremely slim.

Now sitting in my office, I read the message for a third time before finally picking up the phone and calling Brigitte to give her the good news. We were going to the Middle East.

I was posted to the United Nations Truce Supervisory Organization and I was to report to the headquarters in Jerusalem, Israel, on July 15, 1987.

CHAPTER 13

Dealing With a New and Dangerous Reality

The first full day in Jerusalem seemed to go by in a blur of paperwork. When we got back to the hotel I fell into a dead sleep as my body tried to adjust to the eight-hour time difference. Brigitte could remain at the hotel, but I would have to return to the headquarters early the following morning and sit through an endless series of briefings on everything my new job would entail.

We eight Canadians were far from alone in the crowded conference room. Everywhere I looked there were officers from virtually every corner of the globe. Based on the flags sewn on each man's uniform, I could see officers from Australia, New Zealand, Ireland, Chile, France, and Argentina. The Russians all sat together in the back of the room. They didn't say much, but continued to stare at the Americans sitting near the front. During one of the breaks I was introduced to a Chinese officer, but when I tried to shake his hand, he just bowed. After a moment I withdrew my hand and we both stood there smiling awkwardly. Although one of the main prerequisites for work with UNTSO was the ability to speak English, when I spoke to the Chinese officer, I could tell he had no idea what I was saying.

The group from the Scandinavian countries seemed the friendliest. Because of their boisterous and outgoing nature we soon began referring to them collectively as the "Scandahooligans."

One of the first people I met that day was Captain Anders Perrson. Little did I know at the time that he and I would end up working together for the next twelve months. Anders was a Swedish army reservist who had taken a leave of absence from his job as a motorcycle cop in Stockholm. He may have been a part-time soldier, but as I soon discovered, he was a thoroughly competent officer and a true gentleman.

The first speaker was a U.S. Marine lieutenant colonel who held the position of chief operations officer. He was certainly a commanding presence. With his perfectly fitting uniform and highly shined boots, he looked like he just stepped off a recruiting poster. Judging by the multiple rows of ribbons on his tan shirt, he had seen service in practically every corner of the world.

The aim of his presentation that morning was to give us a broad overview of U.N. operations in the Middle East, with particular emphasis on our role as military observers. If there was the slightest doubt as to why we were here in the region, his opening remarks were to set the tone for the remainder of our tour.

"Gentlemen, welcome to the headquarters for the United Nations Truce Supervisory Organization. After we are finished these briefings most of you will depart here and begin your duties at one of our five stations spread throughout the Middle East. Whether you are working in Egypt, Israel, Jordan, Syria, or Lebanon there is only one crucial point I want you all to remember about your job." The colonel paused for a moment to scan the room. "You are there to observe and report any and all infractions of the ceasefire agreement." Again the colonel paused to pick up a measuring stick and position himself in front of the huge wall map of the region. "Depending on which station you work in, you will find that there are a variety of tasks you will be required to perform. If you are in Syria or Israel you will probably be manning an observation post on either side of the Golan Heights. Every other week or so you will find yourself visiting either Israeli or Syrian positions to count troops and equipment each side is holding. In Egypt, you will be conducting periodic patrols through the Sinai Desert between Cairo and the Suez Canal. In Lebanon you will be manning a number of observation posts along the Israeli border or conducting patrols throughout the region." After placing the pointer down on the lectern, he turned to face his audience. "Remember, gentlemen, regardless of where you are or what type of duty you are asked to perform, you are there to observe and report. There are no good guys or bad guys as far as you are concerned. If we as military observers are to maintain our credibility, we must remain impartial at all times, regardless of who we are dealing with."

Again the colonel paused to scan the faces in the room. I can't speak for anyone else in the audience, but I found his next statement rather unnerving. During my three previous U.N. tours in Cyprus, I had always carried a weapon for self defence, so naturally I assumed that this would be the standard practice on any U.N. mission.

"Gentlemen, there is one other important point I want to ensure you clearly understand. UNTSO policy prohibits the carrying of any type of weapon by its observers. This ban includes everything from knives to bayonets, as well as any type of firearm." Judging by the low grumbling throughout the room, I was not the only person caught off guard by the colonel's comments. After waiting a moment for the room to settle down, he went on. "There are a number of other U.N. organizations throughout the Middle East and all of them are fully armed. You may from time to time have to work with these other U.N. groups and at times they may even request transport in one of our vehicles. There is no rule preventing you from working with these groups or even giving them a ride, but under no circumstances will they be allowed to carry arms once they enter our vehicles." The colonel just stood there in silence, waiting once again for the room to settle down. "Gentlemen, I want to leave you with one final thought. The fact that we are an unarmed organization of military observers is well known by every interest group in the Middle East. Whether you are dealing with Sunni Muslims, Amal militia, the Israeli army, or even Hezbollah fundamentalist groups, they all know you are unarmed and, as such, you present no threat to them. Your best defence is to simply do your job in a fair and impartial manner and you should have no problems."

Later on in the tour I would become a station operations officer and have to report to the colonel in Jerusalem each month. I always looked forward to these opportunities to talk with him. He possessed an uncanny ability to listen to what was being said and then dissecting that information to come up with the answer to most problems. I rarely left the headquarters without gaining some new perspective on how to better do the job.

Each afternoon the colonel would make time to go for a five-mile run around the outskirts of the city. It had been a particularly hot summer day and he was roughly halfway around his running route when he collapsed from a heart attack. By the time help arrived, he was already dead. He was only a few weeks away from going home.

There were two more briefings that morning, but nothing as thought provoking as the colonel's lecture. The mid-morning coffee break was a noisy affair with everyone seeming to have an opinion on the colonel's lecture. I was still a little apprehensive about the concept of entering hostile territory without a weapon.

It wouldn't take me long to get used to the new reality. Over the next few months, the concept of travelling around without a weapon would rarely cross my mind. It would take a fatal incident, late in the tour, to make me think that perhaps the policy was flawed.

Every so often during the long morning, another group of a dozen officers would be called from the room. Just before noon, I literally leapt from my chair when I heard my name being called. I was just happy to get out of the stuffy room and into the fresh air. Because our new jobs all required a great deal of driving, each of us would have to endure a short road test.

After being divided into groups of four, we boarded the CJ7 Jeeps and headed down the road to Bethlehem. Out first driver was from New Zealand, and after being reminded to stay on the right side of the road he did just fine. Once we turned around in Bethlehem, I managed to get us through the outskirts of the town without hurting anybody. We had all passed and it was left up to the fourth member of our group to get us safely back to the headquarters. I would be faced with some very scary situations over the next few months, but I cannot remember anything quite as frightening as that last few kilometres that morning, as we hurdled down the highway with a Chinese officer barely in control of the vehicle. Maybe someone should have asked beforehand, but nobody did. Now it was far too late to find out he had never driven anything in his entire life. We could smell the gears burning as he tried jamming forward on the stick shift without engaging the clutch. At last the instructor in the passenger seat managed to reach over a slam his foot down on the brake pedal. The vehicle came to a sudden stop and all of us were thrown forward like rag dolls. For a moment there was silence as we all tried to take a deep breath and assess the damage. Smoke was billowing out from under the hood, but thankfully no one appeared hurt. The Chinese major just sat there smiling, while our Dutch instructor looked pale and shaken, with his foot still firmly planted down on the brake.

When I next saw the Chinese officer, some six months later, he was at the headquarters in Jerusalem, where he had been given a cushy office job where absolutely no driving would be required.

It had been an extremely long day, filled with briefings. As four o'clock approached, we all waited anxiously for the final speaker of the day. You could actually feel the sense of anticipation as the Irish captain entered the room, took his place behind the lectern, and began reading off the list of names and locations. We were about to find out where each of us would be sent for our first six months of duty.

This was one of those times when I was more than happy to be a Canadian. There were a total of sixteen countries represented within UNTSO, but only twelve, including Canada, could serve in any outpost without restrictions. I don't profess to understand the politics involved, but all those observers from the Soviet Union, United States, France, and China had some rather strict limitations on where they could serve. The Russian and Chinese officers could serve in most of the Arab countries, but were not allowed to work on the Israeli side of the Golan Heights. The French and American officers could work in Lebanon, but only in areas close to the border and controlled by the Israeli army.

I have to admit that as I sat there listening for my name, I didn't really give much thought to these rules and restrictions. It would be many months later before we all understood why these rules were in place and just how dangerous and deadly things could be for those members of the group known as the "superpowers."

As Brigitte and I prepared for dinner that night, I could not have been happier. We would be leaving for the town of Nahariya in northern Israel the following morning, where we would live while I worked in South Lebanon.

CHAPTER 14

Trial and Tribulation on the Echo Road

JULY 1987

The town of Nahariya sat nestled against the shores of the Mediterranean, just a few kilometres south of the Lebanese border. At first glance it looked like any one of the many seaside resort towns dotting the Israeli coastline, but as we were soon to learn, this town was distinctly different from those we passed on our drive north from Jerusalem.

After driving through the outskirts of Tel Aviv, we took the coast highway north through the port city of Haifa. At first it seemed that each beach we passed was literally teeming with tourists. Stretches of white sandy beaches with rows of brightly coloured umbrellas were all we saw. Only after we passed through the ancient city of Akko did we see things slowly begin to change. The beaches along the coastline all appeared deserted.

The U.N. headquarters building sat just off the beach at the western edge of Nahariya. Even as we alighted from our minivan I could not help but notice that other than the odd person out for a stroll, the entire shoreline was completely empty. Looking north I could see the very edge of the town and beyond that the ground began to gently rise toward the east. Much of the land looked brown and desolate in the summer heat, but a few large patches of green seemed oddly out of place in these parched surroundings. Our driver told me that these green plots of land were part of a much larger kibbutz farm that stretched along the border. As I shielded my eyes against the sun, I could just make out the faint outline of a fence snaking along the far ridge. The Israeli border fence began right at the edge of the western shoreline and continued in an unbroken line until it disappeared in the rolling hills to the east.

When I asked the driver why the beach was so deserted, he just pointed once again to the north. "You won't find a lot of tourists here because of our proximity to the border with Lebanon. There have been several incidents over the past few years where either individuals or groups have fired mortars and even rockets over the fence into northern Israel. Just a few months ago four heavily armed men were killed just a kilometre or so off shore when they tried to infiltrate using a small rubber boat. If you look closely at the houses around here you will find that practically everyone has a bomb shelter nearby."

While we were talking I could see an Israeli patrol boat prodding through the waves just a hundred metres off shore. Later, when we moved into our apartment by the seashore, I could sit on my balcony and watch what the locals called "The Beirut Milk Run." You could actually set your watch by it. Each morning at precisely six o'clock and again at four in the afternoon, two F4 Phantom jets would appear from the south. At barely a hundred metres off the coastline, the Star of David was clearly visible as they streaked low over the water. Once they reached the border we could hear a thunderous roar as each pilot fired up his afterburners and broke through the sound barrier. Within a matter of seconds they would disappear from view as they continued their patrol run along the Lebanese coast.

Once again I would have to leave Brigitte waiting in a hotel while I headed for Lebanon the next morning. Our need to find a place to live would have to wait while I commenced one final round of training.

As we made the short trip north toward the border, I could not help but notice how very ordinary everything appeared to be. The waters of the Mediterranean on our left looked calm and peaceful, while the farmland off to the right was bustling with activity. It was just past six in the morning and already it was hot and sticky. A long line of tractors made their way across the fields, each dragging its own irrigation tank behind. A steady spray of misty water saturated the landscape as the tractors slowly made their way across the field and around the edges of an orange grove.

The large sign suspended above the road warned us to slow down as we approached the border. We finally came to a complete stop in front of a massive iron gate dissecting the entire highway. Earlier that morning our small band of trainees had been issued with identification cards, which we now held up for the Israeli gate guard to see.

The change in the landscape once we crossed the border was absolutely startling. We were barely a kilometre inside Lebanon and already it looked like we were on a different planet. The first few hundred metres were completely barren of all vegetation. The Israeli army had bulldozed everything flat. A single continuous minefield stretched east from the water's edge to the horizon. The narrow asphalt road we drove on was the only piece of safe ground in the entire area. After passing the minefield we came across the ruins of what had once been a small village. Every house had been flattened, every tree cut down, and every boulder removed by the Israelis to ensure that no one could approach the border without being seen. Two kilometres down the road we came across the first signs of life inside Lebanon.

The village of Naqoura consisted of a long line of squat little buildings stretching along the eastern side of the road. These cinder-block structures looked like they had been thrown together overnight. Signs advertising restaurants, T-shirt shops, liquor stores, and even video rentals littered the front of every building. Obviously all of these establishments had been set up to make a quick dollar from the men who lived behind the six-metre wall on the opposite side of the street. Squeezed between the stone wall and the Mediterranean shoreline sat the headquarters for the United Nation Interim Force in Lebanon.

UNIFIL consisted of an armed force of six battalions whose job it was to control all the access routes leading into southern Lebanon. Working north from the border, the Israelis controlled an area roughly ten kilometres deep and running the entire width of the country, from the Mediterranean shoreline in the west, all the way to the Syrian border in the east. Immediately north of this Israeli controlled area (ICA) there was another buffer zone manned by soldiers from six nations, all working as members of UNIFIL.

*Map of
the entire
Middle East
region.*

Collection of the
author.

A battalion each from Fiji, Nepal, Ghana, Finland, Ireland, and Norway were spread across the entire country from west to east. These soldiers had the difficult job of controlling a huge swath of territory in order to maintain an area of separation between the Israelis in the south and the numerous hostile groups inhabiting all of northern Lebanon.

The headquarters for UNIFIL consisted of just two or three permanent buildings surrounded by a sea of trailers. Tucked away just inside the perimeter wall sat a single line of three trailers, which housed our tiny independent headquarters.

After some quick introductions to the staff, we took our seats in the conference for what we hoped would be a short briefing. The border clearance had taken a little more time than normal and we were already behind schedule for what we knew would be an extremely long day of on-the-job training.

Our Belgian operations officer stood before the huge wall map and began his briefing with some facts and figures. "Good morning, gentlemen, and welcome to Observer Group Lebanon (OGL). Our station is the largest in the United Nations Truce Supervisory Organization and has the strength of eighty officers from sixteen different countries. Eighty officers may sound like a lot, but considering we must provide the manpower for seven patrol teams and six observation posts, we are in fact stretched quite thin." He picked up a long pointer and turned to face the map. "Later on in your tour, once you have gained some seniority, you may be employed on one of the four man teams working within the UNIFIL battalions, but for the first few months your primary job will be to man any one of our six observation posts stretched across the buffer zone." He carefully pointed to each position on the map as he spoke. "Starting in the west and moving east these locations are known as OPs Hin, Ras, Mar, Khiam, and Chateau. After we are done here, you will be departing to visit each of these positions, where you will receive yet another briefing from the officers on duty."

He stopped for a moment and moved his pointer along the thin blue pencil line connecting each of the observation posts. "This blue line is vitally important for your own personal safety." He continued to slap the pointer against the map. "This line indicates what we call the Echo

Road, and it is the only route you will use when travelling to and from the observation posts. As you can see on the map, there are markings known as Echo points, approximately ten kilometres apart all along the route. Each of these points is numbered consecutively, starting at Echo One here in Naqoura and continuing east along the entire Echo Road. Driving at normal speed it should take you approximately fifteen to eighteen minutes to travel between any two of these thirty points. Regardless of whether you are moving east or west on the Echo Road you must contact the traffic control station on the radio and report when you pass one of these Echo points. If more than twenty minutes passes and you fail to call, the traffic control will attempt to make radio contact with you. At the twenty-five minute mark, if there is still no response from you, the control station will declare a mayday, at which point all other activity

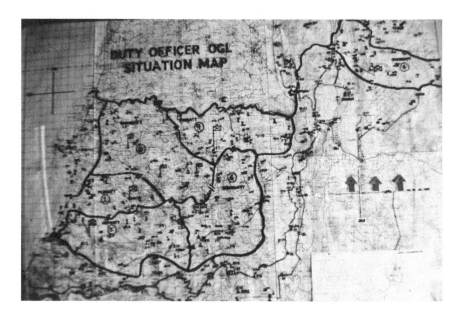

The duty officer's map in Observer Group Lebanon. The line at the bottom of the map indicates the border fence between Israel and Lebanon. The thick black lines depict the boundaries between the six battalions belonging to UNIFIL. The top black wavy line indicates the Litani River, which was the boundary for all U.N. operations.

Collection of the author.

will cease while every U.N. vehicle operating in South Lebanon will be dispatched to your last reported location in an effort to find you."

Up to this point in the briefing the operations officer had been smiling, but now his demeanour changed as he moved away from the map and stood staring at each of us in turn. "I know my English may be a little unclear, but it is imperative that you understand what I am about to say. South Lebanon is a very dangerous place. The economy has almost completely collapsed and any form of government control has all but disappeared. There is no law and order and every day there are reports of shootings, roadside bombs, and even armed robberies. This system of Echo points was devised to ensure we know where you are at all times. Should your radio break down, you still have a portable Motorola set you can use to contact us, but if you simply forget to call in, I can guarantee you it will not happen twice because you will leaving Lebanon and going home on the next available transport."

After giving us a few minutes to absorb everything he said, we were each handed a map, flak jacket, and helmet and began to prepare for our training tour on the Echo Road.

Our Dutch training officer was not one to waste time on small talk. As we stood waiting to depart his first words caught us by surprise. "Please take out your wallets and let me see what you have." He took just a moment to look inside each wallet before hand them back to us. "You all have too much money on you and I suggest you either leave some behind or hide it somewhere on your person."

Lebanese pounds may have been the country's official currency, but after the collapse of the economy, the pound was almost worthless. The U.S. dollar was the currency of choice throughout the country.

I had about thirty U.S. dollars, plus another twenty Israeli shekels. "There is about a fifty/fifty chance we could get held up sometime today, and if that happens I want you each to have at least ten dollars in your pockets and wallet. These guys all have guns and the last thing we want to do is piss them off by having nothing to turn over." I knew his next comment was directed at me. "If you have anything on you with Israeli or Hebrew markings, including money, please get rid of it now, because that could certainly get you shot." After turning over all our extra loot, I thought we were ready to go, but he had one more point to make before boarding the truck. "If you are wearing any type of Christian cross or Star of David or any expensive jewellery, get rid of it now."

We were only a few kilometres into our journey and already we could see that travel on the Echo Road could be treacherous in more way than one. The road was barely three metres wide and what remained of the asphalt surface had not been repaired in years. Every few metres we had to slow down and manoeuvre back and forth to avoid yet another pothole. Some of these holes were more like small, deep craters that could not be avoided without leaving the hard surface. In most cases there was enough room to get around these obstacles, but with mines and roadside bombs always a threat, we were told to remain on the hard surface wherever possible.

Aside from the road itself, the flow of oncoming traffic presented the other serious threat. Unlike us, the civilian population seemed to have no concern about swerving around potholes and flinging dirt and rocks in the air as they sped past on the gravel shoulder of the road. At one point we had to slam on the brakes as we watched an old Mercedes come barrelling toward us. At the last minute the driver slowed down just long enough to wave and smile as his tires caught the hard surface and disappeared behind us. The Mercedes had no doors and the driver looked to be no more than eleven or twelve years old.

At least with an oncoming car we were left with a little room to pass, but later on when it was my turn to drive, we ran into a M48 armoured truck, which left us no choice other than to move well over onto the soft shoulder. It was still a very tight fit as the halftrack edged by. As soon as there was an opening, the training officer told me to floor the gas pedal and get out of there as quickly as possible.

These odd-looking vehicles were used by the South Lebanese Army. With standard rubber tires on the front and tracks on the rear, they were quite capable of manoeuvring through the roughest terrain. They may have been Second World War vintage vehicles, but the .50 calibre gun mounted on top still made it a formidable weapon. Because these South Lebanese soldiers were paid and equipped by the Israeli army, most of the locals looked upon them as the enemy. Both the South Lebanese and

Israelis were under constant threat of attack. We were warned that whenever we came across them, we should stay as far away as possible. Even if we came up behind a military convoy, we were told to stop and wait until they moved off well into the distance.

It was only twenty kilometres down the Echo Road to the first observation post, but it had taken a full forty-five minutes before we finally spotted the whitewashed building perched on the hillside just off the road.

Major Jim Coats was the first Canadian I met in Lebanon. He was one of the two officers working on OP Hin when we arrived. After offering us a coffee, we were all taken to the roof for the first of our six operational briefings that day. As Major Coats explained the situation and gave us the lay of the land, we each took a turn at looking through the thirty-power binoculars mounted on a tripod in the centre of the roof. Just to the south we could clearly see the border fence and a gate leading into Israel. This was in fact two fences, separated by a six-metre-wide dirt track running down the middle. These double gates were one of only a few used exclusively by the military when entering or exiting Lebanon. About ten minutes into the briefing, we watched as an Israeli Jeep made its way slowly down the dirt track between the fences. Small clouds of dust were kicked up by what looked like a long, flat board being dragged along the ground behind the Jeep. As our host explained, this was the hourly patrol searching for any signs of intruders. As the Jeep moved steadily forward the crew commander would scan the soft dirt surface ahead, looking for footprints or anything that might indicate that someone had been in this no man's land between the fences. Once the vehicle passed, the long board would act like a rake and smooth over everything, including the tire tracks. It may have looked crude and simple, but according to the reports, the Israelis had caught many men trying to infiltrate Israel by using this basic method.

Once we got back downstairs, the other officer in the two-man team gave us an excellent briefing on everything to do with the daily routine.

When the training ended and we began regular duty, we would work on any one of the six observation posts. Our two-man team would be out there for seven days at a time and would have to bring enough food and bottled water to last the entire period. Once during the week the

OP Hin was one of five observation posts operating along the Israeli-Lebanese border. Each OP was manned by two military observers who would remain there for a seven-day shift.

Collection of the author.

five-hundred-litre tank on the roof would be filled with wash water and at the same time we would receive a supply of propane tanks to run the stove and refrigerator.

The shed outside contained a generator, which provided all of the electricity needed to light the OP and run the all-important radio. Other than the occasional visit from one of the patrol teams, the radio would be our only means of contact with the outside world.

Our trek continued throughout the morning. At first the steady breeze blowing in off the Mediterranean kept the temperature at a comfortable level, but as we journeyed inland the heat and humidity continued to increase. Wearing a heavy flak jacket in the tight confines of a CJ7 Jeep only added to our discomfort.

After spending just thirty minutes on OPs Ras and Mar, we had actually managed to get back on schedule. Each time we rounded a curve, all eyes would scan the road ahead, looking for any signs of trouble. Our training officer had warned us that as we moved further to the northeast and away from the border, the likelihood of being robbed would increase with every kilometre.

Numerous villages dotted our route along the Echo Road. Just as we came to the outskirts of the first large village, we were met by gangs of children playing near the roadway. As soon as they spotted our bright white vehicle, they sprung into action. Each of these barefoot kids picked up a rock and quickly formed a gauntlet along both sides of the road. As soon as we got within earshot the yelling began. "Give me money, give me cigarettes," they would scream in perfect English. At first we might have thought that these kids were just playing, but we soon learned that this was not a joke. They may have been smiling and yelling as they held out one hand, but their other hand held a rock ready to take out our windshield if we failed to respond to their request.

After our first encounter, our training officer offered us some rather cold-blooded advice on how to deal with these types of situations. "First off, if you have cigarette, give it to them. Even if you don't smoke, start carrying them or you could lose your windshield. These kids will often get very close to your vehicle, but whatever you do, just keep moving. If you do run over one, your safest bet is to keep on going. Stopping could get you killed by the villagers." His words sounded so matter-of-fact, he could have been talking about running over a dog or a cat, rather than a child. When one of the trainees questioned what he was saying, the discussion went on for quite a while before he finally relented. "If you run over someone, the official policy is to stop and help. However, what I am suggesting is that you have to be careful. If the child is a girl, you may be okay to stop, but if you kill a boy, the best advice I can give you is to just keep going and report it when you get back to headquarters."

As we topped the rise and made the final turn into OP Khiam, I could see the mountain range far off to the east. The snow-capped peak of Mount Hermon dominated the area and marked the boundary between Lebanon and Syria.

Standing on the roof of the observation post we had a commanding view of the valley below. Again we received an excellent briefing by the officers on duty, but what we found most interesting was the large fenced enclosure sitting behind the OP. Just a hundred metres to the rear, we could easily see the long squat building surrounded by multiple rows of barbwire.

Khiam Prison derived its name from the tiny village nearby. The heavily guarded prison was run by the South Lebanese Army and it was said that few of the political prisoners who entered there ever got out again. According to the U.N. intelligence briefings, it was very near the top of Amnesty International's list of the most notorious places on earth. Since the prison has opened in 1982, Amnesty International and the Red Cross had been trying to inspect the place. To the best of my knowledge, they never succeeded in gaining entry or confirming what, if any, atrocities went on there. Although officially the U.N. could not get involved, all you had to do was ask any of the officers on duty at the OP and they would tell you about the screams and howls of anguish they heard emanating from the building almost every night. At first I thought they may have been exaggerating, but just a few weeks later when I was on duty I would be awakened in the dead of night by the tortured sounds of screaming coming from the other side of the barbwire.

Oddly enough, OP Khiam was considered the safest of all our observation posts. The very presence of the of South Lebanese Army guarding the prison made it a place to be avoided by the many hostile groups operating in the area.

In an ironic twist some years later, the OP was mistakenly hit by fire from an Israeli jet aircraft. The observers on duty had taken shelter in the bunker just moments before a bomb struck the roof of the structure. All four of the observers, including a Canadian major, were killed instantly by the blast.

Even before leaving OP Khiam, we could already see our next destination sitting on the high ground off to the north.

Chateau de Beaufort Castle had been built by the crusaders in the eleventh century with the sole purpose of controlling the southern entrance to the Bekaa Valley. Eight hundred years may have elapsed, but this particular valley was still the most strategically important piece of ground in the entire region. The Bekaa Valley ran straight south from the interior of Lebanon and its rugged terrain provided good cover and a relatively direct route for insurgents trying to access the Lebanese/Israeli border area.

OP Chateau sat perched on the slopes directly below the castle walls. Using the thirty-power binoculars mounted on the roof, the officers on duty could easily see all the roads and trails leading into the valley from the north.

The location of this OP may have been ideal for observing deep into the valley, but its isolation also made it a very hazardous place to work. Although the American officers in our station were allowed to work in the other five OPs in the buffer zone, their government had decreed that they could not work on OP Chateau. Being an American in the Middle East was considered dangerous enough, but allowing them to work in such an isolated location would only make them all the more vulnerable to being kidnapped or killed by any number of PLO or Hezbollah factions inhabiting the area.

The Litani River snaked its way along the valley floor, just a kilometre or so south of OP Chateau. The river itself had no tactical significance, but it did denote the borderline between what was referred to as "The Two Lebanons." With the exception of OP Chateau, the near bank of the river marked the boundary for all U.N. operations in South Lebanon. Everything beyond the Litani and right up to the city of Beirut was completely outside the jurisdiction of the United Nations. Taking a line from an old western movie, most of the observers simply referred to the area as "The Badlands" or "Injun Country."

All of the villages in the surrounding area were aware of this isolated OP and the riches it contained. The shed inside the compound always had a large store of gasoline for the vehicle and diesel for the generator, and with only two unarmed officers there to protect it, break-ins became almost a nightly event. As soon as darkness fell, the observers on duty could do little more than lock themselves inside the building for the night. The frequent robberies may have had more to do with simple economics rather than the political situation, but this gave little comfort to the officers who had to deal with these armed thieves scaling the fence and making off with practically anything that was not nailed down.

Months later, I would be there to witness the final closing of OP Chateau. After years of indecision, the U.N. headquarters in New York had at last decided that the danger of working this far beyond the U.N. boundary far outweighed the benefits achieved. I had been fortunate enough to only have spent one week in that particular hell-hole, but like every officer in Observer Group Lebanon I was happy to watch as the U.N. flag was lowered for the last time on OP Chateau.

The U.N. flag on OP Chateau was lowered for the last time in November 1987. Chateau was the most dangerous OP for the military observers to work.

Collection of the author.

CHAPTER 15

A Week of Looking and Cooking

Almost as soon as we alighted from the Jeep back in Nahariya, the operations officer greeted us with a duty schedule. I only had to drag my finger part way down the paper before finding my name pencilled in for duty on OP Mar. I had exactly one day to sort everything out, including the all-important need to find a place to live.

Aside from providing a rear headquarters for our station, the U.N. building in Nahariya also doubled as a gathering place for all the observers and their families. From the small bar near the back of the building, it was just a few steps to the patio where you could enjoy a cold drink while watching the sunset over the Mediterranean.

It had been a very long and stressful day on the Echo Road, but we had managed to get through it without being hijacked. The very next training tour, three days later, would not be so lucky. Shortly after leaving OP Ras they had been stopped by two men armed with AK-47 rifles. They had managed to get off a mayday message on the radio, but as one of the victims told me later, when you have a rifle barrel shoved in your face there is little else to do other than turn over your belongings. All told they had lost about fifty dollars plus one rather cheap Timex watch, but at least nobody was hurt.

Brigitte and I returned to the headquarters early the next morning to meet up with the housing officer. One of Captain Petain's main jobs was to assist new families in finding a place to live. He and I had met at the bar the night before, and although he would prove very helpful in finding us an apartment, it was easy to tell that this was one man who truly hated the job he was forced to do. Judging by the ribbons, commando badges, and jump wings adorning his chest, he had obviously seen and done a lot of things in his career. Because he was a French Army officer the restrictions imposed by the U.N. prevented him from working in Lebanon. In the six months I knew him, the only time I ever saw him smile was the day he finally received the message posting him to Cairo, where, as he put it, "I can finally get back to being a real army officer."

Almost as soon as we entered the front door, we both knew that this was the apartment we wanted. From the balcony we had an unobstructed view along the entire coastline. Other than a narrow strip of sandy beach, nothing stood between us and the shiny blue waters of the Mediterranean.

The French Canadian couple who lived in the apartment were just days away from moving to their next duty station in Damascus, Syria. The situation seemed perfect for all concerned. They were anxious to get moved and we were equally anxious to get our living arrangements sorted out before I departed for Lebanon the very next morning. Only one small problem stood in our way. Captain Gilbert Marin was currently on duty with one of the patrol teams, somewhere deep inside Southern Lebanon. His wife Claudette was a very nice lady, but unfortunately she spoke not a word of English. It took a little time, but with our French housing officer translating back and forth, we finally came to an arrangement. Once again Brigitte would be stuck in a hotel for the next four days, and when the other couple departed she would have to make the move by herself.

As we left the apartment building, I could not help but smile when I thought about the irony of the situation. Even though Claudette Marin and I were from the same country, we could not speak a common language. We were Canadians, but could only communicate with each other with the help of a French Army officer.

As we drove away from the headquarters in Naqoura, I have to admit to having a small case of nerves. My jittery partner in the driver's seat was anything but reassuring as we commenced our journey up the Echo Road. Each of us had different reasons for our nervous behaviour.

Other than the training tour, this would be my first time navigating along the Echo Road and all I could think about was getting through this first trip without screwing anything up. With the map spread out on my lap and the radio handset clutched firmly in my right hand, we began our long journey east to OP Mar. During the first few kilometres my head never stopped bobbing up and down between the map and the road ahead. There may have been all kinds of danger out there, but right now I didn't care. My only concern was making sure I didn't miss any of the all important Echo points.

My partner for the week was a U.S. Air Force major who had been in the station for two months and already completed three tours on the observation posts. He was more than familiar with the Echo Road, but, like all the Americans, he was understandably nervous every time he entered Lebanese territory.

Like all the officers in our organization, the Americans wore their national flag on the left sleeve of their uniform. At first their flag was the normal red, white, and blue, but they soon found that this brightly coloured symbol was far too conspicuous. Many of the locals may not have known the Canadian red maple leaf or the green, white, and orange of the Irish flag, but the stars and stripes was instantly recognizable to almost everyone we met.

Any time we had to stop in a village or town in Lebanon, it wouldn't take long before the locals began to gather around the vehicle. Most would just smile and ask for cigarettes or chocolate, but if they spotted an American flag their demeanour would quickly change from friendly to hostile. Americans may have been loved in Israel, but throughout the Arab world they were almost universally hated.

We may have only been two people, but as we departed Naqoura our vehicle was literally jammed with all the personal kit, baskets of food, bottled water, and coolers of perishable goods we would need to sustain us for a full seven days. Being the new guy, I had probably brought far too much, but I knew full well that if we were about to be locked away in the middle of nowhere for a week, running out of food was not an option.

My partner and I had not done much talking throughout the two-hour trip, but as soon as we rounded the last curve and spotted OP Mar, we both could breathe a sigh of relief, at least for the moment. I had missed one of the Echo points, but thankfully I managed to catch my error before the twenty-minute time limit had elapsed. There had been one minor incident involving a pack of rock-wielding kids as we neared the village of Hasbaya, but after flinging half a dozen L&M cigarettes out the window we managed to escape with our windshield still intact.

The Austrian and Irish officers both had immense smiles on their faces as we drove through the gate. Every observer I had met up to this point had proved to be a thorough professional and these two officers were no exception. Even though they were anxious to get home after a long week, they understood that I was the new guy and would need a little more of their time before departing.

OP Mar sat deep inside Lebanon and just a few hundred metres from an Israeli artillery position. Shells were frequently fired directly over the observation post at their targets somewhere inside Northern Lebanon. Note the blast protection wall surrounding the OP.

Collection of the author.

Aside from the all the operational aspects of working on an observation post, there were still a large numbers of critical issues we had to understand if we were to make it through this first week of duty.

The stove and refrigerator both worked off propane. Large propane tanks sat just against the outer walls of the OP. Every couple of days we would have to undo the hoses and valve connecting and thread them through the recess in the wall. Feeding the two hoses through the tiny hole and then reconnecting each could be quite time consuming. Great care had to be taken to make sure everything was snugly in place and there were no leaks in the system. If nothing was detected after sniffing the air and listening for the telltale hiss of leaking gas, I could then perform the final delicate task. Lying on the floor, I would slowly open the valve and reach under each appliance, carefully placing a lit match next to the pilot light. Every second the valve was open the gas continued to pour out, so any hesitation in finding and lighting the burner could result in an explosion. After I managed to do this for the first time without blowing up the OP, I felt a great sense of relief. I was aware that there had been some minor explosions in the past; I just didn't want to be the first person to actually launch a refrigerator through the roof of an observation post.

As the junior man on duty, I was also responsible for filling and maintaining the two generators. These particular machines were without doubt the most important pieces of equipment on the entire OP. Without them we would be in the dark and without any means of communication. If the generators did go down, the back-up battery for the radio was good for roughly four hours, but after that we would truly be cut off and completely alone.

After breakfast each morning I would make my way out to the shed to commence the job of checking the oil levels and filling each generator with diesel fuel. Once each week, when a generator reached one hundred hours running time, I would have to do the long and dirty job of changing the oil. A set of work gloves sat on the nearby post, but before putting them on I would first have to shake each one. For good measure I would then place each glove on the ground and stomp on it vigorously. Just a few weeks earlier, an observer had forgotten to shake first and only discovered the scorpion when it bit into one of his extended fingers. Within a few minutes his entire hand had swollen up to twice its normal size. The headquarters was too far away to help, but they did manage to contact the Finnish battalion, who were able to dispatch an ambulance to the site. The officer would recover after two days spent in the Finnish Army hospital, but there was a more serious problem to deal with. The other officer could not be left alone on the observation post, but it was already approaching early evening and U.N. rules prohibited any travel on the Echo Road during the hours of darkness. Fortunately, Team India, one of our mobile teams who worked with the Irish battalion, was just a few kilometres away and able to reach the OP before dark and remain there for the night. All of these problems had occurred simply because an officer had forgotten to check his gloves before putting them on.

I soon learned that it was not just gloves that had to be checked. The entire area was infested with all manner of potentially deadly insects and snakes, and it soon became almost second nature to be constantly checking your surroundings as you went about your daily tasks. Every type of insect, from the tiny black widow spider to the tarantula, could be found roaming the compound. I often encountered these brown hairy beasts we called Camel Spiders scurrying about. Between their legs and large, rounded bodies, they looked to be about ten inches in circumference. I have no idea if they were poisonous and I had no intention of getting close enough to find out. Fortunately they seemed to be as frightened of us as we were of them, so we each gave the other a wide berth.

There were many types of snakes in the area, but the Palestinian Viper was certainly the most dangerous. According to the warning literature, a bite victim had roughly one hour to reach medical assistance. Failure to treat this poisonous bite would result in unconsciousness, followed by death within two to three hours. Of course these time estimates were based upon a full-grown man. The few cases I had heard of all involved small children and most had died within the hour.

It only took a few days to make the necessary adjustments to life on in this new and unpredictable environment. At first we were always alert for any signs of the creatures that shared our small world, but soon the precautions become almost automatic. Before going to bed each night, you had to first draw back all the covers and look under the mattress. In the morning, before getting dressed, it was best to shake out your shirt, pants, and boots. Any movement outside the building, especially at night, required the wearing of boots. It may have been an emergency, but throwing on a pair of open-toed sandals and heading for the outhouse at three o'clock in the morning could prove to be a disastrously stupid thing to do.

Thankfully the first three days on OP Mar passed without any major incidents. My American partner was proving to be one of the most competent and articulate officers I had ever met. Back in the real world, as he called it, Major Steve Spence was an F-16 pilot. He and I would spend many hours discussing a vast variety of subjects.

If there was one thing we both had in common, it was our complete lack of cooking skills. I may have been a master at frying or boiling eggs, but beyond that I was completely lost. Brigitte had put together a complete lasagne casserole for me to take. After taping the cooking instructions across the top of the tray, she had taken great care to make sure my five-pound frozen lasagne was well wrapped and stored in my cooler before leaving Nahariya. Unfortunately because our trip had taken longer than expected, when we finally reached OP Mar, the July heat had done its work. I will admit that I did briefly consider refreezing the entire thing, but then thought better of it. Having myself or my partner evacuated due to food poisoning would not be an auspicious start to my first week in Lebanon. Only one option remained — the entire casserole would be cooked and eaten that day. The lasagne actually turned out to be one of the best meals of the week, but once it was consumed I was on my own.

It would have been nice to get a bit of a crash course in cooking, but with the little time available, Brigitte had written down some rather basic steps aimed at helping me prepare the simplest of meals.

After Steve put together a very tasty beef stew the following night, it was my turn again. The fried pork chops may have been a little greasy and I definitely put too much salt in the water for the boiled potatoes, but at least I hadn't cut myself when I opened the can of peas and carrots.

They may not have been the healthiest of meal choices, but we did manage to get through the whole week on a steady diet of fried eggs, fried meat, and boiled potatoes. On our final night, as I stood there looking at the disaster I made of the kitchen, I promised myself that I would come better prepared for my next duty.

Steve and I spent many hours on the roof scanning the area through the big binoculars. OP Mar sat just a few metres off the Echo Road. Our rooftop lookout gave us a commanding view of the surrounding terrain. To the north the land gradually dropped away, giving us an unobstructed view far into Lebanon. The territory to the west was partially blocked by a deep ravine running away from us and toward the sea. Just a few kilometres to the south, we could easily see the double fence line running along the border. The high ground just beyond the fence and inside Israel was the area that commanded most of our attention. Two full batteries of mechanized artillery sat lined up along the ridge. These eight M109 howitzer gun carriers were arranged in two staggered lines, with all their 155 millimetre gun barrels permanently pointing north.

At first I thought it was the sound of thunder that woke me from my deep sleep, but after the third crack in a row I realized that the deafening noise was coming from the Israeli artillery position to our south. By the time Steve and I reached the roof, the guns were once again silent. As we stood there in the darkness, we both agreed that there had been a total of six shots fired. The minutes ticked by as we waited.

A few lights had come on down in the valley, but other than that the entire area seemed to be cloaked in total blackness. I don't know why, but Steve and I were both whispering in the dark, trying to decide if we should call it in or wait a little longer. At the ten-minute mark the decision was made for us when the big guns once again opened fire. Now we could see the flash in the distance even before we heard sound of each gun firing. We couldn't see the shells, but we could hear the distinctive whizzing sound as each of these ninety-eight-pound projectiles cut through the night sky above the OP. We could only hear the very faint sound of rumbling as each shell detonated somewhere deep inside Lebanon. Each salvo of six rounds would be followed by a few minutes of silence before the guns once again opened fire. By the time it finally ended just before dawn, we had a total of twenty-four rounds to report.

Every few days the Israelis would open fire without warning. We never found out why they were firing or even if they had hit their intended target. Once in a while we would hear Arab newspaper reports stating that "some peaceful village had been hit and many innocent civilians had been killed in an unprovoked attack." Newspapers in Israel rarely give any details, but would only state that "a successful attack had been launched against some terrorist camp deep inside of Lebanon." All we could do was report the facts as we saw them. Once we transmitted our report to Naqoura, it was forwarded to Jerusalem and then on to U.N. headquarters in New York. It was a slow, cumbersome process, but from our perspective our job was to be absolutely sure our reports were as accurate as possible.

It was perhaps three weeks later when I first heard the reports of an accident on the Israeli artillery position south of OP Mar. According to the observers on duty, the big guns had started firing into Lebanon just after midnight. During the third volley of fire, the two officers on duty reported what looked and sounded like a massive explosion from within the Israeli position. Once daylight arrived and they could use the rooftop binoculars, all they could see was a large blackened spot on the ground where one of the M109 gun carriers had been sitting the night before. Whether it was sabotage or some sort of ammunition accident that had destroyed the howitzer, we never learned. Sometime before dawn the wreckage had been removed and barely two days later, another shiny new M109 was driven into position alongside the other seven gun carriers. Based on the size of the explosion, one would have to assume that any Israeli soldier working on or near the gun would have been killed. As with all things involving military operations in Lebanon, the Israelis said absolutely nothing about the incident. I often wondered if the families of these dead soldiers were told the truth about how their sons, daughters, fathers, or mothers had died while fighting on the very edge of the Israeli-Lebanese border.

Dawn was always my favourite time of day on any of the observation posts. Throwing back the covers and placing your feet on the cold cement floor took a little bit of self discipline, but once I was up and moving, the worst was over. The first order of business was to fire up the stove. One burner was used to boil the coffee water, while the other three were lit in an effort to try and get some much-needed heat back into the cool, damp building. After performing the mandatory inspection for bugs and reptiles, it was time to get dressed, grab a coffee, and head for the rooftop lookout.

If I timed it right, I could just catch the first rays of light in the eastern sky as the dawn broke over Mount Hermon. At first the land seemed deserted. Even the normally busy Echo Road was completely devoid of traffic. Nothing moved in the darkness. For those few moments I could forget where I was and just sit there quietly sipping my coffee and watch as the grey shadows of morning slowly gave way to the sunlight.

The sound of armoured vehicles approaching from the southwest told me that the quiet time was over and a new day was about to begin.

At precisely six o'clock each morning the armoured patrol would begin. The convoy of three Merkava tanks, followed by a section of South Lebanese soldiers in an M48 Halftrack, would make their way down from their hilltop position and cautiously turn onto the Echo Road. The ultra modern lines of the Merkava tanks stood in stark contrast to the old dilapidated halftrack travelling at the rear of the convoy.

The Israeli Merkava was a fast and highly manoeuvrable piece of equipment. Its low, sleek design and ability to fire on the move made it a very formidable weapon on the battlefield. The wide cylindrical device attached to the front of the lead tank always made it difficult to execute that final pivot turn onto the road. This heavy metal roller was there to detect any mines or explosives that could have been planted during the previous night. Long metal arms kept the mine roller well out in front of the tank hull. The weight of the cylinder would be enough to detonate anything in its path, while still making sure the crew were protected inside the tank.

Once this armoured mine detector was on the road and moving north, the second and third tanks would swing into position behind. The halftrack full of soldiers would always remain a few hundred metres to the rear. Their only purpose in being there was to provide ground support in the event of an ambush. The 105 millimetre gun on the lead vehicle pointed straight ahead, while the big guns on tanks two and three each pointed to opposite sides of the road to covering the left and right flanks.

An M48 Halftrack manned by soldiers of the South Lebanese Army. The device on the front of the vehicle could be lowered and rolled along the ground to detonate mines.

Collection of the author.

The Israeli Merkava tank with mine roller attached.

Collection of the author.

Much of the equipment, like this Soviet T-55 tank, had been captured by the Israelis during the Yom Kippur War and given to the South Lebanese Army.

Collection of the author.

With all the hatches battened down we couldn't see anyone in the tanks, but the gunner in tank number three obviously had a rather sardonic sense of humour. Just as his tank drew even with the OP, he would traverse the big gun directly toward us and wave good morning by moving the barrel slowly up and down. It would take a few minutes for the sound of tank engines to fade and the dust to settle, but once the patrol moved north, the area surrounding our compound would again spring to life. The locals may have hated the Israeli and South Lebanese armies, but they were always willing to allow these soldiers to clear the dangerous terrain each morning before they themselves set foot on the Echo Road.

Being confined inside a small compound for days on end could be rather monotonous. You could only stay on the roof and stare through the big binoculars for so long before the lack of activity and the sweltering heat forced you back inside the building. Whether inside or outside the OP the heat was equally oppressive, but at least the interior offered some shade from the sun. One had to be especially cautious and alert during the early afternoon. Touching any exposed metal could lead to serious burns. A large piece of canvas had to be draped over the binoculars before going inside. If you did leave them uncovered for even a few minutes the metal frame would became too hot to touch. Moving around the compound during the afternoon presented its own particular brand of danger. This was the time of day when all snakes and reptiles lay basking in the sun. Visitors to the OP were always a welcome sight. Even the mid-week arrival of the U.N. field service truck with its fresh supply of water and fuel was a brief opportunity to break the monotony.

Our mobile team working with the Finnish battalion made a rare visit late in the week. Their ability to move about the entire area gave them far better insight as to what was actually going on out there. Even with the most powerful binoculars, there was still a great deal of territory hidden from our view. My OP partner and I spent the better part of an hour poring over the map and peppering these two members of Team Foxtrot with questions. I had only been in Lebanon for less than a week and there was still much I had to learn, but at least now I could take some comfort in knowing what lay over the next hill.

Although I had heard mention of these mobile teams during my initial briefing, this was the first time I would actually get the chance to find out what their job entailed. The Italian member of the team was new to the job, but his Australian partner was more than happy to sit and answer all my questions.

As Captain McCarthy explained, there were a total of seven mobile teams operating within our station. One team was assigned to each of the six battalions that made up the United Nations Interim Force in Lebanon and the seventh team worked independently in and around the coastal city of Tyre. Each team consisted of five officers, two of whom would always be on duty with their respective battalion in South Lebanon. The U.N. mandate prevented the members of UNIFIL from dealing directly with the Israelis or any of the many political or military in South Lebanon, therefore our mobile teams were created to act as a liaison between all the parties involved in the conflict.

As Captain McCarthy continued to speak, I could tell he truly enjoyed his job. Team Foxtrot had been at the OP for over an hour when a radio transmission called them away. I still had many questions but they would have to wait until another time.

After Team Foxtrot left, I could see the frustration building up in my OP partner. He already knew that as an American he could never work on any of the teams.

Like most of the Australians I met in Observer Group Lebanon, Captain Peter McCarthy was a friendly, outgoing individual. On duty he was a consummate professional, but off duty he was one of those people who knew how to relax and enjoy life.

During his OP visit I had mentioned my concern about Brigitte. She and I both understood that this was the nature of the job, but nonetheless I still felt guilty. Not only had I left her alone in a strange place, but she would also have to deal with all the problems associated with moving into our new apartment.

By the time I arrived back in Nahariya, I had forgotten about the comments made to Peter, but he had not. Almost as soon as I stepped out of the truck, I was met by Brigitte, along with the entire McCarthy family.

He had only gotten back from duty two days earlier, but Peter and Catherine McCarthy, along with their two young daughters, had already helped Brigitte with the move, taken her shopping, and even had her over for dinner. Over the next few months we would all become close friends. Rarely a week went by when we didn't have dinner together. Whenever I went on duty, I could relax knowing that Brigitte always had someone looking out for her.

CHAPTER 16

The Best of Times

The locals called it a "Khamseen," which loosely translated into "desert wind." Call it what you will, but for those of us who had to work in it, the conditions were almost unbearable. Normally the temperature remained moderately hot, as the winds blew in from the west off the Mediterranean, but every so often the winds would switch completely around and bring with them the heat and dust from the Syrian Plains. As the hot dry wind swept across Israel and Lebanon, it brought with it the sand of the eastern desert. Even with the windows and shutters closed tightly, the sand could always seep in through each crack and crevice, covering everything in a fine layer of grit.

Other than the incessant heat, it had been a productive week on OP Ras. We were already well into September and I was just two days away from completing my sixth and final OP duty. Once I returned to Naqoura, I was looking forward to a few days off before assuming my duties as the newest member of Team Foxtrot.

My partner for the week was an Austrian major doing his first OP duty and he and I had not gotten off to a good start. Other than reporting the Echo points, he and I hardly spoke on the long drive to OP Ras. Initially I just assumed he was simply nervous and unsure of himself like all new observers. Even after we arrived and settled in at our temporary home, he seemed disinterested as I tried explaining our duties and responsibilities for the week. His behaviour seemed truly odd. My first

The powerful binoculars we called "big eyes" sat on the roof of each OP. Note the mixture of nationalities we had in Observer Group Lebanon. The officer looking through the binocular is from Denmark. Against the wall from left to right are officers from Austria, Australia, and Sweden.

Collection of the author.

day on the OP had been a long series of unending questions; he asked nothing and only grunted in response to my attempts to start a conversation. When I finally confronted him, his answer was straightforward and rather surprising.

He was a highly experienced major who did not believe he should be taking direction from a captain. He went to great pains to explain that it had nothing to do with me being Canadian, but because he outranked me, he felt he should be in charge. "Back home in Austria I commanded a company of a hundred men, which included three captains." The bland expression of his face never changed as he spoke.

I took a few moments to consider his point. I didn't wish to appear hasty or upset when I answered. "You're right," I finally answered. "Whether we were operating in Austria or Canada you would be the one in command, but the fact is we are here in Lebanon where my experience outweighs your rank. The job out here is completely different from what we do at home, and regardless of your rank we all have to start with the basics. I would suggest you give it a week or two to see how the station operates and then if your opinion is unchanged, ask to go home."

Even though all the domestic chores were shared equally between both men on the OP, I have to admit that the first time I had been faced with some of the more menial tasks I had done a little grumbling myself. There was certainly nothing glamorous about having to scrub dinner pots, mop a floor, or clean a toilet, but I soon realized that these jobs had to be done.

It didn't happen right away, but over the next two days he slowly became more talkative. He and I never discussed rank again, but as our week together came to an end, he at least seemed more interested. At times his tone could become rather condescending, but at least he was asking questions.

In retrospect I believe my behaviour was rather spiteful, but I have to admit that when I looked at the duty roster a few months later, I had to laugh out loud when I saw that my Austrian friend was about to be given a lesson. Our new commanding officer had just arrived in the station. Before assuming command of Observer Group Lebanon our new boss would first have to do a couple of OP duties, just like any new member of the station. This highly experienced Marine colonel and Vietnam veteran had absolutely no problem with this arrangement. Maybe it was just a coincidence or perhaps others had witnessed his arrogant behaviour, but I do know that my former Austrian partner was rather nervous and upset when he was tasked with the job of running an OP with a lieutenant colonel under his command.

The problem of inflated egos was certainly not isolated to the Austrian officers. Practically every one of the sixteen nationalities represented had its share of individuals who arrived with their own particular brand of bias.

Naturally the American and Soviet officers always looked upon each other with a great deal of suspicion. There was some limited contact between the groups, but usually only when it came to work-related matters. We were still in the midst of the Cold War and the paranoia was evident on both sides. Each of the two groups believed the other to be

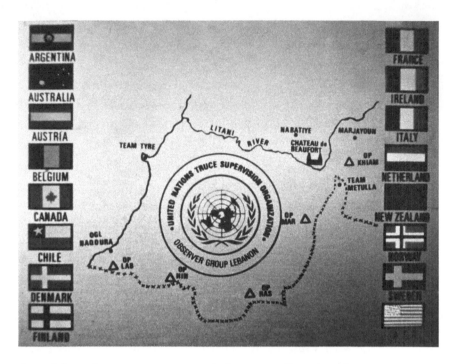

One of these plaques was given to each departing officer. Note the sixteen different nations all represented within Observer Group Lebanon.

Collection of the author.

either CIA or KGB. Only the Chinese officers seemed to take it seriously, while the rest of us just found the whole topic rather amusing.

Later on I was to work with Russian and Chinese officers, and although we all got along well, the two of them would frequently get into long, heated discussions about which of them was the better communist.

The four Chinese officers in Observer Group Lebanon all lived together in one tiny apartment. Although English was the working language of the U.N., most of the Chinese seemed to speak and understand very little. They were a friendly and cooperative group who would always nod and smile when you spoke to them, but you could tell they did not really comprehend what was going on. Spending a week on an isolated OP with someone who could not communicate could be a long, excruciating affair. They were the only national group who were not allowed to bring their families into the mission area. One of the Chinese officers told me that their families remained in China to ensure the officers returned home, rather than defect at the end of their tours.

In spite of having so many diverse personalities and mixed ideologies, we did somehow manage to get along, but it could lead to some rather odd situations.

One morning, about five months into my first tour, a British major arrived in the station to conduct an inspection tour. He had been sent by U.N. headquarters to see if any of our observation posts needed structural repairs. By sheer chance the team designated to escort him through the area was commanded by an Irish captain.

An outsider may have difficulty understanding the deep-seated mistrust the two groups felt toward each other. The south of Ireland had gained its independence from England decades earlier, but Northern Ireland still remained under British control. The rest of the world may have considered the north to be part of the British Isles, but for many of the Irish living in the north, the British were little better than an occupying force in their country. There had been some minor skirmishes between the IRA and the British Army during the first half of the twentieth century, but by the middle of the 1960s the situation had escalated into a full-blown confrontation. Soon the British Army arrived in force and Belfast and Londonderry took on the appearance of a war zone. Over the next three decades there would be brief periods of calm, but with neither side willing to compromise, the hostilities would begin anew.

The Irish officers in our station may have been a long way from home, but the ongoing conflict was never far from their minds. Rather than place either man in an awkward situation, the decision was made to have the Irish officer step back and allow his Argentinean teammate to complete the escort task. What we didn't realize at the time was that both men had fought in the Falklands War and the Argentinean captain had been taken prisoner by the British. Needless to say, once they discovered their mutual connection the remainder of the long inspection tour was completed in awkward silence.

Even the normally friendly demeanour of the Irish officers could quickly change when the subject of the British came up. Having been born in Ireland, I was treated like one of their own, but that didn't protect me from their frequently good-natured ribbing about being a member of the "British Commonwealth" forces. I would of course remind them that they in fact lived in an area that was commonly referred to as the "British Isles."

None of the comments were ever taken seriously, but on one occasion, I did find myself stuck in a rather delicate and awkward situation.

After a year in command of the station, our Australian CO was scheduled to return home. I was tasked with setting up a mess dinner in his honour. There are a number of formalities associated with these types of affairs, not the least of which is a formal toast at the end of the dinner.

A Canadian mess dinner usually consists of a four- to five-course meal. Once the food is out of the way, each man will be given a glass of port with which to toast the Queen.

Obviously, with sixteen different nationalities represented in the station, this particular tradition would need to be altered somewhat. After a lengthy discussion, the decision was to have the senior member of each nation stand and offer a toast to their own head of state. Other than having to refill the port glasses three or four times to accommodate all these toasts, this seemed like the most diplomatic method of doing things.

Everything seemed ready to go, until about fifteen minutes before the dinner was scheduled to start, when the senior Irish officer approached me with what he saw as an insurmountable problem.

All told there were five member countries of the British Commonwealth present and each of those would be making a toast to the Queen. His complaint was quite clear; the Irish officers were willing to do it once, but were not about to stand up five times and toast the British Monarch. After some serious debate and a good deal of running around, I managed to arrange for the senior Australian officer to stand up and offer one collective toast to the British Commonwealth. Not toasting the Queen may have been a breach of etiquette, but at least I was able to stave off what could have been an international incident.

With my last observation post duty out of the way, I finally had a few days to relax before returning to Lebanon as the newest member of Team

Foxtrot. Peter McCarthy had taken over as commander of the team and he would be the one to take me out for my first few days of training in the Finnish Battalion (FINBAT) area.

We may have been close friends, but that didn't prevent him from treating me like the rookie that I was. He and I could share a laugh on the drive north, but as soon as we crossed the border, Peter once again became the consummate professional.

After a brief introduction to the Finnish commanding officer, we were off for my first look at the battalion's area. There was much for me to learn.

The FINBAT area of operations was roughly six hundred square kilometres. The terrain was generally hilly, with numerous small villages scattered throughout the area. Some of the villages looked bright and prosperous, with children playing in the schoolyard and market stalls full of fresh fruit and vegetables. The next village we entered could be nothing more than a collection of dark hovels and dilapidated ruins with few signs of life.

As Peter explained, if you drove into a village with unpaved roads, shattered buildings, and no electricity, chances were good that you had entered a hostile environment. A village that cooperated with the Israelis would be rewarded with paved roads and a steady supply of electrical power. Any town or village that was openly hostile to the Israelis would sit untouched and in the dark. If the Israelis suspected that any building in the village was being used to harbour what they called "terrorists," they would quickly move in and evict families, before blowing up their homes.

The Finnish soldiers in the forward checkpoints had the most difficult and frustrating job of all. Any civilian vehicle trying to enter South Lebanon would first be subjected to a thorough search. If weapons or explosives were found, the vehicle was turned around and sent back. A car could drive up to the checkpoint literally bristling with guns and ammunition. It could even have a rocket launcher strapped to the roof, but all these soldiers could do was turn the car around and send the occupants on their way back north. If a car containing weapons was stopped inside the FINBAT area they could arrest the occupants, but at the checkpoint, while the car was still technically outside the U.N. area of control, they could simply keep their guns, turn the car around, and go home. There were always hundreds of tracks and trails they could use to move their cargo south in the dead of night. The soldiers were doing the best they could under the circumstances, but as they often said, "it was a little like trying to stop a flood by sticking your finger in the dyke."

That first week on Team Foxtrot felt a little like trying to take a drink from a fire hose. The information just kept coming. From early morning until just before sunset, Peter and I would be constantly on the go. Almost overnight the incessant heat was gone and now the sky was filled with dark clouds and the sounds of thunder. Each day we were faced with steady rain. Our CJ7 Jeep certainly took a beating, as most of the roads turned to rivers of thick grey mud. Even in four-wheel drive it was difficult to maintain traction as our vehicle fishtailed through the slippery mess. Erosion had turned the potholes into small water-filled craters. Each of these obstacles had to be approached with great care. Sometimes the muddy water would reach above the doors before we felt the tires touch bottom. It was important to maintain a steady forward momentum and not become bogged down. Once the tires touched the far side, we would gun the engine and hang on as the Jeep shot forward and over the lip of the crater. We always carried at least two spare tires to fix the flats we had each day. Sometimes it must have been difficult for onlookers to tell that we were actually members of the United Nations. Our distinctive white Jeep would be completely encased in the grey pasty substance. Even the large blue flag mounted above the back door would be barely recognizable, weighed down by the mud flying up from the tires.

If there was one thing that made the job worthwhile, it was the people we dealt with on a daily basis. The locals may have been hostile to the Israelis and South Lebanese Army, but most of them understood that the U.N. was there to help. Even when we entered a known hostile village, I never felt seriously threatened by the civilians we met. Every day our team would make a point of visiting a few of the villages in the area. We even kept a log of our visits to ensure we stopped and visited each place at least once per month. Protocol required that we first went to see the *Muctar*, or mayor of a village, before doing anything else.

Most of the homes were little more than four cinder block walls, with a door in front and a single framed window on the back wall. A few of the homes may have had two or three separated rooms, but most had just one large space, with curtains strung up to divide the sleeping and sitting areas. If there were women and children around they were usually banished behind the curtain so the men could talk alone. Other than a few mattresses and seat cushions spread around the walls, most homes were sparsely furnished. A small propane cooking stove provided the only source of heat to the interior. Numerous multi-coloured rugs were scattered about the cement floor in an effort to hold back the dampness. Even if the home had electricity, the power would not be turned on until sunset.

Soon the village elders would arrive and a new round of handshakes and greetings would begin. On the very odd occasion when a woman was introduced, we would simply nod our head and look away. Offering your hand or even maintaining eye contact with an Arab woman was simply not done.

With all the formalities out of the way, we could all sit down to tea. Conversation was usually limited to a few common words and a good deal of hand gestures. "Welcome, welcome," the home owner would continually repeat as he waved for us to take a seat.

The tea I had been drinking my entire life bore little resemblance to what was placed before us. Our host would pour boiling water into small glass cups and immediately heap three large spoonfuls of sugar into the hot liquid. Most of the sugar would sit undissolved at the bottom of the tiny cup. Refusing the tea would be considered very impolite, so we just sat there smiling and sipping on the sickly sweet concoction. The cups were about the same size as a shot glass, so at first I tried downing the entire thing like bad-tasting medicine. That was a mistake. Our host just assumed that I obviously liked it and immediately filled my cup with more tea and heaping amounts of sugar.

We may not have been able to affect the military situation in the area, but these informal meetings did give us the opportunity to speak to the local civilians and learn a little more about their daily problems. Maybe we couldn't resolve the big issues, but there were always a number of small humanitarian problems to keep us busy.

Some of the local farmers were having difficulty getting into their fields to harvest their crops. Their land was perilously close to an Israeli position and if the farmer came even within a few hundred metres the sentry would open fire.

Civilians were never allowed to approach an Israeli position, and even for us, in a U.N. vehicle, it was never an easy thing to do. The roads leading into these fortified positions were frequently mined. The young Israeli soldiers on sentry duties at one of these remote locations, surrounded by hostiles, tended to be very nervous and ready to open fire at anything or anyone approaching.

As soon as we came in sight of the position, we would move to the very centre of the roadway and begin to drive forward very slowly. Even though it was the middle of the day, we had to ensure our headlights were on high. Our slow movement forward gave the sentry ample opportunity to see and recognize our U.N. vehicle. It also allowed us to carefully inspect the road surface for any signs of mines or trip wires. Once we got within fifty metres or so, we could see the sentry standing there, his weapon held into his shoulder and the barrel pointed directly at us. We

If the Israelis suspected a house was being used to harbour the enemy, they would evict the occupants and destroy the building.

Collection of the author.

always stopped well short of the gate and moved forward on foot, making sure our hands were away from our bodies and clearly visible. We could only hope at this point that the sentry finally relaxed the aim on his weapon. Once the position commander arrived we could have our little meeting through the gate. We were never invited inside.

When we first explained the problem of the farmers accessing their fields the Israeli commander was far from sympathetic, but after some lengthy negotiations he finally agreed to a compromise. There could be no more than two people in the field at any one time and they could never come closer than a hundred metres from the fence. They could not enter the field before ten in the morning and they must be out by four in the afternoon. It may have only made a tiny dent in a much larger humanitarian problem, but the farmers were overjoyed when we gave them the news.

Unfortunately, the arrangement fell apart just a few weeks later. Apparently the new position commander had not been briefed and ordered his soldiers to open fire at what he thought were enemy combatants. The informal truce had lasted just over a month, but soon we were back on the same road, trying to broker another peaceful solution.

Whether it was negotiating a localized ceasefire, arranging an escort for refugees, or simply delivering medicine to an isolated village, we never seemed to have enough hours in the day. We may have been tired after each long, exhausting day, but no one complained. Most of us believed we were making a difference. Each day brought a new challenge and another chance to help.

Having to drink gallons of that sweet syrupy tea everywhere we went was a small price to pay, considering how fortunate we felt at having this unique opportunity to interact with these people.

When the operations officer called me into his office in December, I assumed it was to tell me I would be moving to another station. My six months in Observer Group Lebanon was coming to an end and I fully expected to be posted to one of our other U.N. stations. I wasn't particularly happy, but I had resigned myself to leaving what was considered by most to be the best station in the Middle East. All of the stations were manned by capable officers doing important work, but nothing matched the excitement of working in South Lebanon.

Just a month earlier I had gone through the formalities of filling in the paperwork and listing my posting preferences. As a Canadian officer my choices were somewhat limited. Cairo would have been an interesting place to live and work, but because of limitations in other stations, Cairo was usually reserved for the French, American, and Soviet observers. The city of Beirut in Northern Lebanon had a small liaison office with a staff of ten observers, half of whom were Canadians. Beirut would have been right at the top of my list, but to work there one had to be fluent in French. This left me with the choice of serving out the balance of my tour in either Tiberias or Damascus.

Both of these stations did excellent work patrolling and observing on opposite sides of the Golan Heights area separating Israel and Syria. I would eventually end up working on both sides of the Golan, but not just yet. The operations officer was about to give me a third choice, which up to that moment, I had hardly considered as a viable option.

Not only was I being asked to stay in Observer Group Lebanon, but they wanted me to take over as the leader of Team India, working with the Irish Battalion. He suggested I take a little time to consider, but I was already nodding yes before he finished speaking.

It just seemed that all the stars were aligned in my favour. I would get to finish out my one year tour as a team leader, doing what I considered very worthwhile work. I knew Brigitte would be happy to stay in a place where she had made so many friends. I was rarely there myself, but our apartment was always full of wives and kids who came to swim in the back garden pool.

My friend Peter McCarthy received some good news as well. He would be leaving the team and taking over as the station training officer. He and I would get one more shift together on Team Foxtrot before each of us started our new duties in January 1988.

On my very first day with Team Foxtrot, Peter had told me of one particularly isolated Finnish position that we would have to visit. Every officer in the station had heard of this position, but few had actually ever seen it. Poor weather conditions throughout the autumn had prevented us from going and now I was left with one last opportunity to get it done. It wasn't because the position was of any particular strategic importance. It was just a small hydro dam and relay station guarded by two Finnish soldiers. What made this position so unique was its complete isolation at the very bottom of a steep gorge. Reaching the dam was both time consuming and difficult, but if you wanted to be considered a true member of Team Foxtrot, it had to be done at least once.

It was just after nine when Peter and I reached the top of the cliff at the southern entrance to the gorge. From here we would have to proceed on foot down the narrow dirt path. The dam was roughly 275 metres below, but because of the steep terrain, we would have to follow the zig-zag pattern of the trail as it cut back and forth across the cliff face. As we descended deeper into the gorge, the sunlight disappeared, making the ground damp and slippery. Each step had to be carefully calculated as we continued our downward journey. When we finally reached the bottom the ground flattened out and allowed us to move out of the shadow of the cliff and back into the sunlight.

It had taken just over two hours to reach our destination, but the view was worth it. The valley floor was barely a hundred metres wide, with steep cliffs flanking both sides. It felt like we had entered a new world, totally different than what we had left behind. Unlike the barren and dry landscape above the cliffs, here the cool, moist temperatures had created a thick blanket of vegetation. Bulrushes grew as tall as a man near the edge of the stream. A thick carpet of lush green grass and wild flowers covered the valley floor.

As we approached the stream we could hear the distinct sound of spinning turbines and the water rushing up and over the dam. The white foamy water seemed to disappear in a wall of mist as it dropped straight down on the far side of the dam. Once past the obstacle, the current would slow and resume its steady journey through the valley.

The normally quiet and reserved Finnish soldiers were more than happy to see us. The two sentries were already at the halfway point of their ten-day shift and our visit was a welcome break in their otherwise dull routine. When they offered to make us coffee and sandwiches, Peter and I were at first hesitant to accept their kind offer. We both knew just how difficult it was to get food and water to such a remote location.

All the supplies had to be brought in using the same path we had just travelled. Simply walking down the steep trail was one thing, but having to lug a hundred pounds of supplies was a difficult and dangerous undertaking. When each new set of soldiers left the headquarters to begin their duty, they were joined by one of the local civilians and his two donkeys. These animals would be used to carry the heavy load of rations, water, and fuel these men would require for the next ten days. Once they reached their destination, the donkeys would shed their burden and immediately take on a fresh load of garbage and empty fuel cans. With the turn over complete, the outgoing soldiers and their donkey train could begin the long journey back up the cliff.

Peter and I did not wish to cut into their meagre food supply, but we finally said yes to a cup of coffee.

It was already well past noon and we both knew our time was quickly running out. Obviously the journey back up the hill would be much more difficult and time consuming. The Finnish operations centre had given us permission to go, but only with the strict understanding that we would be back to our vehicle and reporting on the radio well before dark.

I could see Peter looking at his watch, but there was just one more thing I had to do before we left. Peter had already done it on his first trip down the mountain, now it was up to me to continue the team tradition.

I sat down on the bank and began to quickly undress. With Peter and the two Finnish sentries cheering me on, I knew that this was not the time to hesitate. After kicking my socks and underwear to the side, I took one deep breath before plunging head first into the cold black water. It only took seven or eight strokes to reach the far shore, but already it felt like pins and needles were stabbing every inch of my body. As soon as my hand touched the bank, I swung around headed back across the stream. The entire ordeal had only taken about thirty seconds, but by the time I leapt out of the water my hands and feet were numb.

As we began the ascent we both knew that we were already behind schedule. My little stunt had cost us precious time. We had less than four hours to reach the summit and make that all-important radio call before sunset. If the sun dropped below the horizon before we made contact, we would be responsible for placing the entire United Nations Force in Lebanon on alert. We may not have been in any immediate danger, but they wouldn't know that.

The midway point in the trail was the most difficult. Some places were so steep we would have to grab on to roots and hoist ourselves up the embankment. Every few hundred metres I simply had to stop and catch my breath. Peter seemed unfazed by the ordeal. He would sit there on a rock, casually drinking from his water bottle while I stood bent over, just trying to breathe. "Are you okay there, old man?" he asked with his usual wry smile. My birthday had been two months earlier and I made the unfortunate mistake of telling Peter I was turning forty. Even though I had only four years on him, he soon began referring to me as the "old man." Normally I was ready with a quick comeback, but right now I could barely breathe. "Don't worry mate, I'll make you a nice Vegemite sandwich when we get back and you'll be as good as new."

All I could manage to do was give him a disgusted look and a one-word reply. "Yuck," was all I said, as we both began to laugh.

Vegemite is a yeast extract paste that is spread on bread. Most of the Aussies and New Zealanders absolutely loved the stuff, but the rest of the civilized world wouldn't touch the foul-smelling concoction. It may have been very good for you, but after trying it once, I found the smell and the taste equally disgusting.

We finally made the summit with just minutes to spare. It took a while, but by the time Peter finished the call, my breathing was slowly returning to normal.

By now our drinking water was lukewarm, but it still tasted good as we clicked our canteens together in a toast to our accomplishment. Looking down over the edge of the precipice we could no longer see the valley floor. The sun was just touching the horizon and the evening shadows were already creeping along the cliff face.

I have many great memories of my time in Lebanon, but that day, that moment in time, will be forever etched in my mind. It was the best of times.

I had almost forgotten about my camera stuffed deep in my pocket, but just before the sunset I took one final picture of Peter standing at the very edge of the cliff, with the last rays of light slowly fading behind him. As we stood there laughing and celebrating the end of a perfect day, how could we have known that so many things were about to change. The best of times were nearly at an end and many dark days lay just ahead.

CHAPTER 17

The Worst of Times

Christmas in South Lebanon was a day like any other. Someone had placed a few bulbs and some tinfoil strips on a potted plant just outside the Finnish battalion headquarters. A large rock had been wedged against the front of the pot to prevent it from toppling over in the wind and rain.

My Danish partner and I laughed and joked as we cautiously manoeuvred our way along the slick roadway. Normally spending Christmas driving through the mud and rain would not be considered a pleasant experience, but at least we could take solace in knowing that our efforts were helping make this a better holiday for others. Both of us had volunteered to spend these extra days on duty so that those on the team who had children could have this time with them. For me the decision was easy. Working in Lebanon was definitely more enticing than sitting alone in an apartment in Nahariya. Days earlier Brigitte had departed Tel Aviv airport and would spend the next few weeks with our children in Canada.

It promised to be a relatively easy day. I had already finished my last official duty with the team, and these extra days would give me one final opportunity to say goodbye to the many civilian contacts I had made during my time with Team Foxtrot.

The normally tight communication procedures were surprisingly lax that morning. The radio waves were filled with all forms of unnecessary chatter. We all knew it would only be a matter of time before the traffic control station finally put a stop to all the Christmas greetings. We wouldn't have long to wait.

"Control, this is Team Zulu. Mayday, mayday, mayday, over!" The sudden panicked call jolted all of us back to reality. My teammate quickly pulled the Jeep over to the side of the road. Precious seconds ticked by as we just sat there listening to the sound of radio static. We all understood the importance of following the emergency procedures, but nonetheless it was extremely frustrating to just sit there helplessly waiting for something to happen. One of the observation posts tried to come on the radio, but was instantly told to get off the air by the duty officer at the Naqoura headquarters. Right now Team Zulu owned the airwaves, and until they reported their situation everyone else in the area could only sit and listen to the dead air and perhaps say a silent prayer for their safety.

It only took about ninety seconds for Team Zulu to come back on the air, but you could almost feel the collective sigh of relief all across the radio network. I didn't recognize the caller, but considering the situation, the voice sounded quite calm. "Control, this is Team Zulu. We wish to report a total of six shots fired at our vehicle from the vicinity of map reference 2389, in the hills just south of Tyre. One of the rifle shots struck the taillights of our vehicle, while the other five appeared to strike the roadway. We are not injured and are currently moving south on the coast highway toward your location, over."

The ancient city of Tyre sat nestled against the western shoreline of the Mediterranean, just fifteen kilometres north of the Israeli border. The city itself was generally peaceful, but the main highway leading in and out had become the scene of many serious incidents over the past few months. There was a single U.N. checkpoint manned by soldiers from the Fijian contingent roughly five kilometres north of Naqoura, but once you passed that position there was nothing other than isolated road all the way to Tyre.

This two-lane highway followed the coastline and was the only route in or out of the city. With water on one side and steep cliffs on the other, a driver had literally no place to go if trouble arose. The many blind curves and isolated stretches of road were proving to be ideal locations for hijacking vehicles and armed robberies. Team Zulu had actually been lucky. The robbers had not blocked the road, but rather opened fire from the hillside, allowing the team to speed away from the danger area.

It wasn't the first time, nor would it be the last time a team was fired upon in that area, but the fact that it happened on Christmas Day seemed to put everyone on edge. Gone was all the friendly banter on the radio as each of us came back to reality. This was Lebanon, after all, and regardless of what the calendar said, this was never a place to relax and feel safe.

By early afternoon my partner and I had resumed our patrolling routine. Already my stomach was feeling a little queasy from the many glasses of sweet tea that had been pushed upon us. The constant sway of the Jeep from the slick roads was not helping. Even the antacid tablets I chewed like candy seemed to do little good.

We still had many places to visit, but all of that would have to wait, as the radio suddenly sprung to life. The Finnish duty officer requested we return to headquarters. Apparently there were two women at the front gate asking to speak to us.

As soon as we saw the unit interpreter standing beside these women, we knew this was not a casual meeting. Based on their dress and uncovered heads we knew immediately that these women were not Muslims, but probably Arab Christians from one of the nearby villages. After a curt introduction, our little group moved under the cover of a small verandah. The older woman stood rigid and unsmiling. She did all the talking, while the younger one looked nervously about. My teammate and I just stood there silently as the old woman and the interpreter talked in hushed whispers.

As the conversation went on, I could see the younger girl becoming more and more upset; she slowly moved to shield herself behind the older woman.

At last the interpreter turned and spoke to us.

It turned out that the pair were in fact mother and daughter and ran a small cafe just down the road from the main Finnish camp. The daughter had taken up with one of the Finnish soldiers and now she was pregnant with his child. Once the unit found out, the soldier had been immediately shipped home to Finland, leaving the girl to suffer alone. Both women realized that they would never see the baby's father again, but they still needed our help before it was too late. Aside from our little group, only the unit doctor and the commanding officer knew of the pregnancy. As the interpreter continued to translate, the mother kept nodding anxiously, as if she understood what was being said. The problem was very straightforward. If you looked closely, you could already see a slight bulge in the girl's stomach. Once the bulge grew into the unmistakable signs of pregnancy, the girl and her baby would quite probably be killed by her male relatives.

It took a few days to arrange, but with the approval of the unit commanding officer and a doctor's certificate, we were able to take her to the Tyre hospital. From there she was handed over to the World Health Organization and taken to Beirut.

In the weeks and months that followed, we tried to get information but found nothing. We often drove by the cafe where she had lived, but the place was boarded up and empty. The last time we saw the mother she had been crying as we drove away with her daughter. Now all evidence of them just seemed to disappear. Whether any of them were still alive, we would never know.

That first week of January 1988 brought many changes to the station. Our Australian station commander was heading home at the end of his tour and Lieutenant Colonel Rich Higgins was taking over as the new commanding officer. Colonel Higgins had already been in the station for over a month, but like all new officers he had first to complete some training by doing a shift or two on the observation posts. He had even spent a few days travelling around with the teams. For any incoming CO this would have been considered quite routine, but when the new boss was an American, the situation was far from ordinary. Working on any of the mobile patrol teams would take him deep into Lebanon and well beyond the relative safety of the Israeli controlled area. His initial request to accompany a team was met with a flat out "no." If the headquarters in Jerusalem thought the matter was closed, they didn't know Colonel Higgins. After a number of rejections he finally got the chance to make his case in front of the major general commanding all U.N. forces in the Middle East.

His argument was simple. How could he command a station and ask officers to work in dangerous areas when he had never done it himself? The general finally agreed to let him go, but only under some very strict conditions. He could not remain in any one area for more than twenty-four hours and he was not allowed to enter any hostile villages or meet with any of the team's political contacts.

Colonel Higgins may have been satisfied with this arrangement, but many of the team members were less than happy about the prospect of driving around South Lebanon with a U.S. Marine officer sitting in the back. There had already been a number of abductions in Lebanon throughout the 1980s, and the consensus among most of the officers was that any attempt to capture Higgins would mean an immediate death sentence for any non-American who happened to be with him. Americans were important political targets. The rest of us were not.

I must admit to being a bit nervous as I took my seat in the conference room for the morning briefing. I had attended many of these meetings in the past, but this time things were a little different. I was about to take command of Team India and begin working with the Irish battalion in what many considered some of the dangerous territory in all of South Lebanon. The eastern flank of Irishbatt (Irish Battalion) sat open and exposed at the mouth of the Bekaa Valley. The rough and hilly terrain and numerous hidden trails made the area very difficult to control. The Irish had been given the task simply because they were the best and most professional troops in the entire U.N. force, but even they were having trouble stemming the flow of armed insurgents. For every one they caught, at least one other was getting through and causing major havoc along the Israeli border.

As soon as we took our seats in the conference room that first morning, the new CO had announced an upcoming meeting for all teams in Tyre. I had just three days to learn all I could about my new job.

If I thought that my Irish upbringing was going to get me some special treatment, I was wrong. My first meeting with the commander of Irishbatt and his senior staff did not go as expected. Their initial greeting was friendly enough, but once the briefing began, I immediately knew that our working relationship was going to be problematic. The Irish battalion had been doing a very difficult job for a long time and did not necessarily trust outsiders. For some unknown reason my Norwegian predecessor had chosen to withhold certain information from the CO and that had led to a complete lack of trust between the Irish staff and the team.

From that very moment I knew that if I was to succeed as a team leader, my first priority would be to repair that rift. I was well aware that these things take time. If our team was to regain the trust, it would only happen by doing our job well over the next few weeks and months.

Unfortunately, we would never get the opportunity. In a matter of weeks, Team India would no longer exist.

By the time my partner and I showed up for the team meeting in Tyre we were both exhausted. In my first three days on Team India we had visited every outpost, seen every inch of Irishbatt territory, and put roughly fifteen hundred kilometres on our Jeep. Fortunately for me, I had the most experienced member of Team India to show me the ropes.

When I first encountered Pekka Kovisto I was a little concerned about how he would react to me being named the new team leader. He had already been on Team India for four months and he seemed to be the logical choice to take command. I need not have worried. Pekka was just weeks away from returning to Finland and was only too happy to be going home. This would be his final duty in Lebanon and my last opportunity to pick his brain and learn from his experience.

I know it was a quite unrealistic for me to think I could glean so much information in just three days, but I was just vain enough to try. I knew the team meeting in Tyre would be my first real test and I had no intention of sounding like a rookie.

I had read a good deal about Tyre and the surrounding area and now I would finally get the chance see this ancient city.

Two thousand years ago the city of Tyre was an integral part of the vast Roman Empire. Endless caravans carried trade goods from Persia, through the Arabian Desert and across the Syrian Plains before reaching this eastern Mediterranean port. From Tyre, these goods were carried across the sea to Athens and Rome and all the cities in the known world. By the beginning of the twelfth century Tyre had become one of the main assembly points for a crusader army coming from Western Europe. Once disembarked at Tyre, the crusaders would march south through Palestine, laying waste to every city along their way to Jerusalem.

Today the city of Tyre was barely a shadow of its former self. Years of war and a collapsed economy had left the inner city in ruins. A few rusted out ships were all that remained in the once busy harbour.

Our destination that morning was a former Lebanese Army barracks, known as the Tyre Logistics Base. Aside from a small U.N. supply unit, the base was also the home of Team X-ray.

The standard format for these meetings was for each team leader to give a short briefing on their area of operation. The meetings I had attended as a member of Team Foxtrot had been rather dull and boring. Some of the team leaders would simply stand up and say there was nothing to report, while others would tend to ramble on for a few minutes before asking if anyone had a question.

Most of us had assumed that our new boss would start out slow on this his first full day in command of the station. We couldn't have been more wrong. Perhaps some of the previous station commanders had been laid back and allowed teams to do as they pleased, but as we soon discovered, this guy intended to hit the ground running.

I actually felt a little sorry for the first two team leaders. They were obviously unprepared for the steady flood of questions coming from the colonel. It didn't take long before everyone was wide awake and making copious notes before it was their turn to stand up and face the barrage of questions from our new boss.

Maybe it was because I was new to the job or perhaps it was just luck, but I was the last to give a briefing. I hardly got past the introduction before the colonel interrupted me for the first time. "Are you familiar with the Metulla Gate?" The colonel was holding a pointer next to the wall map as he spoke. His question caught me by surprise and it took a second to register. Other than driving by the gate a couple of times I knew practically nothing about it, but that was not the answer he wanted to hear.

"Yes, I believe so," was my half-hearted response.

"I want your team to arrange a meeting with the gate commander and see if we can start using the Metulla crossing to relieve our teams and observation posts in the northeast."

If our new commanding officer was disappointed in our briefings, he didn't show it. His parting words about having a meeting every month put all of us on notice. The era of lacklustre briefings ended that day. This guy knew his stuff and you had best come prepared to answer his questions.

It had been a long, intense morning of non-stop briefings. Even as the colonel was making his closing remarks, you could hear the sound of chairs being pushed back from the table. Most of us were anxious to get out of there as quickly as possible. Normally after a meeting like this, all of the teams would hang around for some coffee and friendly conversation before returning to duty, but now most just wanted to get away from this man and his incessant questions.

Just as we thought we had him figured out, his demeanour suddenly changed. "Right, gentlemen," he said, slamming his notebook shut. "That's enough business for one day. Now I want us all to have a little fun." We all just looked at each other, not sure of what to do next. "I have often wondered whether my Toyota truck could beat a CJ7 Jeep in a race and now we have the perfect oval track to find out." One after another people began to whistle and applaud as we headed out the door and mounted our Jeeps.

Sitting near the edge of the city were the ruins of a former Roman coliseum and chariot track. Most of the structure had disappeared as the city closed in over the centuries, but the huge oval track still stood at the very centre of the complex of columns and arches. There were many roman ruins spread throughout Lebanon, but this was the most well known, simply because it had been used back in the 1960s to film the famous chariot race scene in the movie *Ben-Hur*.

We didn't actually race because there was barely enough room to line up our Jeeps eight abreast, but we certainly had fun trying to maintain a straight line as we moved around the oval track at twenty kilometres per hour.

In hindsight, I have always found it oddly perplexing to think how such a small gesture can change peoples' attitudes. By the time we parted ways that afternoon, it was like someone had flicked a switch. Gone were the grumbling complaints and sour faces. Most were actually looking forward to our next get-together. Maybe we were all becoming far too complacent and needed someone to shake us out of our rut. The job was important, but it shouldn't become all-consuming. Somehow we had to find a middle ground between doing a better job while still allowing ourselves to relax and enjoy life.

The Metulla Gate looked more like an armed fortress than a border crossing point. Machine guns protruded through narrow slits in the two large cement pillboxes on either side of the gate. Four heavily armed Israeli soldiers roamed back and forth along the fence line.

Aside from the Naqoura gate near the coast, this was the only civilian border crossing between Israel and Lebanon. Every morning a steady procession of Lebanese civilians made their way from the surrounding villages and took their place in the long line waiting to enter Israel. Most of them had jobs as domestic help or picking crops on one of the many kibbutz farms just over the border. They would stand there for hours holding on to their identification papers, just waiting to get through the first barrier. Sometimes they could wait all day, only to find that the crossing was closed because of trouble in the area. If they did manage to get past the first fence and into the compound, they were then subject to a thorough body search before stepping through the second gate into Israel. Once they returned in the evening, they would once again face a full search before being allowed to re-enter Lebanon.

Obviously these civilians hated the entire degrading procedure, but with the entire Lebanese economy in ruins, they were left with little choice. They needed the money to feed their families.

Using the Metulla crossing to relieve our teams and observation posts would certainly make our job easier and a good deal safer, especially for those of us working in the eastern interior of Lebanon. Instead of having to stay inside Lebanon while driving fifty kilometres to or from the Naqoura crossing, we could save a great deal of time and remain much safer by crossing at Metulla.

My team partner and I were kept waiting for over an hour before we were finally allowed to drive into the compound. We may have been in a white Jeep with a U.N. flag flying from the roof, but none of that seemed to matter as all of the weapons in the compound remained pointed directly at us. Even after the barrier closed behind us, the sentries never relaxed their aim. After a few more minutes of indecision, we were directed to drive over a narrow pit in the centre of the compound. The Israelis had these cement pits at every border crossing, and although I had done it many times, I always dreaded this part of the procedure. The three-metre-deep pit was only slightly narrower than the wheel base of the Jeep. Once the vehicle was lined up, I slowly moved forward, making sure the tires remained perfectly straight. Too far to the left or right would cause the Jeep to drop sideways into the open pit. As soon as we were directly over the centre of the pit, we were told to stop and shut off the engine. There we sat waiting while the sentry proceeded down the steps and under our vehicle. Once he satisfied himself that there were no explosive devices attached to the undercarriage, we could then drive forward and back onto solid ground.

When we were first introduced to the Israeli commander, he seemed rather suspicious, but as soon as he spotted the Canadian flag on my sleeve everything changed. As it turned out, he had spent a good deal of his youth living in Toronto. After turning eighteen he had felt obliged to return to his homeland and serve in the Israeli Defense Forces (IDF). His story was not unusual. Many of the soldiers I met were not Israeli born. Some had come from Europe, while most came from North America, but as Jews they felt it was their obligation to serve and defend Israel.

Team India had made the initial contact, now it would be up to Colonel Higgins and the staff to hammer out an agreement. The negotiations went on for weeks and our team would be called upon to escort the colonel to and from each meeting. I had not met many U.S. Marines but the few I had known tended to be rather stiff and formal. The long drives to and from meetings gave me ample opportunity to learn that Rich Higgins was not your average Marine.

He was a Vietnam veteran with over twenty years of experience. Prior to coming to Lebanon, he had been a special military advisor to the

American secretary of defence. When it came to soldiering he certainly knew his stuff, but he was far from a one-dimensional man. He and I spent many hours talking about everything from world politics to sports and books. I soon found out that we both enjoyed historical fiction, especially the novels written by Edward Rutherfurd.

By the second week of January the additional shifts and escort duties were beginning to take their toll on Team India. Even when we returned to Irish battalion headquarters at night, you could never count on more than two or three hours of uninterrupted sleep. Our trailer was just a short walk from the operations centre and rarely a night went by without at least one visit from the duty officer to inform us of some situation happening in the area. Once we closed down and parked our Jeep at the end of the day, we still had to monitor the Motorola radio set in the trailer throughout the night. At first the constant static buzz made it difficult to fall asleep, but like any ambient sound it soon faded into the background. With all of the teams and observation posts using the same frequency, there was never a quiet night. One moment all would be peaceful and then suddenly the radio would spring to life. It could be one of the teams reporting an attack in their area, or perhaps one of the observation posts calling in about artillery fire, but regardless of the reason, everyone across the network was now wide awake and listening.

After nine straight days in Lebanon, I finally returned to the apartment in Nahariya. It would only be a day-long break, but it would at least give me the chance to get a little sleep and get cleaned up before heading back on duty. It wasn't easy doing these back-to-back shifts, but by doing these extra days while Brigitte was still in Canada, I would be able to take a full week off once she returned.

It is amazing how well you can feel after twelve hours of uninterrupted sleep. I felt rested and refreshed as I made my way back across the border for another seven-day shift in Lebanon. With everything that had gone on since the start of January, I had not had a chance to talk to Peter McCarthy about his new job. He had taken over as the station training officer just two days earlier and had yet to make it out of the office. His new position would require him to have a comprehensive knowledge of station operations, and after suffering through an endless series of briefings, he was finally getting back into the field that morning. Peter was already a highly experienced military observer, but to be an effective training officer he would first have to spend a few days working with each team and learning everything about their operation.

Thankfully not much had gone on the night before, so the morning briefing was very short. I had already arranged a meeting with one of the Irish company commanders for that afternoon and wanted nothing more than to get away from the headquarters and back into the team area.

I could see that Peter was equally anxious to finally get away from the office and back to the field. I don't remember what exactly was said as we both made our way down the steps toward our waiting vehicles. I thinking I joked about him being the rookie training officer and reminding him to pay attention to his new Canadian boss.

Major Gil Cote was a Canadian and the commander of Team Romeo. His team worked with the Nepalese Battalion, and he and Peter would spend the next few days going over their entire area of operations.

It was an unusually warm and pleasant morning as my partner and I motored up the Echo Road toward our destination. The rain had let up the night before and it looked like we might finally have our first dry day in more than a week. We were just passing OP Ras when we heard the traffic control trying to raise Team Romeo. We didn't think much about it at first. The team had obviously missed their twenty-minute report time, but for the teams working near the coast, this was not uncommon. Sometimes vehicles moving along the highway could find they were unable to send or receive radio transmissions because of dead spots caused by the coastal cliffs. It had happened a few times before, but usually after two or three minutes the offending team would come on the air and apologize for the delay.

By now we had pulled our vehicle to the side of the road, and, like everyone else in South Lebanon that day, we could do nothing more than sit and wait. According to my watch, Team Romeo had now been out of contact for twenty-five minutes.

I knew the voice of traffic control belonged to Major Mike Sullivan. He was one of the three American Marines we had in the station, all of whom worked as members of the traffic control team. He had done his share of duties on the observation posts, but like all the Americans in the station, he could not work on any of the teams. Mike and I had become friends and shared more than a few beers at the bar. At first he told me how he had absolutely hated the idea of sitting behind a radio and monitoring traffic, but after a while he realized just how important their work was to our safety. Mike may have been a gung-ho Marine, but he could become a bit of a mother hen sometimes, especially if he was on duty and you failed to call after the prescribed twenty minutes. We may have considered him overprotective at times, but we all understood that he and the entire traffic control team shared a genuine concern for our safety.

After thirty minutes had elapsed without a response, we all knew what was coming next.

"All stations, this is traffic control. Mayday, mayday, mayday. Team Romeo is missing. All stations will remain stationary and stand by for further instructions."

It only took a moment, but it seemed much longer. When the radio came back on, I recognized the voice of the station operations officer.

"All stations, this is headquarters. Team Romeo's last reported location was the hill feature just east of the coast highway, five kilometres north of Naqoura. Teams X-ray and Zulu will move toward that location at best possible speed." We could hear the sound of revving engines and wind in the background as both teams acknowledged the order and sped down the highway from different directions. My partner and I were already scanning the map, but we both knew that we were too far away to provide any immediate help. Team Zulu was somewhere near the city of Tyre, and even at top speed it would probably take them fifty minutes to reach the site. Team X-ray was at the Ghanaian battalion headquarters and much closer. Barring any problems, they could be there in less than thirty minutes.

Although I had never been up to the top, I was familiar with the hill where Team Romeo had last reported. If Peter was trying to gain a better understanding of Team Romeo's area, this hill would be the logical place to start. It was the highest and most prominent feature in the area. From its eight-hundred-foot summit you could see for over twenty kilometres in all directions.

Just sitting there listening to radio static was maddening. We all wanted to do something to help, but now was not the time to clutter up the airwaves with unnecessary chatter. At last we received permission to move.

"Teams X-ray and Zulu will continue with the search. All remaining teams will report to this location as soon as possible."

We were only a few kilometres east of Naqoura when we heard the first radio report. "We found them, we found them!" was all the voice said before the radio once again fell silent. The sender had not identified himself, but we already knew it could only be Team X-ray.

What followed was a series of garbled messages back and forth between the headquarters and the unknown station. Based on the frequent breaks in the transmission, it sounded like Team X-ray was out of their vehicle and moving on foot while using the small hand-held radio.

For the first time we heard the voice of Colonel Higgins coming on the air. He spoke in a slow but forcible manner as he tried to get the voice to calm down and explain what was happening. "Team X-ray, this is the commanding officer. Your message is broken and distorted. You will return to your vehicle immediately and contact me on your main set."

The voice sounded breathless from running back to the Jeep, but at least we could hear him clearly. "Headquarters, this is Team X-ray. There has been an explosion. One member of Team Romeo is dead and the other is severely injured. Request immediate medical evacuation."

For a few seconds there was absolute silence on the radio. It was as if nobody knew what to say or do next. Finally the colonel came back on the air.

"Team X-ray, roger. A med vac helicopter is on its way. Estimated time of arrival at your location: five minutes."

By the time we reached the front gate at Naqoura, it looked like the entire U.N. force was mobilized and ready to move. We had to suddenly pull to the side of the road to avoid the line of armoured personnel carriers as they sped through the gate and headed north. We knew this was the forty-man quick reaction force and they were being deployed to the site of the explosion. At this early stage no one knew if this was a random act or a planned attack against United Nations personnel. Until there was a better understanding of the situation, every precaution would be taken to protect the medics and our unarmed teams.

By the time we entered the gate, I had already made up my mind. My teammate was a little surprised when I drove by the headquarters and headed straight for the hospital. Judging by all the Jeeps sitting in the parking lot, it was obvious that many of the other teams had the same idea. Colonel Higgins and the operations officer came to meet us as soon as we stopped. Even before we could ask the question, the CO knew what we wanted to know. "Sorry, there is still no word, but we should know something soon." Almost on cue, we could hear the distant sound of rotor blades beating the air. A moment later we saw the big white Huey Helicopter approaching from the north. Already we could see a team of medics standing ready near the helipad at the back of the building. The instant the skids touched the ground the side doors slid open and the medical team sprang into action. From our vantage point all we could see were white coats pushing gurneys toward the aircraft door. Each of them had to bend forward to protect themselves from the rotor blades still flapping just over their heads.

Only the colonel was allowed inside the hospital. All the rest of us could do was pace around the parking lot, waiting for him to re-emerge. It took a long time, but when he finally stepped through the swinging door, we all stopped and stared, waiting for him to speak.

The Team Romeo Jeep had run over some type of explosive buried in the dirt roadway. It had probably been a land mine, but no one knew for sure at that point. Peter had been killed instantly when the device detonated under the vehicle. The force of the explosion had thrown Major Cote from the Jeep. When Team X-ray found him he was unconscious and bleeding from numerous pieces of metal shrapnel buried in his head and torso.

Even as the colonel was speaking, we could hear the helicopter engine power up again and the rotor blades begin to rotate even faster. If Gil Cote had any hope of survival, he would need to be operated on without delay. The nearest surgical hospital was seventy kilometres down the coast, in Haifa, Israel.

As I stood there listening to the colonel speak I couldn't help but wonder about Catherine McCarthy and her two young daughters. Right now they were just a few kilometres away in their apartment in Nahariya, completely oblivious to all that had just happened. Maybe she was busy doing housework or preparing dinner for Peter? Maybe she was playing with the girls and enjoying a rare sunny January day? In less than an hour, a knock on the door would change her life forever.

I know the colonel would have wanted to wait as long as possible before delivering the news, but these things can't wait. The communications centre in the rear headquarters had heard the same radio traffic as us. At this time of day there were sure to be any number of wives and children on the patio or in the garden just outside the building. If any of them had heard the original transmission, there was no telling where the panic would lead.

In fact, there had been an aerobics class going on in the back garden, but fortunately the music they used to exercise had drowned out Team X-ray's first transmission. As soon as the duty officer heard the broadcast, he had immediately switched off the speakers.

Lieutenant Colonel Higgins had only been in command of the station for a few days and already he was faced with the dreadful task of telling a woman that her husband was dead. Two of the Australian wives stayed with Catherine and her daughters to help her get through the next few days.

For the rest of us, the job had to go on. Each of the teams was ordered to return to their respective areas. At first none of us wanted to leave the parking lot. Peter's body was still inside the hospital and it just felt wrong to drive away and abandon our friend. It took some rather harsh words from the operations officer to bring us all back to reality. Peter was gone and the best way to honour his memory was to get back out there and do our job.

Forty-eight hours later we returned to Naqoura for a memorial service and a last chance to say goodbye. After the service I had only a moment to speak to Catherine before she was whisked away in a staff car. I never saw her again. By the time I came off duty, she and the girls, along with Peter's casket, were already on the long flight home to Australia.

The following day we received one piece of good news. Major Gil Cote had sustained some very serious head injuries, but he was out of danger. When I went with some of the other Canadian observers to see him in the Haifa hospital a week later he still did not look well. Most of his head and face were covered in bandages and his legs and arms were swollen and bruised. He recognized us, but still had no memory of what happened in the moments following the accident. It would take over a month before he was stable enough to be flown home to Canada.

The U.N. military police had started an immediate investigation and each of the teams had questioned their contacts, but still there was no answer to the one burning question. Had Team Romeo been the target of a terrorist attack or had they simply been in the wrong place at the wrong time? The answer finally came from a rather odd source.

The Amal Militia was one of many paramilitary groups within Lebanon. They were far less radical than the Hezbolla organization that wanted nothing less than the complete destruction of Israel. The Amal Militia could care less about the nation of Israel. Their stated goal was to remove all Israeli forces from Lebanon.

On the January 16, just four days after the incident, a spokesman for the Amal Militia came on Beirut radio to announce their responsibility for the explosion. The speaker actually apologized for their part in the death of Peter McCarthy and the injuries to Gil Cote. Apparently the mine had been planted on the road to catch a high-ranking Israeli officer who often went there to hunt wild game.

It took quite a while, but slowly the station routine began to return to normal. Those first few days and weeks you could almost feel the tension and anxiety every time someone reported an incident on the radio. Everywhere you went people seemed to be on edge. No one seemed willing or able to laugh.

The bar and patio in the rear headquarters had always been the gathering place for the off-duty staff. After a long week on an observation post or patrolling on team, it was the best place to go and just relax and enjoy a cold beer. Husbands and wives could sit on the patio and watch their children laughing and playing in the garden. In the days and weeks following the accident, the entire atmosphere of the place changed. You could still find a crowd in the bar each evening, but the laughter and joy had disappeared. Small knots of people would gather near the bar and patio. The playground equipment in the garden sat unused. Mothers seemed unwilling to allow their children out of the sight for even a moment. Children seemed to sense the mood and clung to their parents. There were a few half-hearted attempts to organize some sort of a social function, but each was cancelled for lack of interest.

For a while it seemed that nothing could break through this blue funk that had enveloped the entire station.

The Australian officers, along with their wives and children, had been the group most affected by Peter's death. Now it seemed oddly appropriate that they would be the ones who would finally break the mood and get the entire station back on track.

We were all aware that Australia Day was fast approaching. With so many different nationalities represented in the station, these national day celebrations had always proved a great source of fun and entertainment. There was always a healthy spirit of competition, with each group trying to outdo the other.

Back on the first of July, the Canadian members of the station had hosted a huge pancake breakfast and had even managed to scrounge up a few cases of genuine maple syrup from our embassy in Tel Aviv. Three days later we had celebrated American Independence Day with a big barbeque in the back garden. The St. Patrick's Day celebrations put on by the Irish in March were legendary.

Based on all that had happened in the station, I think most of us just assumed that Australia Day, on January 26, would come and go quietly. It wouldn't be fair to expect the Australians to organize a party so soon after losing one of their own.

When the Australians first announced that they intended to host a party in the mess, no one seemed particularly enthusiastic, but that quickly changed when they told us the purpose of the get-together. The entire event would centre around an auction of all things Australian. Everything from boomerangs to stuffed koala bears and giant Australian flags would be put up for bids. Still some people remained a little skeptical about the event, but that quickly changed when they announced that all money raised from the auction would be donated to a special education fund being set up for the daughters of Peter and Catherine McCarthy.

To say the auction was a success would be an understatement. Once people knew where the money was going, the bidding just went crazy. A set of matching boomerangs probably worth ten dollars went for one hundred dollars. Everything went for four or five times its true value. The last item up for bid was a huge Australian flag, measuring twenty-by-ten feet. After a prolonged round of bidding, I managed to get it for seven hundred dollars. The following day I received a call from some senior official at the embassy, asking me to kindly return the missing item. Apparently the flag had actually been "borrowed" from the roof of the Australian Embassy and they would be happy to give me a small flag in its place.

It didn't happen right away, but I believe that Australia Day auction marked the beginning of the change. Slowly but surely you could feel the positive energy return to the entire station. By the beginning of February, the death of Peter McCarthy was no longer the daily subject of discussion. He would never be forgotten for the good person and true friend he had been, but now it was time to move on with our lives. I am sure Peter would have expected nothing less from all of us.

My Australian friend and teammate, Captain Peter McCarthy. He was killed by a land mine in South Lebanon on January 12, 1988.

Collection of the author.

CHAPTER 18

Mayday, Mayday, Mayday!

When I heard the dull ringing sound my first instinct was to jump out of bed and grab the radio handset. Who could possibly be calling at this time of night? I sat there in the darkness just staring at the small red light on the radio receiver, still half asleep. As I looked at my watch it dawned on me that it was only ten o'clock and I was still fully dressed. It still took a few moments for the haze to lift before I realized I must have dozed off.

My partner and I had gotten back to our trailer in the Irish battalion headquarters after an extremely long and frustrating day of patrolling. It had been one of those days when everything seemed to go wrong. It had rained all the night before and our Jeep simply refused to start in the morning. Another hour was lost trying to find cables to jump start the engine. Shortly before noon we had come around a sharp curve, only to find an Israeli tank patrol barrelling straight toward us. My partner had barely avoided a head-on collision by swerving off the road and into a ditch. Luckily our four wheel drive allowed us to back out of the ditch, only to find that one of our tires had been flattened by the impact. It did little good to curse at the Israelis; they hadn't even slowed down and were already long gone down the road.

By the time we returned to the trailer that evening, I wanted nothing more than some food and perhaps a little rest. The plan was simple, I would just lie down for an hour and then have a quick shower before supper.

It still took a few seconds to register. I had obviously slept through supper and the dull ringing I heard was coming from the field telephone and not the radio.

By the time I switched on the lights and found the receiver, the telephone had already rung for the sixth time. The voice at the other end sounded rather impatient. "Captain Burke, is that you?"

"Yes, it's me," I shouted back into the handset.

"Captain Burke, this is Colonel Higgins. Stand by, I have someone here who wants to talk to you." I pressed the handset hard against my ear, straining to hear through the constant static.

"Happy Valentine's Day," was all she said. Even through all the background noise, it only took me an instant to recognize Brigitte's voice. We only had a few minutes to talk before the line went dead, but that short call at least provided a good end to an otherwise horrible day.

I wanted to ask Brigitte how she had managed to get through to me all the way from Nahariya, but we were cut off before I could ask. Making a call between Israel and Lebanon was difficult enough, getting through on a military field phone should have been practically impossible. Early the next morning, I had my answer.

We were scheduled to meet with the colonel and his operations officer at the Metulla Gate at nine in the morning. After the previous day's problems, we decided it was best to get an early start.

The rain had let up overnight, but as we descended into the valley, we could see the black thunder clouds forming in the west. Soon Mount Hermon would no longer be visible as we watched the curtain of clouds slowly work their way across the valley and up the mountain slopes leading into Syria. It looked like we were in for another day of rain.

I still wasn't sure why we were there for this particular meeting. Other than making the initial contact with the Israeli commander and providing an escort for the colonel for the first few meetings, Team India's job was done.

When I first spotted the two-vehicle convoy approaching, I thought something looked rather odd. Even after they pulled in beside us, it took a moment for it to register. The Operations Officer and his assistant were in the lead vehicle and the colonel was alone in the Jeep Cherokee behind them. Later, when I asked the colonel about this, he just laughed and shrugged it off. "Once in a while it's just good to get a chance to drive again." In his previous job in Washington, DC, he always had a driver. Even here in Lebanon he rarely got the chance to drive his own vehicle, but every once in a while it was nice to get back behind the wheel.

Normally any U.N. vehicle travelling alone in South Lebanon must have a minimum of two people on board. One person could travel alone, but only when they were in convoy with at least one other U.N. vehicle.

Colonel Higgins was his usual energetic self when we greeted each other at the side of the road. He and I moved to the rear of his Jeep to gain a little protection from the constant steady downpour. We joked about "liquid sunshine" and how we both preferred North American snow to a Lebanese winter of mud and rain. When I tried to thank him for arranging the call from Brigitte, he just waved it off as if it were nothing. It was only later I found out that he had gone through three separate switchboards and at least two operations centres before finally reaching me deep inside eastern Lebanon. He had gone through all of that simply because he had happened to overhear Brigitte say she wanted to wish me a happy Valentine's Day.

After all the small talk was out of the way, the conversation finally turned to the purpose of our meeting.

"I don't need Team India here for the meeting this morning, but I am a little pressed for time and I wanted to talk to you face to face while we had the chance." He and I just stood there a moment staring at each other. I had no idea what he wanted to talk about, but based on his stern expression, I knew it was serious. "Based on all that has happened in the past little while, we have had to make some changes to the staff." I was beginning to understand what he was getting at. The death of Peter McCarthy and the injuries to Gil Cote had created some serious shortages to the staff of the station. A new training officer had already been found, but there were still at least four key staff members, including the operations officer, who were fast approaching the end of their tour. If the station was to continue to function effectively, these positions had to be filled quickly.

As soon as he mentioned the staff shortages, I began to realize where he was going with this conversation, but still his words caught me by surprise.

"I want you to be the next operations officer." I just stood there a moment, not knowing quite what to say. Thankfully he interrupted before I could respond. "I know this is sudden, but I will need an answer within the hour."

The meeting was only a formality and took less than forty-five minutes. The Israelis had already agreed to allow us the use of the Metulla Gate, this final get-together was just an opportunity for both sides to hammer out some last-minute procedural details.

Perhaps if I had known I would be the first person to use the gate, I would have paid a little more attention to what was being said. I knew how important this agreement was to all of us in the station, but right then I was more than happy to just sit at the back of the room, pretending to listen, while my mind mulled over the colonel's offer.

I would like to think that I was the best man for the job, but I knew there was any number of men in the station who were equally or better qualified to be the operations officer. When choosing a person to place in a position of authority, most military organizations will make the decision based on experience and ability. However, the United Nations was not your average military organization. When choosing an officer for any staff position, the U.N. always had to consider one overriding factor: "National Balance." Our station had over eighty officers from sixteen different countries. When it came time to fill any position, there had to be equal representation among all the national groups

I could delude myself into thinking that I was the best candidate to be the operations officer, but the simple reality was that I had been chosen because of my nationality. After the evacuation of Major Gil Cote, there were no more Canadians left within the senior staff.

Long before the meeting broke up, I had already decided to accept the position. I had no illusions about why I had been given the job; now it would be up to me to show them that I was up to the task.

I knew the outgoing operations officer was not scheduled to leave until the end of the month, but any assumptions I made about easing my way into the job were quickly dashed as soon as I said yes to the colonel. "I have a meeting the day after tomorrow with the head of the Amal Militia in Tyre and I want you to sit in with the staff. After that you can take all the time you need to brief your own replacement on Team India."

* * *

There were many words you could use to describe what it was like to work as a United Nations observer, but the one word you could never use was boring. I had only been in Lebanon for roughly nine months and already I was starting my fourth new job. After five weeks on Team India I had barely enough time to feel somewhat comfortable in the job, and now I was off again to something completely new and different.

At least I could take some solace in the knowledge that I was leaving Team India in the hands of a strong and capable Swedish officer.

Captain Anders Perrson and I had known each other since day one, in Jerusalem. Our U.N. careers seemed to be following the same basic path. After working together on the observation posts, we had both been selected to go on a team on the same day. Now, after spending three months working with the Norwegian Battalion on Team Sierra, he would assume command of Team India.

When Anders arrived from Naqoura on the morning of February 17, I was truly looking forward to the week we would spend together going over his new duties. But all of that would have to wait for one more day. The priority for that morning would be to get to Tyre for the meeting between Colonel Higgins and the leader of the Amal Militia.

When we left the Irish battalion headquarters, it looked like a typical winter day in Lebanon. The early morning fog had lifted and the sun was trying to break through the clouds over the eastern mountain range. We knew it wouldn't last. It took us two hours to reach the coast, but already we could see the storm clouds forming over the Mediterranean. By mid afternoon the sky would turn grey and the winter rains would return once again. The best we could hope for was a slow drizzle, but judging by the rumble of thunder and the flashes of lighting out over the water, today promised to be a real soaker.

Anders and I had taken the northern route to Tyre. When we finally emerged from the hills, the city was just a few kilometres to the south. Judging by the radio traffic, we had timed our arrival perfectly. Just as we pulled into the Amal Militia headquarters we could hear the colonel's convoy reporting their progress along the coast highway. According to the map, they were less than fifteen minutes away.

It had been over a month since the last incident on the coast road, but the area was still considered dangerous. I remember thinking back to Christmas Day and the incident with Team Zulu. Their Jeep had been hit by a single round, but they had managed to get away from the would-be robbers. At least the colonel and his staff were in convoy together and surely there was some safety in numbers. Still, I couldn't help but have this nagging doubt running through my mind.

I can't speak for the others sitting there waiting, but when I finally saw the two vehicles enter the parking lot, I felt a strong sense of relief.

There was no real agenda for the meeting. This was simply a chance for the colonel to meet with one of the key political and military figures in the region.

After the Israelis pulled back to the border region of Lebanon in the early 1980s, the Amal Militia had quickly moved in to fill the vacuum. This ragtag army now controlled a large swath of South Lebanon, stretching from the Tyre Pocket north to the city of Sidon. Most of their military equipment consisted of a few rusty armoured personnel carriers and civilian pick-up trucks with .50 calibre machine guns mounted in the back. What they lacked in weaponry they made up for in manpower. Even the slightly better-equipped South Lebanese Army tended to give them a wide berth.

The Israelis may have considered the Amal Militia little better than terrorists, but like it or not, they did provide a certain level of stability throughout the area. If it came to an open confrontation, the Israelis could no doubt destroy them in a day, but as long as the Amal remained well north of the border region, the Israelis were content to leave them alone.

For the U.N., it was more like a marriage of convenience. They certainly did not condone their strong-armed methods, but without them the U.N. would have a much more difficult task of keeping the peace in the most volatile region.

The Amal leader looked oddly out of place in his ill-fitting green fatigues. A cloth patch containing three white stars adorned each shoulder of his uniform. Even his green beret looked far too small to cover his large crop of silver-grey hair. The green web belt looked rather snug around his ample waistline. A Colt .45 automatic was protruding from the holster at his side.

As soon as the two men came face to face, the militia leader grasped the colonel's hand and began to speak at length, in Arabic. I didn't understand the words, but based on his serious facial expression and bowed head I had a good idea what this was about. He never let go of the colonel's hand as he continued to speak without pause. The interpreter stood patiently waiting to speak. The speech in Arabic seemed to take two or three minutes, but when the interpreter finally spoke, the translation only took a few seconds. "The general wishes to express his sincere regrets about the death of Captain McCarthy and only hopes we can continue to work together in a spirit of cooperation."

After a few moments of awkward silence, the colonel finally responded. "Tell the general that we appreciate his concern for our loss, and I sincerely hope that he has dealt with those responsible and also taken steps to ensure this sort of thing never happens again." Colonel Higgins never took his eyes off the general as he spoke. We all understood that this was just a polite way of telling this man that he needed better control of his men and he hoped the general had punished those responsible for committing this terrible act.

Now that the formalities were out of the way, we could all take a seat and get down to business. There wasn't a great deal to discuss, but it wouldn't do to simply rush out too quickly.

After another few minutes of small talk, the colonel brought up a rather sensitive point about some militia positions that were causing our officers some difficulty. For reasons known only to them, the Amal had set up checkpoints on some of the roads leading into downtown Tyre. There had already been a minor confrontation the first time Team X-ray had been stopped at one of these makeshift barriers. At first the team had refused to allow a search of their vehicle, but when you have a nervous teenager waving an AK-47 around, it is best to comply.

The discussion went back and forth for quite a while, but neither side wished to alter their position. The Amal may have considered themselves the only law in this region of Lebanon, but as far as we were concerned, they had no right to interfere with or search any U.N. vehicle. After half an hour of fruitless back and forth, the colonel finally agreed to postpone the discussion until a later date.

Once we returned to the parking lot, the colonel pulled me and the operations officer aside to discuss how we would handle the this particular problem at the next meeting. The colonel's message to me was quite clear. He had no intention of allowing the militia to search inside our vehicles. Our next scheduled meeting was in one month, by which time I would have taken over as the station operations officer. In the next couple of weeks the colonel wished to sit down with me and the staff and see if we could come up with some sort of comprise.

After a few more minutes of small talk we each headed for our separate vehicles. Just before climbing into his Jeep, he made his all-too-familiar parting remarks. Every meeting we had always ended with him uttering the same phrase: "Take good care of yourselves and take care of each other."

Those would be the last words we ever spoke.

By early afternoon the sky had turned black and the downpour began. Even with the heavy rain, Anders and I made good time as we headed north through the city. As we turned east and headed into the hills the sky brightened somewhat. It looked like we were just on the leading edge of the weather front and up ahead the skies were still bright and clear. We could hear the Jeep engine labouring as we continued the steady climb back into the hills. Once we topped the rise and the ground levelled out it would be smooth sailing all the way home to Irish battalion headquarters. With any luck we would be back in time for a shower before supper.

That's when we heard the distress call.

"Mayday, mayday, mayday!" Even without hearing the call sign, we both recognized the voice of the operations officer.

Again there was that maddening radio silence, as we sat there on the side of the road just waiting. There was no need to look at the map. We already knew that based on the elapsed time, the convoy containing the colonel and the operations staff was somewhere just south of Tyre on the coast highway. All we could hope for was somehow they had managed to evade the robbers and gotten away safely.

We couldn't possibly be prepared for what came next.

"All stations, this is the operations officer. Colonel Higgins is missing." The poor weather conditions and hilly terrain were creating a lot of radio static, making it difficult to hear, as the voice kept cutting in and out. We could just make out the voice of the duty commanding officer (DCO) as he kept asking the operations staff to repeat the message. The rest of us stayed silent as the operations officer and the DCO tried to communicate back and forth.

From what we could surmise, the two-vehicle convoy had been heading back to Naqoura, with the operations staff in the lead and colonel travelling alone in the rear vehicle. Somewhere along the highway, the two vehicles had lost visual contact. When the staff had turned around, all they found was the colonel's Jeep sitting empty at the side of the highway.

By now I already had the map spread open in front of me. Anders and I did not have to talk. We both understood what was going on. "Come on, come on," I kept mumbling at no one in particular. It had been at least twenty frustrating minutes since we stopped at the side of the road and we both knew that time was the enemy.

The weather front had caught up to us. The Motorola radio cracked with static as the thunder clouds rolled east over our heads. We briefly considered moving undercover, but we didn't want to take the chance of losing radio contact. All we could do was sit and wait.

At last we heard the voice of the deputy commanding officer. "All stations, this is the DCO. Colonel Higgins has been abducted by persons unknown. We assume he is being taken north and all U.N. positions have been ordered to shut down all crossing points leading out of South Lebanon." Anders and I strained to listen to the words of the DCO as his voice continued to cut in and out through the static. Even though we didn't catch every word, the message was clear enough. Whoever kidnapped the colonel would have only one option if they wished to make a successful getaway. They would have to travel north and get out of the U.N.-controlled area as rapidly as possible. The Litani River was just a few kilometres beyond the city of Tyre, and if they managed to get past this boundary line and into Northern Lebanon there was nothing or no one to stop them from reaching Beirut.

More than thirty minutes had elapsed since the abduction, but perhaps the weather had hindered the escape and the kidnappers. Maybe they were still on the south side of the Litani River and desperately trying to get past one of the U.N. checkpoints. With the entire U.N. force now on high alert, there was always the hope that he would be found before it was too late.

Two unarmed men in a Jeep couldn't do much to help, but still we sat there waiting and hoping for something to do.

Only Team Zulu remained in the outskirts of Tyre, while the rest of us where spread across the area to the south and east.

At last we heard the call we had been waiting for. Each of the teams in turn was sent to various locations all across the northern flank of the area. "Team India, this is the DCO. You will go to position Golf Three Zero and report on the status of the search."

This Fijian Army checkpoint was the last U.N. position on the coastal highway leading into Tyre. Colonel Higgins was abducted from his Jeep approximately seven kilometres north of this checkpoint.

Collection of the author.

Golf Three Zero was a Ghanaian position at the very northern edge of their area of operation, about ten kilometres inland from the coast. The bridge over the Litani made it a major artery leading out of the area, but the distance from the abduction site made it an unlikely escape route. We knew all this as we sped through the rain, but still it was a relief to be doing something after all those minutes of indecision.

The radio airwaves were filled with many separate voices, all trying desperately to get to their assigned positions. Team Zulu had only a short distance to go up the main highway, north of Tyre. We were still a long way from the Ghanaian Battalion position, but already we could hear Zulu come on the air to report their arrival at the Litani River Bridge.

For the first time I could hear the sound of panic in the DCO's voice. Every few seconds he would come on the air to check on the status of Team Zulu and confirm they were all right. We could all understand his concern for the team. Right now they were completely alone in an extremely dangerous position. There was no U.N. position on the bridge and until the Ready Reaction Force arrived from Naqoura, they were on their own and unarmed in the middle of nowhere. We all wanted desperately to stop the abductors, but if they showed up on this bridge in the next few minutes, the two members of Team Zulu were as good as dead.

When my teammate and I arrived at the Ghanaian position, we could not believe our eyes. The barrier gate was wide open with cars flowing through unchecked in both directions. This was a platoon-sized position of about twenty men, but all we could see were two soldiers standing under the shelter of a tin roof. Even as we pulled up next to the gate, neither soldier seemed willing to come out and meet us in the downpour.

Anders and I got out of our vehicle and screamed at them to close the gate. One of them wore corporal's stripes on his sleeve, but even when I confronted him, he just turned and disappeared inside the building.

Until then I had only had a few dealings with these soldiers from Ghana. My first impressions were of a highly disciplined force that seemed extremely cooperative. If you drove up to one of their positions, the sentry would instantly spring to attention and execute a perfect salute. It was readily apparent that everything they did and said was heavily influenced by their British Army training.

When the Ghanaian officer appeared from the side of the building, I could hardly contain my anger. The young lieutenant just looked at me with a blank expression as I continued to shout and point at the barrier. Even in the few minutes since we arrived, at least six or seven vehicles had come and gone through the open gate.

In hindsight, I know I should have handled it a lot better, but in that moment it took all my willpower just to keep myself from punching this guy in the mouth. Anders had been a cop back in Stockholm, so he was no stranger to confrontation. He quickly placed his big frame between both of us and easily pushed me backwards.

I just walked away and tried to calm myself down. We were all soaking wet, but I didn't care. After a few minutes Anders joined me next to the Jeep. I could hear the officer begin to shout at his soldiers and I saw the commotion as the Ghanaian soldiers came running from the building and began stopping cars at the barrier.

Thankfully Anders had intervened before I did something truly stupid. As he explained, the officer knew nothing about what was going on. Their radio had been knocked out by the bad weather and our arrival at the position was the first indication that something was wrong.

At least now all of the cars were being stopped and searched, but we all knew it was too late. Considering how far we were away from the highway into Tyre, it is very unlikely that the abductors would have come through here. Still, the thought has plagued me for all these years. Where had he been taken across? Had he slipped past, right under our noses? If we had been just a few minutes quicker shutting down all the exits could we have saved him?

These are questions that will never be answered.

Just after five o'clock the rain finally ended. By then the entire United Nations force in South Lebanon was scouring the area. Every road and trail leading to the Litani River was manned. Some civilian eyewitness said that Higgins had been thrown into the back of a mini-bus and driven north. Another report said that he had been taken to the nearby coastline and spirited away in some sort of motorboat. The U.N. Ready Reaction Force was stopping everything on the highway and already the traffic was lined up for kilometres down the coast. The helicopters from the Italian

Air Group were making constant low level passes all along the coast. An Israeli patrol boat cruised nearby, waiting to board anything the Italian helicopters deemed to be suspicious.

Like all the other teams, Anders and I could do little other than sit and wait in our assigned position. I had apologized to the Ghanaian lieutenant for my earlier behaviour. After we shook hands, he just nodded and walked away. I never saw him again. It was difficult to tell if he had accepted my apology, but I was far too tired to care. Anders and I just sat on the bumper of the Jeep, listening to the crackle of the radio and waiting for the inevitable call. Neither one of us spoke as we sat there staring off into the distant hills. Daylight was slowly fading and taking with it any hope we had of finding Colonel Higgins.

"All teams, this is headquarters. You will cease operations and report to the Tyre logistics base as soon as possible."

Even though we were less than twenty kilometres from our destination, it was already well past dark when we reached the outskirts of the city. It would have been preferable to return to our trailer in the Irish battalion camp, but that was not a safe option. Moving through the interior of eastern Lebanon alone in the dark was far too dangerous. Even the Israeli army patrols stayed off these roads at night. Somewhere out there in the darkness the insurgents were already busy planting their mines and booby traps in the hope of catching any Israeli or South Lebanese soldiers foolish enough to travel these roads at night.

Like all the teams, the events of the day had caught us completely off guard. Now with the approach of night, we were all far from the safety of our home base.

Thankfully, by nine o'clock the last of our six teams had arrived at the logistics base without incident. As each team came through the door, the question was the same. Was there anything new? Had anyone seen or heard any news? Every so often we would all perk up when we heard one of the U.N. outposts come on the air to report their status. The vehicle searches were continuing but there was nothing new to report.

As soon as the operations officer came through the door we all immediately crowded around hoping for any piece of good news. Even before he spoke, we could see from his expression that there was nothing.

We were all tired but he looked positively exhausted. After we sat down, he filled us in on the details of what had happened that morning on the coast highway.

Their two Jeep convoy had left the meeting in Tyre shortly after one in the afternoon. At some point the lead Jeep had rounded a curve and lost sight of the colonel's Jeep in the rear-view mirror. Assuming he had been caught in traffic, they stopped on the side of the road and waited for him to catch up. After a few minutes, they turned around and when back north in an effort to find him. About six or seven hundred metres back they found the colonel's Jeep. The engine was still running and the door was open, but the vehicle was empty.

With sixteen men trapped in the logistics base for the night there was hardly enough of anything to go around. With all that had happened, most of us had not eaten since early morning. The food supply was meant to feed two people and it was long gone. All that remained was a box of stale crackers and a single jar of instant coffee. All we could do was try to get some sleep and wait for morning. Someone had managed to scrounge up a few grey blankets and each of us found an empty space on the floor. Soon there was silence and all I could hear was the steady breathing of those around me. Every so often I could hear someone moving around, trying to get more comfortable. We were all exhausted, but no one slept. All we could do was lay there on the cold stone floor, waiting for the dawn to arrive.

Most of us were up and moving even before those first rays of grey light entered the building. It felt good just to step outside and breathe in the fresh air. A thick mist had rolled in off the Mediterranean during the night and now it was difficult to see anything beyond our small compound. The weather reports promised a clear day and by eight o'clock the rising sun had already burned off most of the lingering fog.

One of the Team Zulu guys had gone to the local market and returned with a flat of eggs and a couple of loaves of bread. Within fifteen minutes all thirty eggs and every slice of bread was gone.

Soon all the teams were busy outside in the parking lots. All of our Jeeps were gassed up and ready to go. Individually we may have all thought that there was little hope of finding the colonel, but none of us would ever say it out loud. We just sat there waiting and listening for the radio order telling us to resume the search. When the word finally came, it was not what we had expected.

The search was over. Colonel Higgins was no longer in South Lebanon.

Some group calling themselves the "Organization of the Oppressed on Earth" claimed responsibility for the kidnapping of Colonel Higgins. Their statement said that the colonel was already in Beirut, where he would be put on trial for spying.

The sun was already high above the horizon, yet still we sat waiting in the Tyre logistics base. Nobody seemed willing to discuss what would happen next. When the four armoured vehicles of the Ready Reaction Force pulled into the compound, we had our answer.

According to the U.N. intelligence reports, it was still unclear if Americans were the only group targeted for abduction, and until a threat assessment could be completed, none of the teams were authorized to re-enter the area controlled by the six battalions of UNIFIL. The Ready Reaction Force was there to escort us all back to the headquarters in Naqoura.

The drive back down the coast highway gave us ample time to consider the situation. Like most of the other officers, I assumed that these restrictions were just a temporary measure and we could soon return to our battalion areas.

Even before I had a chance to park the Jeep in Naqoura, I could see the deputy commanding officer waving for me to stop. It took him a moment to catch his breath before speaking. He had a special task that only Team India could perform because we were the only ones familiar with the Metulla Gate crossing procedure. Within minutes, Anders and I were speeding to the east along the Echo Road. There were still two American officers trapped deep inside Lebanon and our job was to get them out as quickly as possible

I have to admit that with all of the activity surrounding the abduction of Colonel Higgins, I had not given much thought to the other Americans still working in South Lebanon. Within hours of the abduction, all of the U.S. officers working on traffic control and in the headquarters were ordered out of Lebanon. However, by the time the decision was made, it was far too late in the afternoon to remove the two Americans still trapped on the Mar and Khiam observation posts. Two other observers had already been sent to replace them, but by the time they reached the OPs it was too late in the evening to safely move the Americans.

Our team task was very straightforward. We were to use the Echo Road and get to OP Mar as quickly as possible. Once we had the first American, we were to take him to the Metulla Gate, where he could wait with the Israelis while we headed to OP Khiam for the second officer. Once we had both Americans inside the Metulla Gate, it was just a short drive through the second barrier and we were safely back inside Israeli territory.

Neither officer had said much on the tense drive from the observation posts, but once that second gate closed behind us, I could hear them both take a deep sigh of relief. They had spent the entire night sitting in the dark and listening to the radio. I can only imagine how frightening it must have been to just wait there, never knowing if you were the next one to be taken.

It had been two full days since the colonel disappeared and still we sat around anxiously waiting for someone to make a decision.

With the exception of those people manning the observation posts, the headquarters conference room was packed with every available officer in the station. A steady rumble of noise filled the room as we all conversed among ourselves, waiting for the general to arrive. We all knew that this man held the fate of an entire station in his hands. Most of us were still optimistic in our belief that we were about to return to duty with our respective battalions.

Observer Group Lebanon had lost two outstanding officers in just one month, but surely the general could understand that this was not the time to back away from our responsibilities. Had Peter McCarthy or Rich Higgins been standing there that morning, I have no doubt that they would have expected us to get on with the task at hand.

As soon as the general walked through the door, the room fell silent.

At first his words sounded encouraging, but slowly the message began to shift toward the negative. It took him a long time to get to the point. After he finished, he took questions from his audience. A few of us offered suggestions on how the team concept could continue, but our ideas seemed to fall on deaf ears. Someone even mentioned the idea of arming us with pistols, but that suggestion was quickly shot down. The mandate for the United Nations Truce Supervisory Organization did not allow observers to carry any type of weapon. Nothing we could do or say seemed to make a difference.

When the general asked for a show of hands about who would be willing to return to work in their battalion area, every hand in the packed auditorium shot straight up. None of it mattered. The decision had been made.

The observation posts would continue, but all the territory to the north was now deemed far too dangerous for unarmed observers to enter. All the patrol teams were to be disbanded, effective immediately.

I am sure the general thought he was doing the right thing, but to those of us who actually did the job each day, his decision simply put an end to all the good we had ever done. United Nations military observers had been patrolling the region since 1948 and in a single sentence he had managed to put an end to forty years of good work.

It is strange what the mind contemplates in times of crisis. As we left the conference room all I could think about was the Team India trailer back in the Irish battalion headquarters. It had only been two days since we left, but it seemed much longer.

As we left the trailer to begin the day, the routine had been the same as countless other mornings. One quick check to make sure the coffee pot was unplugged, the Motorola radio was switched off, and the windows were closed against the threat of rain. Last but not least, I always took a momentary glance at my bedside table. Even on the worst of days the framed pictures of Brigitte and my kids always made me smile.

When I closed the trailer door that morning how could I have known we would never return. Some of our personal kit would find its way back to us in the weeks following the abduction, but the pictures seemed to have disappeared.

CHAPTER 19

The Magical Mystery Tour

When I finally received the call from the senior Canadian in Jerusalem it should have been cause for celebration. I had been waiting for months for an answer to my request and now I just felt an odd twinge of guilt about my good fortune.

Considering that there are only twenty Canadian officers working within the entire United Nations Truce Supervisory Organization at any given time, it is difficult enough to get even one tour. The end of my one-year of duty in the Middle East was fast approaching and my request to remain for a second year had just been approved.

In the weeks following the abduction of Colonel Higgins there had been absolutely nothing. Even after all this time, we still had some faint hope that there was still a chance that he would be set free. Both the secretary general of the United Nations and the president of the United States had tried to negotiate for the colonel's release, but the kidnappers remained silent until one morning in early April.

According to Jordanian television, the colonel and been found guilty of spying for the Israelis and was about to be executed. Any doubt about the authenticity of the report was put to rest when we saw the film footage. The black and white image of Colonel Higgins holding a newspaper filled the television screen. The camera zoomed in for a moment to show the previous day's date on the newspaper. His uniform had been replaced by a dark grey shirt and he looked pale and gaunt. His unshaven face showed signs of bruising. Two dark hooded figures holding AK-47 rifles stood on either side of him.

Every day we waited to hear more, but once again the kidnappers fell silent. Sometimes we would hear unconfirmed reports, but there was never any concrete information to prove that he was either dead or alive. Soon the newspapers and television reports moved on to other stories.

The approach of summer heralded the start of a new rotation cycle. Some old friends departed for home, while others moved to different stations. Soon the morning briefings were filled with new and unfamiliar faces. Even on the busiest of days, the conference seemed a lot less crowded. Once the teams were disbanded there was no longer a need to keep eighty officers in the station. The increased threat had forced us to double the manpower on each outpost from two to four observers, but with the station strength now set at sixty, we had just enough officers to do the job.

The American officers had remained at the rear headquarters in Nahariya for weeks after the abduction. Neither the U.N. nor their own government seemed to know what to do with them. They certainly could not return to Lebanon, but most of the other stations already had enough observers to do the job. Eventually a few would be sent to work in the Cairo station, while the rest would return home to the States.

The night before Mike Sullivan was due to depart, a few of his friends got together at the bar for a final goodbye drink. Mike was returning home to take command of a Marine company at Camp Pendleton in California. It had only been a few weeks since the kidnapping so no one was in the mood for a party, but we couldn't let this man go home without doing something. Mike had always been that steady quiet voice at the other end of the radio. In times of trouble, he had always been there to help. Most of our maps were vastly out of date and on more than a few occasions an inexperienced observer had gotten lost in the maze of villages surrounding the Echo Road. Mike's voice always remained calm while he helped resolve the situation and got everybody back on the right path.

Just as I was about to leave that night, Mike called me to the side and handed me a small brass medallion. I recognized the square plate immediately. The words "United States Department of Defense" were stencilled just above the engraving of an eagle clutching a bolt of arrows.

It had been left hanging on the key chain in the colonel's Jeep on the day he was abducted. "Here is something to remember the chief." I thanked him, but before I could say anything more, he was out the door and gone into the night.

In the twenty-four years since that night, the medallion has been with me everywhere I go.

By the fall, my job as station operations officer had settled into a routine. When I stood to speak at the morning briefing, I would take a moment to stare at the faces. There had been so many changes I sometimes had to make a conscious effort just to remember the names of those staring back at me.

Each morning I would finish and turn to our new commanding officer and ask if he had anything he wished to mention. Each day he said no. After the meeting broke up, most of us would grab a coffee and take a few minutes to talk informally about the events of the day. Our boss would just enter his office and close the door behind him. Unless I went to him with some pressing issue I rarely saw him.

He had arrived directly from Italy just a few weeks after Higgins disappeared. The first day we met, I knew there was something wrong. He seemed nervous and extremely apprehensive. It was clear to me that he did not want to be there. At first I thought he was just unsure about the prospect of taking over a U.N. station, but as soon as I mentioned the duty roster, I knew we had a problem. At first he said he was simply too busy to go. I knew this was untrue, but this was not the time and place for a confrontation. I needed to choose my words carefully. Like it or not, he was still a lieutenant colonel and I was a captain. I simply told him that the headquarters in Jerusalem expected all new station chiefs to do some on the job training before assuming command. I knew I was stretching the truth, but the mention of headquarters seemed to do the trick. He agreed to do one outpost duty, but insisted on going to OP Hin because it was the closest to Naqoura.

At first the working relationship between the staff and our new boss was rather awkward, but we soon learned to work around him. If someone had an administrative problem they went to the deputy chief. All operational problems came through me. Once or twice each week I would brief the commanding officer on what we what we were doing. He never objected or changed anything. He simply nodded his approval and then went back to whatever he did behind closed doors. We may not have been following proper military protocol, but somehow it worked.

A month or so after I left the station, I heard that he had been caught crossing back into Israel with some contraband liquor and cigarettes. Rather than charge him with smuggling, the U.N. commander simply sent him home to Italy.

Once each month I was required to visit the headquarters in Jerusalem and brief the chief of operations on all that was happening in Lebanon. The meeting would always follow the same format. I would give him a breakdown on any incidents, including roadside bombs, vehicle hijacking, robberies, and any reports of artillery or tank fire in the area. He may ask a few questions, but generally the briefing took about thirty minutes. As soon as I finished I could see the scowl cross his face because he knew what was coming next. Every month I asked the same questions and every month I received the same negative response.

Was there any new information on Colonel Higgins? Was there any new information regarding the reinstatement of the teams back into South Lebanon? Was there anything new on my written request to decrease the number of observers on each of the observation posts?

For the first four months, the chief of operations simply said "no" to all my questions, but after five months of nagging, I finally received a positive response to my last question.

Each of the observation posts had been working with a four-man crew since the day after the abduction and there simply wasn't enough work to keep them all fully employed. At last I was authorized to bring the numbers down to two officers per outpost. Of course, everything comes with a price. Within a couple of months the station strength would drop to fifty officers, which meant we would continue to work with just enough people to do the job.

I knew firsthand just how isolated you could feel when left alone on an OP deep inside Lebanon. When I did my first few outpost duties, we could always count on at least three visits during any given week. These visits were especially important for any new officers doing their first few duties. It was imperative that they understood their duties and the best way to confirm this was to take them up to the roof and have them give you a full formal brief on their area of responsibility. Now with a chief who refused to leave the office and no patrol teams in the area, an OP crew could go a full seven days and never see a soul.

It didn't take long before I could sense a level of complacency beginning to spread throughout the station. There may have been many things outside of my control, but I decided early on that this was a situation that had to change.

My duties during the week kept me busy, but every Saturday morning I would take my Jeep and begin the long haul up the Echo Road. If I could get started at six, this would allow me to spend at least one hour on each OP and still get back to Naqoura just before dark.

The regulation requiring a minimum of two people in a vehicle was still in full force, but in the beginning I had no problem finding a volunteer to join me. However, as the weeks went by I began to notice that people were beginning to avoid me, especially late on Friday afternoon, when they knew I was searching for my weekly volunteer. I am sure there were those who thought I was a little fanatical, but somehow or other I always managed to find someone to join me on what most were now calling "Burke's magical mystery tour."

Sometimes late at night when I couldn't fall asleep, I would stand on my apartment balcony and stare off into the darkness. Leaning against the railing, I could hear the waves lapping against the shoreline just metres away. Looking north along the coast, I could easily see the flood lights along the border fence.

I had been in working in Lebanon for a very long time. I was tired and restless. Most nights I would lie down and close my eyes, but sleep didn't come. Brigitte put up with my nightly wandering for a while, but we both knew what needed to be done. Other than a day or two every couple of weeks, I had been on duty for seventeen straight months. I didn't want to leave, but maybe it was time to move on and do something different. I didn't need a doctor to tell me I was becoming more than a little burned out. Right now I just needed to take some time away from the job and try and figure out what to do for the seven months remaining in my tour of duty.

Fortunately, the answer to my immediate problem came when I met an old friend who had just arrived from a six-month tour in Damascus, Syria.

Captain Don Millwater and I had first met during an earlier tour of duty in Cyprus. While he was there, Don had been admitted to the British Military Hospital, where he would meet his future wife, Maggie. Now that we were all together again, we decided to take a week off for a little rest and recreation. Another Canadian couple, Mike and Josselyn Titus, decided to join us, and together we all climbed aboard our minivan and headed south.

The first hour on the road did not go very well and it was all due to my incessant chattering about work. Even though I had left everything in the capable hands of the training officer, I still found it difficult to relax and just let go. I was so busy obsessing about the job I hadn't even noticed the looks of annoyance I was getting from my friends. Even when Don pulled to the side of the road and stopped, I still didn't realize I was the problem. "Okay, here's the deal. The next person who talks about work has to pay for everyone's dinner tonight." At first it took a conscious effort on my part to keep my mouth shut, but soon I was able to put it from my mind and just relax and enjoy the ride.

It took only three hours to reach the Arab-Israeli border. After that it was a full day's travel through the Sinai Desert before reaching the Suez Canal. After a ferry ride across the canal, it was a short run to our final destination: Cairo, Egypt.

The week spent wandering through the city, seeing the pyramids on horseback and cruising down the Nile, could not have been better. I had been so concerned about abandoning my job and now I didn't want to go back.

The long drive home gave me ample time to consider what I needed to do. Even if I had doubts, they were quickly erased when I returned to work.

Crossing the Suez Canal on the way to Cairo, Egypt. From left to right: Captain Don Millwater, Major Mike Titus, and the author.

Collection of the author.

Mick Withers, the training officer, had filled in for me while I was gone, and from all accounts he had done an outstanding job. Any vain thoughts I may have had about being indispensible were now put to rest. The station possessed a number of capable officers who could step in and do the job.

I still had six months left in my tour of duty, but it was time to leave Lebanon and do something else.

Driving in downtown Damascus is not something for the faint of heart. I have no idea why they even bothered to paint dividing lines on the boulevard when no one seemed to pay attention. When we stopped at the first traffic light, there were at least six cars squeezed into the three lanes. The instant the light turned green all the cars behind us started hitting their horns to urge us forward.

When my Russian guide picked me up at the border, he had not said a word when I asked if I could drive. The traffic on the back roads was relatively light, but as soon as we entered the outskirts of the city the pace picked up. Now my Russian passenger could not stop laughing every time he looked at the frightened expression on my face. By the time we reached the city centre, we were already doing well over the eighty kilometre per hour speed limit, but still the cars whizzed by like we were standing still.

We were just a couple of kilometres from the U.N. headquarters and I thought I could relax. That's when my Russian friend warned me that there was just one major hurdle left to cross.

When I first laid eyes on it, I was not sure what to do. It would have been nice to stop and assess the situation, but being in the centre lane and surrounded by cars left me with only one option. I put my foot on the gas and tried to stay in the lane as we entered the massive traffic circle.

I have no idea what the proper name was for this intersection, but all of the military observers referred to it as "Holy Shit." It would be difficult to find two more perfect words to describe the experience of going through that traffic circle. There were six major roads all funnelling traffic into the centre of the massive roundabout. No one paid attention to the speed limit, as cars cut in and out from every direction. It seemed that the right of way belonged to those with the most guts and the fastest cars. It took me three trips around the complete circle before I finally managed to force my way into the outer lane and find the exit.

By the time I reached my destination on that first morning, I swear I left an indentation of my fingernails in the steering wheel.

After working for so long in the intense atmosphere of Lebanon, it took some time to become accustomed to my new surroundings. All U.N. outposts operate in the same way, but these six observation posts on the Syrian side of the Golan Heights had one major difference.

Each post sat on a narrow strip of no man's land just inside the Syrian border. The entire area surrounding each U.N. position was one vast minefield. Only the main highway and the outposts were safe. Stepping off the road anywhere in the border region of the Golan Heights could kill you.

The Yom Kippur War had ended fifteen years earlier, but still the border region remained heavily fortified by both sides. At least once each month we could witness the Syrian war games being conducted just behind their border. Looking through the OP binoculars we could see great clouds of dust as the Israeli tanks and artillery carried out similar exercises on their side of the line.

From our perspective, it seemed that both sides possessed more than enough weaponry to destroy the other. There was, however, a key clause in the ceasefire agreement that set limits on the numbers and types of weapons each side could have within certain distances from the border. The Syrians and the Israelis both had countless numbers of tanks, but each side was limited to fifty tanks within five kilometres of the border. The same held true for any size and type of artillery piece. The more sophisticated weapons, such as surface-to-surface missiles, had to remain at least fifteen kilometres behind the lines.

Our job was to ensure both sides were following these strict rules.

Twice each month we would depart Damascus in teams of two and spend the day counting all the equipment on the Syrian side of the Golan Heights. Our U.N. station in Tiberias would be doing the exact same thing on the Israeli side. It took every available officer to muster the ten teams it would require to cover the entire area in one extremely long day.

Just after dawn we would make our first stop at Syrian army head-quarters to pick up our liaison officer, who would act as our translator for the day. All of these young Syrian officers were university graduates who spoke impeccable English. They were certainly friendly enough and seemed to enjoy discussing Western culture. I learned early on that it was best to steer clear of all conversations involving politics. Despite their education, most were rather closed-minded when it came to this particular subject. Just a month before I arrived at the station a Danish officer on one of these inspection teams had made the mistake of referring to Assad, the Syrian president, as a dictator. The very next day, the station chief in Damascus received a letter from the Syrian Ministry of Defense stating that the Danish officer had forty-eight hours in which to leave the country.

Living in downtown Damascus did have its own special challenges. Our fifth-floor apartment had no elevator and trudging up and down the stairs each day could certainly raise your heart rate. Someone had actually been kind enough to place a chair on the third floor landing so you could sit a moment and catch your breath. The electrical power would automatically shut down at six each morning and remained off until late afternoon.

During the hotter months, the water was only turned on for brief periods in the evening. Brigitte and I both became expert in the two-minute shower. As soon as we heard the sound of the electrical pump kick in, we sprang into action. I would go last, and as soon as I jumped out, Brigitte was right there scouring out the tub. There wasn't a second to lose. The water could go off at any moment. Once the enamel surface was clean, she stuck in the drain plug and filled the tub with water we might need in the event of an emergency. None of this water was fit for consumption; we always kept a few cases of bottled water handy for drinking or brushing our teeth.

Even the simple act of going to the market needed a certain amount of planning. Brigitte didn't need to wear a head scarf, but women were expected to dress conservatively. Dresses were fine as long as they had sleeves and were cut below the knees. Shorts were never considered appropriate for either men or women. One of the officers had actually had rocks thrown at him when he when he went for his morning run in shorts.

Like most countries in the Middle East, one always had to take extra precautions when it came to food. The rule of thumb was very simple: if you couldn't peel and boil it, you were best to leave it alone. Buying frozen foods at the market could be especially dangerous. With the power going off so frequently, one never knew how many times that cut of meat had thawed out and been refrozen.

Even when you took every conceivable precaution, it was still almost impossible to get through a full six months without picking up some type of intestinal ailment. When I was a kid we called it the "Galloping Trots." The Arabs used the words "Yella Yella" to describe the problem. Literally translated it meant "Hurry, Hurry," which was very appropriate when you consider that this infection kept you running back and forth to the toilet all day. Believe me when I say that spending a week on an isolated outpost when you have "Yella Yella" is not a good thing. It is not just bad for you, but also your poor unfortunate partner who has to share the outdoor toilet.

It may sound strange to say, but in spite of all we went through, Brigitte and I both loved living in Damascus. The civilians we dealt with were warm and friendly. Our Arab neighbours were always asking us over for tea and cake. Based on their sparse surroundings we knew they didn't have very much, but they were always willing to share what little they had.

It had been two fascinating years, but it was time to go home. The plan was to spend a week with Brigitte's family in Germany and then another week in Ireland before finally departing for Canada. I had been busy for so long, it actually felt strange not having any work to do for an entire month. We were both looking forward to spending some time with our kids and our new grandson before heading east. In mid August I would assume command of a company at the infantry school in Gagetown, New Brunswick.

I should have been happy and I was, but I had this nagging feeling of guilt in the back of my mind. The same guilty thoughts had been there when I left Lebanon six months earlier. All of the officers who had been with Colonel Higgins on the day he disappeared were now gone from the Middle East. I was the last one and now I was about to depart. I know it was not a rational thought and my presence could not change the situation, but still I felt that I was somehow abandoning him.

It had been six months since Colonel Higgins was abducted, and other than that single television report in April, there had been absolutely no news. The U.S. Marine Corps still listed him as missing and had even promoted him to full colonel, but the reality was that no one other than his captors knew if he was alive or dead. The nagging question would finally be answered just a few days after we left the Middle East.

It was a beautiful sunny day as Brigitte and I strolled down the main street in Athlone, Ireland. We had spent the morning driving north toward the border with Northern Ireland, and this little town sitting on the banks of the Shannon River was the perfect place to stop for lunch.

Just as we were passing the newsstand I happened to glance over. I tried to block her view, but I was too late. Brigitte and I both stopped and stared, not quite believing what we saw. Plastered across the front page of the *Irish Times* newspaper was a picture of Colonel Higgins. His lifeless body hung suspended from a beam, with a thin wire rope wrapped around his neck.

Many of the locals stared as they walked by, but I really didn't care. I am sure they had no idea of what to make of these two strangers sitting down on the side of the road. All I could do was sit there on the curb and hold on to Brigitte as she buried her head in my shoulder and cried.

AFTERMATH

Like her husband, Robin Higgins was a member of the United States Marine Corps. In the seventeen long months following the abduction of Lieutenant Colonel Higgins, she was relentless in her efforts to achieve her husband's release.

By late March of 1988 she had met with the U.N. secretary general and most of the top officials within the U.S. government. The American representative to the United Nations put forth a resolution demanding the release of the colonel. U.N. Resolution 618 was quickly passed by the General Assembly, but still his kidnappers remained silent.

At last, in the latter part of April 1988, a Beirut newspaper released a grainy black and white image of the colonel. At least the picture proved he was still alive, but judging by the gaunt appearance and obvious signs of bruising around the face, he had been beaten and tortured by his captures. This initial photograph was followed by a series of threats that stated that the colonel was to go on trial for spying. In the weeks and months that followed, the group holding Higgins once again fell silent. Soon the news media moved on to other stories, but at the urging of Robin Higgins, the U.N. and the U.S. government continued to press for answers that never seemed to come.

Finally, on July 31, 1989, his captors released a videotape showing a dangling, inert body hanging from a makeshift gallows. The poor quality of the video made it difficult to confirm the authenticity of the image, but after a thorough analysis by the FBI, it was believed that the image in the video was that of Colonel Higgins. Because there still remained a degree of uncertainty, it took until July 6, 1990, before he was officially declared dead.

Even after his death had been confirmed, Robin Higgins never wavered in her resolve to have her husband's remains returned to American soil.

In late December 1991, an anonymous caller notified the American University Hospital that a body had been dumped along the side of a Beirut roadway. A Danish officer with the U.N. observer stationed in Beirut was quickly dispatched to retrieve the body. After an extensive examination by the Lebanese coroner, the partially decomposed remains were confirmed to be that of the colonel.

It was Robin Higgins's forty-first birthday and what would have been their fourteenth wedding anniversary, but December 23, 1991, would forever be remembered as the day that the body of her husband finally came home in a flag-draped casket. Seven days later Colonel Rich Higgins was laid to rest in the National Cemetery in Quantico, Virginia.

On February 17, 1994, exactly six years from the day of his abduction, the Secretary of the Navy announced that an Arleigh Burke–class guided missile destroyer would be commissioned in his honour. Three years later, Robin Higgins christened the USS *Higgins* and watched as the 8,300-ton ship slid into the waters of the Kennebec River, in Bath, Maine.

As of 2010, the 280 men and women of the USS *Higgins* were engaged in relief operations after the earthquake in Haiti. The colonel would have been very pleased.

EPILOGUE

The Search for Peace of Mind

JULY 1996

When I woke up that first morning it took a long time for the cobwebs to clear. All the windows in the trailer were open, but still the air felt dank and warm. The interior was still in darkness, but through the screen door I could just see the first rays of dawn. As I rolled onto my back I could smell the damp perspiration on the pillow beneath my head. For a moment I just lay there trying to slow my heart rate.

The dream had come again. Sometimes the image was Peter McCarthy standing in the shadow of a setting sun. Sometimes it was a vague image of Higgins standing in the rain. We would be talking but I could never hear the words. I could watch their lips move as they spoke but I knew that none of this was real. They were dead and yet we stood there having this conversation without words. Normally I would just wake up in a sweat. I wasn't so much frightened by the images, but just relieved that it was over. That morning the dream seemed much more real.

As my eyes adjusted to the morning light, my mind flashed back to my time with the Irish battalion in Lebanon. The trailer was the same, but somehow different. Once my heart rate slowed, I sat up and put my feet on the floor. Now that I was fully awake, it only took a moment to realize where I was.

I was on OP 60 Bravo, overlooking the intersection of the Israeli and Syrian borders. It had taken eight years, but I was back. It was July 15, 1996, and I was about to start my first day of duty back in the Middle East.

I have to admit that when the two days of training ended in Jerusalem and they announced our assigned location, I felt a little let down when I didn't get Lebanon. The feeling quickly passed when I realized how fortunate I was just to be back here in the Middle East. I had been in the military for over thirty-two years and my fiftieth birthday was fast approaching. Like it or not, I had just over five years remaining before compulsory retirement. Many officers far younger than me had applied for these few positions each year and never gotten a single tour. How could I possibly complain when I was about to commence tour number five. This was my last chance and I intended to do the best job possible, regardless of where they choose to send me.

For the next six months I would be posted to the station in Tiberias and working on the Israeli side of the Golan Heights.

The observation posts strung along Israel's northern border were uniquely different from any other U.N. positions in the Middle East. Each outpost was tightly sandwiched between the twin border fences that formed the boundary between Israel and Syria. If you were to walk the forty-five metres from the back to the front of the U.N. compound, you were in fact crossing between the two countries. Because of this odd setup the Israelis controlled access to and from the position.

When the two man observer team arrived for duty, they were met by an Israeli officer who would turn off the power and open the main gate leading into the compound. Once the outgoing team departed, the gate was closed, the power switched back on, and the new observers were effectively locked inside the outpost for a full week.

That first week of duty was spent with a Chilean officer who spoke perhaps twenty words of English. He was certainly a capable officer, but the lack of conversation made for an extremely long and boring week. Looking out at the electrified fence and the dense minefields surrounding us always gave me the odd feeling of being a convict in a maximum security prison.

Some past observer had laid out a narrow path just inside the fence line. It took fifty laps to make a kilometre, but at least it gave us some form of exercise.

As the six-month mark approached in my tour, I was offered a staff position in the station headquarters. Tiberias was certainly a nice place to live. As usual, Brigitte had adjusted very quickly to her surroundings and made many new friends. Our hillside apartment was tiny, but comfortable. We could pick oranges and lemons right off the trees in our garden. Sitting on the patio in the evening, we could watch the sun go down over Galilee. The town of Nazareth sat perched on the hillside just to the west. Looking north we could see the mouth of the Jordan River, where it flowed from the hills and emptied into the Sea of Galilee. We were living in the birthplace of Christianity. Work on the observation posts may not have been particularly challenging, but Tiberias was the picture perfect place to live.

The Australian station chief and I got along very well and his offer to make me the training officer was rather tempting, but still I said no. I had already been told that all U.N. tours were now limited to one year, and with only six months left in the Middle East, there was something I simply had to do before it was too late.

As I drove across the border into South Lebanon, it was comforting to see that little had changed. The shacks lining the street in Naqoura still looked like they had been thrown together by a drunken carpenter. The economy had improved, but you could still buy anything from pots and pans to T-shirts or the pirated version of the latest Hollywood movie. That knock-off pair of Nike running shoes may fall apart after a month, but for five dollars you could get yourself a new pair.

As soon as we entered the conference room I went straight to the large map covering the front wall. It was clear to see that little had changed in the intervening years. The Nepalese force had departed and their old area was controlled by a Spanish battalion.

Team Victor was one of three new teams created in 1990. The team used OP Ras as their base of operations. Note the large variety of nationalities represented on the team. Left to right, standing, are officers from New Zealand, Australia, the Netherlands, Ireland, and China. Left to right, kneeling, are officers from China, Canada, and Norway. The officer keeping watch from the roof is from Argentina.

Collection of the author.

There were still no teams living and working within the various battalion areas, but the restriction on movement had been decreased somewhat. Two new teams had been created to patrol the southern area. They both used the observation posts as their base of operation, but were allowed to enter the battalion areas if they needed to meet with the staff. The city of Tyre had been reopened to us, and once again we had a team living and working out of the logistics base.

This last piece of information was particularly important to me. I had been having thoughts of returning to these places for a very long time and now I knew it was possible. My chance would come soon enough, but for now I needed to deal with this first day of training.

I had hoped to remain inconspicuous, but that first morning on the training run up the Echo Road was rather embarrassing. I had only met the other trainees in the vehicle that morning and we were all just getting to know each other. The fact that I had been here before was not important at the moment. Later, if they asked, I would be happy to talk about the past, but right then we were in the middle of our first day of learning a job. Travelling on the Echo Road was still dangerous, so focusing on what the training officer had to say was all that really mattered.

I took the wheel for the first stage of the drive and after ten kilometres I took over the job of radio operator. Everything remained routine until I came on the air to make my first location report. Before the traffic control station could respond, they were cut off by a Canadian on one of the observation posts. "Training team this is OP Mar. Welcome back to Lebanon."

The training officer looked only slightly annoyed, but before he could say anything the radio came on once again. This time the voice was different but still distinctly Canadian. "Captain Burke, this is OP Ras. It is good to have you back." Now the training officer was truly upset and he grabbed the radio handset from me. The other trainees found the whole thing rather amusing, but all I could do was shrug meekly and try not to smile.

"Unknown stations, this is the training officer. You are interrupting an important exercise. You will get off the air and stay off the air immediately!" The remainder of the tour was accomplished in an uncomfortable silence. I had only initiated one call, but that was the end of my time on the radio, at least for that day.

As soon as I dismounted the Jeep that evening, I was handed a note telling me to report to the station chief. This was not the way I wanted to begin my tour of duty in Lebanon. The moment he opened the office door I was ready to defend myself. I immediately began to apologize about the radio chatter, but he cut me off mid sentence. That's not why I was there.

"I believe these belong to you?" As I opened the large manila folder, I couldn't help but smile when I saw the contents. Judging by the dust on each photograph, they had been laying around for a very long time, but still it felt so good to finally see them again. It had been over eight years, but those pictures of Brigitte and our two children I had left in the Team India trailer that fateful morning where now back in my hands.

It didn't take long for the other officers in the station to find out about my past. At first people were curious about Peter McCarthy and Rich Higgins, but after a couple of weeks the questions just stopped. That was fine with me. I had grown tired of answering the same questions. Sometimes I found it necessary to skip over some of the details. I didn't want to lie, but, by the same token, when I was approached by two of the Australian women I thought it best not to share all the facts surrounding Peter's death. I simply told them that Peter had been killed when his Jeep ran over a mine. At the very moment we were talking about the incident, their husbands were out there somewhere in Lebanon. Describing the carnage would have been cruel and totally inappropriate.

I had always been bothered by the arbitrary nature of Peter's death. Soon after returning home in 1988 I had gone to Ottawa where I met with the Canadian major who had been in the Jeep with Peter that day. It had only been eighteen months since the accident, but Major Cote looked surprisingly well considering the extent of his injuries. As we sat down to talk I could see the large shrapnel scar on his forehead had still not fully healed. He told me that he still remembered everything up until the moment the mine exploded. After that everything was a blank.

They had gone to the high feature in order to get a good view of the surrounding terrain. The dirt track leading to the top was only slightly wider than their Jeep. After surveying the area, they got back into the Jeep and headed back down to the highway. They were just a few hundred metres from the bottom when the mine exploded beneath them.

Had the Jeep been even a fraction left or right on the uphill journey, perhaps Peter would still be alive today. Captain Peter McCarthy's death could be measured by a matter of inches.

When it came to Colonel Higgins, there was no real need to gloss over the facts. The entire incident from start to finish had been well documented in newspapers throughout the world. Sometimes I would listen in to conversations at the bar. The majority of people knew how he had been abducted, so most of the discussion seemed to revolve around the reasons why he had been taken. Some believed that the abduction had been meticulously planned, while others put it down to simple bad luck. He had been in the wrong place at the wrong time.

To me the causes had always been straightforward. Colonel Higgins had been the perfect political target. He was a high-profile American who happened to work in an extremely dangerous area. In my mind there was never really a doubt as to why he had been abducted. The question that dogged me constantly was more abstract.

Why had we not recognized the threat and done more to protect him?

Some days I could convince myself that it no longer mattered. After all, these men were dead and should be left to rest in peace. I could force myself to think of other things, but eventually the doubts would return. How could I talk to others about this when it hardly made sense to me?

I had been having the same recurring dream for many years, but since my return to the Middle East the images had become much more vivid.

Deep down inside I knew it wasn't logical, but somehow I believed that if I could only get back there, I could find the answers I was looking for. If I could stand on the spot where Higgins had been abducted, perhaps I could finally put an end to the dreams.

When I saw the Norwegian major standing by the bar late one evening, I knew he was the commander of Team Tyre. According to the duty roster, he and his teammate were scheduled to depart for the area the very next morning.

When I first asked if I could spend the day with the team, he didn't seem to keen on the idea, but once I explained he became genuinely excited. He knew the story of Colonel Higgins's abduction and had travelled the highway many times, but never really knew the exact spot where everything had happened. Now he had me to fill in the details.

As soon as I stepped out of the Jeep and stood staring at the spot where the abandoned vehicle was found, the events of that day all came flooding back to me.

From the moment I first heard the mayday call on the radio until this very moment, I had always believed that the abduction of Colonel Higgins was not a random act. The entire event had been planned in detail.

The meeting in Tyre that morning was well publicized. The kidnappers knew that the coast highway was the only route in and out the Tyre

Pocket. Perhaps they had watched him pass that morning, alone in the vehicle, as he made his way north toward the city. They must have known that it was just a matter of time before he came back down this same road. There were a number of twists and sharp bends on the coast highway, but the point where Higgins was taken was far and away the largest and most secluded curve on the entire route.

The weather that day had been terrible, but even standing there in the bright sunshine I could not see more that a few metres in either direction. This had been no chance encounter. The kidnappers had chosen the perfect spot to execute their plan.

Standing there I suddenly realized that I had deluded myself for all these years. I didn't need to be here to find the answers. I had known the truth all along. Maybe that was what the dreams were meant to tell me.

Could we have done more to protect him? An armed escort would have been easy to arrange. The idea had been mentioned once or twice, but never seriously considered. Having an escort that day would probably have saved his life, but what about all the other days and the other meetings? We all knew that the colonel was not the type of man who would allow himself to be surrounded by a protective bubble. From the first moment he stepped across the border into Lebanon he understood the danger. Perhaps the outcome had been inevitable.

I could not help but think back to a day in early February 1988. Colonel Higgins was being interviewed by a Norwegian television correspondent. The reporter asked him his thoughts on the dangers of working in South Lebanon. His answer was almost like a prophecy of what was to come.

"We can be kidnapped. We can be shot at. We can be robbed. But all of these things are just a part of our daily lives."

As we drove down the highway back to Naqoura, I took one final glance in the rear-view mirror. I knew I would never return to this place, but the image of the tiny isolated spot would be forever etched in my memory.

Perhaps all those dreams were meant as a reminder that it was time to move on. I may not have found all the answers I was looking for, but somehow I knew that things would get better.

Peter McCarthy and Rich Higgins were gone, and nothing could change that. Eight years of constant doubt was long enough. Maybe now I could finally put all of this behind me and get on with the rest of my life.

Also by Terry "Stoney" Burke

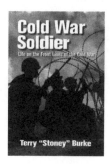

Cold War Soldier
Life on the Front Lines of the Cold War
9781554889594
$22.99

Terry "Stoney" Burke paints a graphic picture of military life at the height of the Cold War. The danger of participating in live fire exercises, the realism of NATO manoeuvres in Western Europe, the sordid behaviour of soldiers on leave in Amsterdam, and a Christmas spent in a military prison are all described in detail.

Visit us at
Dundurn.com
Definingcanada.ca
@dundurnpress
Facebook.com/dundurnpress